THE
TAKEDOWN

THE TAKEDOWN

A Suburban Mom, a
Coal Miner's Son, and
the Unlikely Demise of Colombia's
Brutal Norte Valle Cartel

JEFFREY ROBINSON

Thomas Dunne Books
St. Martin's Press
New York

THOMAS DUNNE BOOKS.
An imprint of St. Martin's Press.

THE TAKEDOWN. Copyright © 2011 by Jeffrey Robinson.
All rights reserved. Printed in the United States of America.
For information, address St. Martin's Press, 175 Fifth Avenue,
New York, N.Y. 10010.

www.thomasdunnebooks.com
www.stmartins.com

Book design by Rich Arnold

Library of Congress Cataloging-in-Publication Data

Robinson, Jeffrey, 1945–
    The takedown : a suburban mom, a coal miner's son, and the unlikely demise
of Colombia's brutal Norte Valle Cartel.—1st ed.
        p. cm.
    ISBN 978-0-312-61238-2
    1. Cartel del Norte del Valle.   2. Drug traffic—Investigation—Colombia—
Case studies.   3. Drug traffic—Investigation—United States—Case studies.
4. Drug control—United States—Case studies.   I. Title.
    HV5840.C7R62 2011
    363.4509861—dc22

                                                                    2011005981

First Edition: August 2011

10   9   8   7   6   5   4   3   2   1

This story is forever dedicated to

Adele and Herbert Klapper
and
Mary Wallo, Josephine Wallo, and Romedio Viola, Sr.

Your kids did real good

Author's Note

This is a story about a long and complex investigation of an international criminal enterprise. A number of people in this book have been charged with—and prosecuted for—heinous crimes, which has been enough to see them sent to prison for many years. Allegations of other crimes were brought to the investigators' attention, and some of those allegations are reported here. Where a suspect has not been prosecuted and convicted for an alleged crime, he is, of course, presumed innocent until found guilty.

THE
TAKEDOWN

Introduction

April 2007.

Assistant U.S. Attorney (AUSA) Bonnie Klapper convenes a grand jury in the new federal courthouse at Central Islip, New York—in Suffolk County, in the middle of Long Island—to indict a group of dangerously violent Colombians for their part in a massive, international drug-trafficking organization.

She explains to the twenty-three men and women sitting in the large, comfortable light wood–paneled room, exactly who these men are and precisely what they've done. The vote is in favor. The indictment is sealed by the court and arrest warrants are issued against the men, all of whom are two thousand five hundred miles away in Colombia, hiding in the mountainous villages in the northernmost corner of the Cauca Valley.

None of these men has ever heard of Central Islip. But, by now, they have heard of Bonnie Klapper.

The attractive, stylish, brunette in her late forties and mother of two boys—one of whom is a special needs child—has stubbornly spent twelve years pursuing this gang.

April 2008.

One of the indicted men is sitting in Combita Prison waiting to be extradited to New York. He knows that this woman—in that town he has never heard of—intends to prosecute him on multiple charges, including international drug trafficking, which could put him in jail

1

for thirty years to life. He has convinced himself that he must stop the extradition process.

He even tells some of his fellow inmates that he is dealing with this, "The Colombian way."

Unbeknownst to anyone in New York, a gun that cannot be traced back to the man in Combita Prison, or anyone associated with him, is delivered to a secret place in the Brownsville section of Brooklyn.

Once it is in place, a thirty-two-year-old man checks in at El Nuevo Dorado International Airport in Bogotá for an Avianca flight to Madrid, Spain. At the counter he produces a Colombian passport in his own name. In Madrid, he plans to transfer onto an Iberia flight to John F. Kennedy International Airport in New York, using a Spanish passport with another name.

The man in Combita Prison is paying the thirty-two-year-old a rumored $1 million to assassinate Bonnie Klapper.

1

Phones were always ringing and people were always shouting across the room.

"Who's got a spare ticket for the Knicks' game tonight?"

And, "Where's my goddamned phone book?"

And, "The marshals just cancelled so we've got to deliver the fucker to jail ourselves."

The huge open-plan office took up a third of the entire fifth floor at No. 6 World Trade Center—referred to in those days as WTC6—an eight-story building off Vesey Street, in the shadow of the North Tower. The smallest building in the complex of seven, it housed the U.S. Commodities Exchange, the New York City headquarters of the U.S. Customs Service, and the El Dorado Task Force.

"Who ordered pizza?"

And, "Where's Forbes?"

And, "My old lady is crazy."

A joint venture of Customs and the Internal Revenue Service

(IRS), El Dorado was created in 1992 specifically to target drug-money laundering in the greater New York metropolitan area.

In theory, the mission was sound. Drug trafficking is a business and like any business, it requires cash flow and reinvestment to survive. Money is the oxygen. Therefore, if you can cut off the trafficker's cash flow and prevent him from reinvesting, you can suffocate him. If he suffocates he goes bankrupt. And a bankrupt business means no product on the streets.

The group was made up of 140 investigators from the two lead agencies plus the Secret Service, the New York Police Department, the U.S. Postal Inspection Service, the New York State Police, the New Jersey State Police, and several local law-enforcement agencies. The investigators, all of whom were handpicked, combined drug savvy with street-smarts and a background working money cases. They were backstopped by forensic accountants; authorities from the New York State Banking Department; intelligence analysts from other agencies; plus prosecutors from the U.S. Attorneys' offices in Manhattan, Brooklyn, and Newark, New Jersey; the district attorneys' offices of all five New York boroughs; and the DA's offices in both Nassau and Suffolk counties on Long Island.

As soon as they opened their door, they hit the ground running. Their first big job was a classic undercover sting code-named "Wire Drill," that focused on the money remitter industry.

Money remitters are "nonbank" financial institutions that use the global banking system to transmit funds around the world. Western Union and American Express MoneyGram are the best known. But there are dozens of others, all of whom subcontract to agents, many of them operating out of ethnic neighborhood storefronts to serve the great "unbanked."

Made up of recent immigrants, these are people who work at low-paying jobs and may not trust banks, may not have the proper paperwork to open an account, may find banking too expensive, or may be—and many are—illegal. Instead, they purchase money orders with cash to pay rent and utility bills, and to send funds home to their families.

Storefront agencies catering to this clientele also usually offer foreign currency exchange, mailboxes, travel facilities, parcel shipping, and pay phones for international calls. They sell beepers, cell phones, and insurance. When a client buys a money transfer, the agent forwards his name, address, and phone number, plus the name, address, and phone number of the recipient, to the licensed remitter. He deposits the cash into the licensed remitter's bank account, and the licensed remitter then transfers the money to another agency at the other end, where the recipient collects the money.

For drug traffickers and their laundrymen, remitters are a fast, reliable, cost-effective way to move dirty money. Either they find a friendly agent who creates false invoices and ignores reporting requirements or, better still, they set up their own agency.

There were, at the time that El Dorado was formed, forty-two licensed remitters in New York State operating through thirteen thousand franchised storefront agencies. Nineteen of the forty-two, catering primarily to Latino communities, were wiring well in excess of $1 billion a year to South and Central America. Just along the two-mile stretch of Roosevelt Avenue in Jackson Heights, Queens, a generally quiet Colombian neighborhood running from the Brooklyn Queens Expressway to Grand Central Parkway, there were 328 storefront agents.

Looking closely at those storefronts, El Dorado surveillance teams began by identifying thugs and money mules loitering at pay phones, waiting for cash pickup instructions that came via pagers. Undercover agents then moved in and developed informants to infiltrate the pickup business. Once they were inside, they planted cameras, and videotaped deliveries of duffel bags and suitcases filled with cash, sometimes as much as $500,000 per drop. They tapped phones and recorded conversations with remitter agents willing to take drug cash and falsify invoices. Finally, they funneled $1.5 million of undercover funds through target storefronts and followed the money directly back to traffickers in Colombia.

Then in June 1994, El Dorado took down the Vigo Remittance Corporation.

This was a big score because Vigo was one of those nineteen licensed remitters. The task force arrested fourteen people, picked apart the Vigo network, and seized financial records from several companies. A federal grand jury charged Vigo with money-laundering violations and two years later Vigo pleaded guilty to structuring financial transactions with the intent to avoid reporting requirements. The case documented significant collaboration between remitters and money launderers and also uncovered correspondent bank accounts used by remitter agencies to put drug money through offshore accounts. But, perhaps most significantly, the Vigo bust provided El Dorado analysts with an enormous amount of statistical information on the wire remitter business.

Once those numbers were crunched, they spoke for themselves.

Census figures for 1995 put the number of Colombian households in New York City at 25,521, and established their median income at around $27,000. Multiplying households by income put the gross income at just under $690 million. But, based on payment data obtained from licensed remitters, analysts established that over $900 million had been remitted that year alone from New York City to Colombia.

In other words, these storefront remitters were sending more money to Colombia than the total annual income of every Colombian household in the city!

By law, remitters had to report all cash transactions to the government in excess of $3,000. But with numbers like that to support their petition, El Dorado asked the Treasury Department to issue a Geographical Targeting Order (GTO), which imposed stricter reporting and record-keeping requirements for a limited period of 60 days.

That first GTO focused on 12 licensed remitters and 1200 agents and lowered the reporting requirement for them to $750. Over the next 14 months, El Dorado's GTO would be renewed every 60 days and expanded to include 22 licensed remitters and 3,400 storefront agencies.

Now El Dorardo's investigators saw storefronts all over New York—particularly in the Colombian neighborhoods of Queens and the Colombian and Dominican neighborhoods of Washington Heights in Upper Manhattan—restructuring drug money wires. Of the original twelve licensed remitters subject to the first GTO, eight were indicted, pleaded guilty, or were convicted and had their license revoked. There were over one hundred individual arrests and convictions, and $13 million was seized.

Using that as a springboard, by the end of summer 1996, El Dorado began moving against forty more remitters. In what would become a nonstop marathon, they launched raids at the rate of one a week from their fifth-floor perch at WTC6.

"Who's on for golf Sunday?"

And, "Anybody remember where we hid the witness?"

And, "Who took my fucking tape recorder again?"

Large windows along the side of the big room looked into office windows across West Street and, if you craned your neck to see beyond the corner of those buildings, the Hudson River was right there, and so was New Jersey. No windows faced south, which meant there was no Statue of Liberty view, because on that side of the floor they'd put up partitions to create the "money room," a space with nothing but two very long wooden tables, so that when the team confiscated drug cash they could pour it all out onto those tables—in view of everybody and with no place to hide anything—to sort it, count it, and bundle it.

At any given time during the day there were sixty to seventy men in jeans and shirtsleeves or sweatshirts, and fifteen to twenty women in jeans and shirtsleeves or sweatshirts, constantly moving in, and out of, and through the room. At any given time during the night, there were ten to twenty men and women doing much the same thing, although doing it more slowly.

Many of the men and women working there were street agents, who dressed to belong on the street. At one point, some higher-up from headquarters—a man who clearly didn't understand what the street was all about—dictated that if agents wanted to dress for the street when they were on the street, that was one thing, but when they were in the office they needed to dress appropriately for the office. So the senior Customs supervisor, John Forbes, himself a former street agent, went to the nearby discount store, Century 21, and bought a dozen dress shirts—one size fits all—plus a dozen striped ties. Now, when that higher-up from headquarters stopped by, at least some of the scruffier street agents could throw on a shirt and tie.

Except, all they did was put the shirt on over their street clothes—they didn't bother to tuck it in—and only half-knotted the tie, and after a couple of weeks, they stopped doing even that.

A few senior managers, like Forbes, had their own tiny private office, just large enough for a desk, two chairs, and a secure file cabinet. In Forbes's office there was also a large green sign that read, AUTHENTIC IRISHMAN.

But the rest of the task force sat together in the big neon-lit room where beat-up old metal desks were pushed together two-by-two and sometimes two-by-three.

Wherever you looked, bulletproof vests hung off chairs. There were low-backed chairs on wheels, straight chairs with no wheels, and a couple of ergonomic kneeling posture chairs. Agency-crested baseball caps—Customs, IRS, NYPD, NJSP—dangled from lamps. Desktops were littered with individual computer terminals, coffee mugs, framed photographs of kids, telephones, more baseball caps, nameplates, computer games, cell phones, pagers, floppy disks, putters, golf balls, Walkmen, headphones, hand weights, magazines, half-eaten sandwiches, milk cartons, water bottles, soda cans, wrapped and unwrapped candy, trophies for bowling and tennis and fishing, and how-to books on investments. Three basketballs lay on the floor beneath a hoop fixed to the partition that was the east wall, next to the main door. Nearby, two big and much-too-noisy shredders were forever needing to be emptied. Personal weapons had to be stowed away in gray-metal, combination-lockable filing cabinets that were scattered all over the office, but there were plenty of empty holsters and handcuffs on desks, too.

In the middle of this, Romedio Viola sat at his desk typing a statement, trying to cut out all the noise around him.

A small, wiry fifty-year-old street agent, he always dressed like a street agent in jeans and short sleeves and a baseball cap, and even when he had to throw on one of those shirts and a tie, he still looked like he was dressed for the street.

Known to everyone as Rooney, someone, somewhere along the way had decided that Romedio was too difficult to pronounce. Everyone else agreed, so the nickname stuck. Even though he didn't like it and was constantly reminding them, "My name is Romedio."

"Okay, Rooney," they'd say, "no problem."

"I'm too old for nicknames," he'd tell them.

"Okay, Rooney," they'd repeat, "no problem."

It wasn't that he eventually gave up, it was that, after a while, he just stopped talking to some of those people who insisted on calling him Rooney to his face. "Fuck 'em," he'd say.

But behind his back, no one called him Romedio.

The son of an Italian immigrant, his father had come to America in 1929. With no education, he found work during the Depression as a coal miner in West Virginia and married a local Appalachian woman. They named their first son Carlo. Ten years later, they christened their second son Romedio.

By the time he was two, the coal mines were shutting down, so his father moved the family north to Brooklyn. Five years later, his mother died. She'd come from a family of thirteen and, after a while, his father married his own sister-in-law Josephine, making Rooney's aunt—who also happened to be his godmother—his stepmother.

When he was twelve, Rooney's father died. Then, two years later, while Rooney and Josephine were visiting West Virginia, she passed away.

Josephine's last wish was that her younger sister Suzy would look after the fourteen-year-old, so Rooney was transplanted back to West Virginia and into a house that had no plumbing and only barely had electricity.

Aunt Suzy was married to a German immigrant who staunchly

believed in reincarnation and swore that he was Jesus incarnate. He was convinced that his mission in life was to survive the inevitable Russian attack on America, and then to create the next generation. The man was so certain that a Russian invasion was imminent, he spent the last twenty-seven years of his life converting a swimming pool into what was officially proclaimed, "the finest fallout shelter in West Virginia."

Absolutely state of the art, with beautiful oak pillars holding up tons of cement for the roof, there was a filter to bring in fresh air, a well to bring in fresh water and enough stocked food to last for years.

Rooney's uncle told him that he planned on living in the shelter for however long it took. But Rooney decided that just two days stuck down there would be so stifling and claustrophobic, anyone would surely want to kill himself.

Still, with little else to do in the backwoods of West Virginia, he helped his uncle build the thing, and spent days filling five-gallon jugs with lentils to stock the shelter's pantry.

When he wasn't working on his shelter, Rooney's uncle tended to the fields of his small farm. But, every hour on the hour he came into the house to listen to the news from a Pittsburgh radio station on his transistor radio, almost as if he was hoping that the announcer would say the Russians had arrived so that he could hide in his shelter.

After one week of this, Rooney decided he'd had enough and walked five miles to the nearest five-and-ten cents store, in Morgan-town, where there was a telephone. He called his brother Carlo in Brooklyn and said, "I've got to get out of here."

Carlo said, "Come back," and a few days later Rooney was on a bus for New York.

He lived with Carlo and his wife, but both of them worked, which meant Rooney pretty much raised himself. He went to Catholic high school and got into Queens College, but quit during his first year because he didn't like it. He and a few friends then bought a pickup truck and drove around the country for a while. When he returned to New York, he worked as a cab driver, until he got fired because he kept getting into accidents. He reenrolled in Queens College—this time found school more to his liking—and three years later graduated with a degree in history, the first member of his family ever to attend college.

He took a job in a local hospital, got bored, and joined the Air Force. He was stationed for a time in California, liked it, and when he got out decided that's where he'd wanted to be. He got himself a job there as an IRS tax collector. "Everybody hated me," he remembers, "they were always trying to kill me."

A year later, he transferred home to Brooklyn, where he spent five more years collecting taxes—"They kept trying to kill me in New York, too"—until he heard that the Treasury Department was looking for enforcement agents. He passed the test, was hired by U.S. Customs, and spent a few years sorting through luggage and freight at Kennedy Airport. When El Dorado formed, he applied for a job there, worked first in intelligence, then moved onto a street action group.

A loner by nature—"I'm not particularly sociable"—Rooney played on the team when he had to, but never hid his feelings that he preferred not to. He always did his best work when he was left alone. So everyone pretty much left him alone.

He wore his dark hair short, had wire-rimmed glasses, and spoke with a slight twang. He also seemed to have a permanent sleepy expression on his face, which made sense to a lot of people on the task force who were convinced that Rooney never slept. He was always either in the office, or running off somewhere to bring back a fugitive. He was married, his wife was trying to become an actress, but he collected stray cats, and so did she, and because his cats didn't like her cats, they lived in separate apartments.

Only five eight and 160 pounds, Rooney didn't automatically strike fear into anyone, at least not until he got angry. And when that happened, most people—if they were smart enough—got out of his way.

That he kept his weight constant was no surprise to anyone on the task force, especially the same people who were convinced that he never slept, because they were equally convinced that Rooney never ate. He hardly ever went out for lunch with the other guys, and when he did, he only ordered coffee. Whenever food was brought in, he'd just sit there drinking coffee, waiting for everyone else to finish before he'd wrap up what was left to take home. "For my cats," he'd tell them. "They'll love this."

He always wore jeans, and his shirt was, more often than not, falling out from under his belt. It was rare that he went anywhere without a baseball cap pulled low across his face. His favorite was a University of West Virginia cap, but he had a whole collection and changed them frequently, sometimes wearing different caps on the same day. "It changes your appearance. You never want too many people to recognize you."

Averse to cold—"A West Virginia thing," he'd say—other agents never minded riding with him in a car in winter because the heat was always on. But they went out of their way to avoid riding with him in summer because he categorically refused to turn on the air-conditioning. It could be the hottest, most sweltering New York summer day, and when someone invariably said, "What about the AC?" He'd complain, "Too cold," so it stayed off.

While everyone else on the team carried a 9mm Glock semiautomatic pistol, Rooney still wore an old-fashioned Magnum 44. Some agents joked behind his back that if they were busting down a door, Rooney had to go first because nobody wanted to be in front of him when he drew his gun. But that wasn't a joke they shared with him.

"Why do you use that?" young agents sometimes dared to ask about his old-fashioned pistol.

He'd mumble back, with just enough disdain in his voice, "Because . . . it works."

Now someone in the room called out, "My computer died."

And someone else said too loudly into the phone, "What do you mean the hearing date has been moved up?"

And Danny Min stopped at Rooney's. "I don't believe it."

Rooney looked up at the stocky, powerfully built thirty-three-year-old Korean American. An ex-Marine who still wore his "fat head" crew cut, Min had been an IRS agent for only a few years, but like Rooney, he, too, was an original member of the El Dorado team. "What don't you believe?"

"We've got this remitter . . . three businesses, all tied together in

Queens . . . so Toby and me . . ." he said, referring to his IRS partner, Toby Barbero, ". . . we put everything together for a warrant. These guys in Queens have moved a total of $70 million to Colombia. We got it all. So we take what we have to Brooklyn and some AUSA there says no. Just like that. No."

Four months earlier, a tip-off had come in through one of the El Dorado Task Force undercover agents who'd turned a street-level money drop-off guy into a confidential informant (CI). According to the CI, bags of cash were being delivered every day to a money remitter agency at 70-13 Austin Street, a block off Queens Boulevard in the heart of Forest Hills. The CI said that as soon as the money arrived, the owner of the place would order the young women who worked for him to fill out false documentation—always keeping amounts below federal reporting requirements—so that the money could be wired to Colombia without the government finding out. What's more, the CI added, this had been going on for a number of years.

Min and Barbero landed the case.

A simple drive-by established that the address was a three-story building with several shops, where steps led up from the sidewalk to a narrow walkway. Right there on the left, a storefront had a neon sign in the window that read, "Tele-Austin Travel."

The El Dorado intelligence unit quickly came up with a name for the owner—Ignacio Lobo, a forty-year-old Colombian who'd legally been resident in the United States for more than ten years. A further search discovered that Lobo was also listed as the owner of a second Tele-Austin remitter agency five miles away. That office was on the ground floor of a three-story building on the southwest corner of Broadway and Forty-third Street in Astoria, with an awning over the doorway. Those locations were now referred to as Tele-Austin I and Tele-Austin II.

Lobo's name then popped up a third time, as the manager of another wire remitter agency, Around the World Communications. This one was on the second floor of a two-story building at 37-66 Junction Blvd. in Corona, one block north of the elevated subway tracks that run along Roosevelt Avenue.

As Min explained to Rooney, he and Barbero—a stocky fellow about Min's age but with dark hair and a big smile—spent weeks sifting through reports of money wired out to Colombia, and found very clear violations at these three locations. They strongly suspected that Lobo was structuring drug-money payments to avoid reporting requirements.

To prove it, early one morning, the agents took Min's personal video camera to Queens. The best vantage point for Tele-Austin I was from the roof of the movie theater directly across the street, so they got permission to go up there and stayed on the roof all day, videotaping the front door.

It turned out to be a long, very boring day because only two people went inside.

The following day, they did a similar customer head count, minus the camera, at Tele-Austin II. No one at all showed up.

They planned to watch Around the World Communications, but the entrance was on the side of the building, and another business used the same entrance, so they didn't bother. They knew that, even if they saw someone going inside, it would never hold up as probable cause for a warrant because they had no way of knowing which business that person was visiting.

A month later, Min told Rooney, they received official reports on the wire activity coming out of those business for the same days they'd watched them. Two people had gone inside Tele-Austin I, and yet Lobo had reported dozens of clients wiring out thousands of dollars. No one had gone inside Tele-Austin II, but Lobo was showing similar numbers for that business.

Min and Barbero took their case to John Forbes, who agreed that the task force had "multiple areas of interest" in Mr. Lobo, and the decision was made to go inside his businesses.

So the two agents bundled their evidence into stacks and drove to Brooklyn, to the office of the United States Attorney for the Eastern District of New York—which handled cases located in Queens—and dumped everything onto the desk of an Assistant U.S. Attorney in the narcotics division. They pitched their case to her, went through the numbers, showed her what they'd uncovered, and told her what they expected to find once they got inside the three businesses. They even played the videotape for her. In their minds, this was a slam dunk.

The woman listened to what they had to say, looked at what they had to show her, expressed some doubt about particular aspects of the evidence and, just like that, told them, "No. I'm not taking it to the magistrate."

Both agents were shocked.

She repeated, "No."

They argued that the warrant was really important.

But she wouldn't budge. "There's no hard evidence that the Tele-Austin money is directly tied to cocaine."

Other agents had run into this attitude before. Narcotics prosecutors like cases best when they can be photographed next to a table filled with bags of white powder, guns, and piles of money. Those are the elements that make their case obvious. Money laundering and paper trails didn't have sex appeal. To make this case, she'd have to get creative. But, for overworked prosecutors, getting creative takes a lot of effort, at the risk of too little result.

"I'm too busy," she told them. "We close one remitter, six more open. It's never-ending. Sorry guys . . . a waste of time."

Back at WTC6, Min now looked at Rooney and kept shaking his head. "Can you believe it?"

Rooney simply mumbled, "Bonnie."

Min said, "What?"

"Bonnie," he said again, as if it should have been obvious. "Bonnie Klapper. She works out of Hauppauge. Next to Central Islip. On Long Island. Nobody in narcotics likes money cases, except her. She loves this shit."

Min was hardly impressed. "Hauppauge? That's one hundred miles away. Philadelphia is closer."

Rooney had been one of the agents working on Vigo in 1994. Bonnie was one of the prosecutors who took the case to court. That's when they met, when Rooney needed someone to understand a complicated money angle and one of the agents on the team assured him, "Bonnie's the only one who gets it."

As Rooney explained to Min, although she was officially assigned to the U.S. Attorney's Office in Brooklyn, Bonnie worked out of a little office in Suffolk County because she had two young children and there were family reasons why she needed to stay close to home.

Min said, "We have to schlep all the way out to Hauppauge?"

Rooney nodded. "I'm telling you, she'll do it."

Realizing that this was his only chance, Min asked Rooney to make the call.

For just about everyone else, getting Bonnie on the phone was next to impossible because she was either in court, or in a meeting, or proffering witnesses, or driving between one place or another. Her oldest son took up a lot of her time, and because she knew what it was to be "the other child," she tried to devote just as much time to her second son. When you dialed her office, you got voice mail. When you dialed her cell, you got voice mail. When you rang her at home you got the answering machine. Sometimes she'd phone back the same day. Usually it would be later.

But not when Rooney called.

She saw his number on her caller ID and answered the phone. "Romedio . . ."

Bonnie was probably the only person who didn't call him Rooney.

"Two guys need a warrant," was how he started the conversation. "It's a money case. They'll even come to you to get it. I'll bring them out."

She made arrangements to see them the next day.

When the four of them sat down, Min and Barbero made their case. "$70 million!"

Rooney admitted, "Nobody at Brooklyn would take it, so I promised them you would."

Bonnie stared straight-faced at the three men. "You can't get it anyplace else . . . everyone else says no . . . so you come to me. You figure I'll give you what you want. What am I, your local warrant slut?"

2

Hauppauge, Long Island, was never part of Bonnie Klapper's master plan.

When her paternal grandfather arrived in America from Hungary sometime after World War I, he started a small sewing machine factory. The business did all right, but he couldn't really compete with the likes of the Singer Company, and quickly realized that there was more money to be made in generic sewing machine parts. Back then, no one was buying anything from China, so he regeared to make and supply parts for industrial sewing machines and, over the years, steadily built up his business.

When Bonnie's father got out of the army after World War II, he went to college, hoping to become a doctor, but her grandfather took ill and her father had to drop out of school to run the family business.

Bonnie was born in Brooklyn in 1957. By the time she was three, her father was well on his way to becoming the biggest industrial sewing machine parts supplier in the country, and had moved the family to North Woodmere, a manicured village in the affluent south shore area of Long Island known the "Five Towns." A few years later, Bonnie's sister was born, but she suffered health problems when she was very young.

Because Bonnie's mother dedicated most of her time to Bonnie's kid sister, and because her father was usually at work, Bonnie had to invent her own world. She studied music—took seventeen years of piano and classical voice lessons—and became a vociferous reader. "Basically," she admits, "I was a nerd."

At Lawrence High School, she also got involved in student government. "It was either that or sports, and I'm not at all athletic. I was always the last to be picked for every team. The megaklutz."

She hoped to go to Juilliard, New York's celebrated conservatory of music, intending to sing opera or, second choice, to appear in Broadway musicals. But Juilliard turned her down and when Yale accepted her for January admission, she announced to her parents that she'd wait to go there. Except that her parents didn't like the idea of their teenaged daughter sitting around doing nothing for six months and, as long as she'd also been accepted at the University of Pennsylvania, she started there that fall.

Unfortunately for Bonnie, she never really fit in. Especially coming from the Five Towns, she felt she was supposed to look a certain way, to act a certain way, and to hang out with certain people. Unlike some of the young women she met at Penn, Bonnie wasn't convinced that the primary reason for this exercise was to find a husband. What's more, Penn, in those days, was a big drug school, and that didn't work for her, either.

Intent on doing everything she could not to be "that girl from the Five Towns," she spent a lot of time studying. Then, every summer she studied abroad. She attended the Sorbonne in Paris and the University of Madrid, and also worked on a kibbutz in Israel. In her senior year, she announced that she wanted to do grad work at the Columbia School of Journalism and eventually, maybe, find a job at the United Nations. "I was going to bring about world peace."

But her parents suggested she should think about law school. In their minds, that meant some old established Eastern-seaboard law school. Maybe, they said, it was time for Yale.

Instead, Bonnie escaped to the University of California at Berkeley where, famously, the flame of counterculture and radical liberalism has burned brightly since the early part of the twentieth century. Not exactly what her parents had in mind for their Five Towns daughter. "It was an incredible place, exactly the right time to become a feminist."

Suddenly finding herself in a campus culture with "rights' movements" for everybody and everything on every corner, she got involved with just about every nonconformist, radical, off-the-wall movement she could find. She also found time to graduate in the top 10 percent of her class and with the honor, "Order of the Coif."

In her mind, Berkeley Law was only one short step away from defending the poor and downtrodden with Legal Aid in San Francisco. But her career as a public defender was derailed when she was offered the opportunity to clerk for Justice A. Wallace Tashima, who sat on the U.S. District Court for the Central District of California in Los Angeles. He would later became the first Japanese American to be appointed to a United States Court of Appeals.

While she was in Tashima's office, he presided over the "Grandma Mafia Case." The defendants were three seemingly respectable old ladies who used the clothing company they ran as a front for a drug trafficking ring which was laundering more than $2 million a month.

Fascinated by the money aspect of the trafficking world, Bonnie fast came to the conclusion that prosecutors have the most fun. So when her year of clerking was up, she applied for a job with the U.S. Attorney's office in LA. But they turned her down because they wanted people with a lot of trial experience. To get that, she went to work for a small corporate litigation firm, and hated every minute of it. In fact, she only stayed long enough to land the AUSA job, where she could specialize in money-laundering cases, one of the few AUSAs to do so.

Around that same time, Bonnie met a good-looking young lawyer who'd just moved to California from back East. He figured the weather was better in LA, found himself in a firm doing real estate law, and didn't like it. They fell in love and by the time they decided to get married, the two of them also agreed to move back to New York.

The Justice Department wouldn't allow Bonnie to transfer to another office—"That would have been too easy"—so she applied to both the Southern District, which is in Manhattan, and the Eastern District in Brooklyn. She settled on Brooklyn because it was one of only two offices in the country with a dedicated money-laundering unit.

That was in 1987.

Bonnie and her husband planned to stay in New York just long enough to build a nest egg so that they could move back to Southern California. Two sons and a whole bunch of Havanese dogs later, they still haven't made it.

The eighteen-page document she drafted for Min and Barbero, requesting permission to search all three of Lobo's premises, hung on the claim that Tele-Austin I, Tele-Austin II, and Around the World Communications were deliberately structuring wires to avoid federal reporting.

What Min and Barbero had established—which became the basis of Bonnie's affidavit—was that before the GTO came into effect, from July 1, 1996, through August 5, 1996, Tele-Austin I sent 86 wires to Colombia, worth $190,390, averaging $2213.84 per wire. The post-GTO totals, for the period August 6 through August 31, came to $68,250 in 108 wires, bringing the average down to $631.94. At Tele-Austin II, 95 pre-GTO wires totaled $223,340, averaging $2350.94, while 55 post-GTO wires, totaled $37,340, averaging $678.90. The figures for Around the World Communications were not very different. There were 73 pre-GTO wires for $182,715, which is an average of $2530, and 20 post-GTO wires totaling $13,100 which is an average of $655.

In other words, every single wire sent by the three locations always fell below reporting requirements, both pre- and post-GTO. The only conclusion possible was that all three locations were "structuring" the remittances.

In the document she'd prepared Bonnie argued that because structuring wires to avoid any cash transaction reporting is a crime under the money-laundering laws, structuring to circumvent GTO reporting is also a crime.

A magistrate agreed and signed the search warrant on January 9, 1997.

Surveillance on the locations was ratcheted up. Layouts were checked to determine if there were any dangerous entry or exit points. Covert photos were shot from parked cars so that the entry teams could see what to expect. Undercover agents visited each location— pretending to be customers, or passersby looking for directions, or shoppers asking for change for a parking meter—to see for themselves who and what was there.

After those officers reported back that only two or three young women worked at each store, it was determined that the possibility of violence was very low. Still, the teams would follow standard procedure and go in wearing body armor and with guns drawn.

Five days after the warrant was issued, El Dorado agents took down all three businesses at precisely the same time.

Tuesday morning, January 14.

The day began at 11:15 A.M. when nineteen men and five women arrived in unmarked cars at a remote corner of the large private parking lot, hidden from public view, behind the art deco Bulova Watch building, where the Brooklyn Queens Expressway meets Astoria Boulevard, just off Grand Central Parkway, not far from La Guardia Airport in Queens, New York.

It was cold. The temperature had dipped down into the twenties and there was still a little weekend snow left on the ground. Everyone was dressed for winter, but most of them didn't pay any attention to the weather—except for a few who mumbled with steamy breath, "It's fucking freezing"—because they were too busy checking everything that needed to be checked, one last time. Assignments. Tactics. Warrants. Equipment. Call signs. Weapons.

Executives at Bulova had, a few of years before, agreed to allow the group to use the parking lot, but no one from Bulova knew when they were there or why.

The plan was that two agents would secure each location, two agents would conduct interviews—at least one of those two had to be female because they knew that several women might be arrested—two agents would search each location, one agent would record and deal with whatever evidence was seized and the team leader would be available to stopgap wherever he was needed.

Standing there in the parking lot, clapping gloved hands and shuffling feet to stay warm, the team studied the surveillance photos again. And were shown the floor plans of the storefronts again. And were reminded, again, where the nearest hospital was and where the nearest police station was. They were told, again, which phone numbers to use—to talk to the other teams, to talk to Bonnie in her office in Hauppauge, to talk to Forbes and the other El Dorado senior managers back at the World Trade Center, and to reach the Customs Operations Center in Florida where outside assistance—NYPD backup, SWAT teams, medical evacuation, the bomb squad, hostage negotiators—could be coordinated if that suddenly became necessary.

They went over everything, step by step, again, until everyone was sure that everyone else had it right, and until, finally, one of the team leaders asked, "Any questions?"

Either there were none, or nobody could be bothered because it was just too damned cold to be outside like that, so one of the team leaders said, "Synchronize your watches," and they all did that, and then he said, "Saddle up," and that's when everyone headed for their cars.

Trunks flew open and body armor came out, and once everyone was wearing a vest—with large letters across the front and back, spelling out US CUSTOMS or IRS or NYPD—they all climbed back into their cars, and turned on the heat, then pulled out of the parking lot, heading for the three target locations.

Min and Barbero took a team into Tele-Austin I. Rooney led a team into Tele-Austin II. An NYPD officer took a team into Around the World Communications.

And at each location it was the same thing.

Teams stormed into the storefronts screaming, "Federal agents . . . police . . . we have a warrant . . . get away from the desks . . . get on the floor now . . . move away from the desks . . . keep your hands in sight . . . get down on the floor . . . now!"

The women working at the locations—all of them Colombian and all of them in their late teens—became hysterical and started crying.

The female agent on the team got the women to lie down on the floor with their fingers clasped behind their heads, while the other agents secured the place. Agents pulled storm shutters and blinds across the windows and doors so that no one could see in from the street, while the female agent did her best to calm down the young women. The others then helped the women get up from the floor and sat them down on chairs in front of the desks.

It was several minutes before these young woman stopped shaking in fear and stopped crying.

The search agents then started going through files and the interviews began.

At Tele-Austin I, there was a safe in the back and Min wanted it opened. But none of the women could open it. Either they couldn't, or they were too afraid, so Min called for an NYPD drill team. It was several hours later before they arrived and when the drill team opened the safe, they found cash inside, but not a lot.

There was also some cash on hand at Tele-Austin II and Around the World Communications, but again, the amounts were comparatively small.

Throughout the afternoon as the search progressed, agents briefed each team leader on their interviews with the young women. The three team leaders then reported by phone to Bonnie, telling her what the women were saying. These women needed to be properly identified and based on what they were saying to the agents, Bonnie had to decide who needed to be brought back to WTC6 for further questioning, and who could be released.

Two items were uncovered that amused the agents. At Tele-Austin I, Min found a local phone book, in Spanish, with page after page of names and addresses circled or underlined in ink. Hundreds of names had been highlighted. It would later turn out that these names and addresses were used to falsify clients sending money to Colombia. And at Tele-Austin II, Rooney found a school report card—it was for Ignacio Lobo's son—which showed that the poor kid had been struggling.

Then, something happened that no one took much notice of.

It was one of those forks in the road that might have changed how Bonnie and Rooney would spend every working moment for the next twelve years.

At around 1:20, a man outside Tele-Austin I started banging on the closed shutter.

One of the agents inside shouted, "Go away."

The man continued banging on the shutter. "What's going on? Let me in."

Making the mistake of assuming that this was just a customer, the agent shouted, "Go away. Federal agents. This premises is closed."

The man outside turned and left as fast as he could.

While Rooney, Min, Barbero, and the others spent two weeks after the raids sorting through and analyzing all the evidence they'd bagged, Bonnie was busy interviewing the young women who worked for Lobo.

There were a dozen, but two had already disappeared—probably back to Colombia—and three others, Bonnie decided, were of no interest. Of the seven remaining, she interviewed three women several times and concluded that some of them were lying to her.

By now, each of the women had lawyers which made it increasingly difficult for Bonnie to find out everything the women knew about the remitters. She couldn't talk to them without their lawyers being present and, because it was increasingly evident to everyone that these women were in real jeopardy, the lawyers had no interest in allowing their clients to talk to Bonnie without first putting a deal in place to secure their safety.

So the lawyers argued with Bonnie that the women were innocent victims of the system, nothing but clerks filling out forms, and that she should cut them a lot of slack.

Bonnie knew that, eventually, she would work out a deal to help these women, but playing that card too soon was bad poker. So she agreed that they were victims of the system, but insisted that they had, nevertheless, violated the law.

The lawyers said, if you're not going to give them a free pass—"Come on, Bonnie, they're only kids"—the most you should think about is a slap on the wrist.

She tried to show genuine sympathy toward these young women, but her usual friendly, up-front style wasn't going to change the fact that she was intent on finding out what she needed to know.

Foolishly, a couple of the lawyers mistook her otherwise laid-back approach as a sign of weakness and decided to call her bluff. They dug in their heels. "It's a free pass or nothing," one of them said.

"Okay," she answered, "then it's nothing."

Another one dared her, "Give it your best shot because no judge is going to convict these teenaged girls of anything."

"Watch this space," she told him, summoned a federal grand jury and subpoenaed five of the women to testify.

That got everybody's attention.

A couple of the women were illegals, which meant they were facing deportation. But they had babies born in America, so deportation meant separating them from their children, who were otherwise entitled to stay. The others feared that they could be sent home to Colombia, while their lawyers worried that, in addition to deportation, some of the women might wind up in jail before they were deported. After all, if Bonnie's grand jury indicted them, the women would be locked up as flight risks awaiting a trial, which could take two to three years. It didn't matter that none of these women had ever heard the term "money laundering." Technically, they were in violation of various statutes and could face long prison sentences.

On the surface, an indictment seemed like a heartless act, especially for an old Berkeley radical. Except that Bonnie never had any intention of putting the women before a grand jury. Or of deporting them. Or of throwing them into jail. She understood that they were just lowly clerks being paid two to three hundred dollars a week. Her real targets were the owner of the Tele-Austin businesses—Ignacio Lobo—and his major clients. But to get to them, she needed these women to tell her the truth, which meant playing chicken with their lawyers.

And it worked.

Defense lawyers were suddenly lining up outside her office to protect their clients, offering information in exchange for a deal.

Unfortunately for a few of the women, this was a double-edged sword. Bonnie knew that if they cooperated with the government, or if someone thought they were cooperating, there could be violent retribution against them or their families back in Colombia. If they didn't cooperate, they believed that they risked jail and deportation. So she sat down with each of the women, one by one, to assure them that protection could be arranged. But, she explained, they could only be protected if they accepted the deal she was putting on the table. She promised to grant them immunity from prosecution. But they had to tell her everything she wanted to know. And it had to be the truth. If they lied, she warned, the deal was off.

For three of the six, even a guarantee of protection was not enough. They were still too afraid to talk. But the other three were willing to take the deal, and one in particular—call her Isabel—had a lot of information to offer. She spoke about Lobo and his operation in great detail. She said that Lobo had only taken over in about 1993, after the manager of Tele-Austin II, a Bolivian woman who can only be identified as Confidential Witness 7 (CW7), went home to South America.

That was of particular interest to Bonnie for two reasons: first, because Lobo was listed as the owner of Tele-Austin II, not the manager, which meant Isabel might be lying; and second, because CW7's name was already in the system. She'd been arrested in 1986, attempting to smuggle cocaine into the United States. Eight years later, she'd been arrested again, this time carrying $62,600 concealed on her person en route from New York to Colombia.

Isabel also spoke about a woman named Maria Vega who ran a remitter called Telefolklor, saying that when there was too much money for Lobo to handle, he sent cash to her.

Bonnie asked Rooney to take a close look at Vega and Telefolklor. In the process, Rooney discovered two more storefront remitters accepting cash overflows from Tele-Austin. One was Tele-Lapaz. The other was called Universal. Those two businesses were also used by Maria Vega when her remitter had excess cash to process. And both of them were owned by CW7.

Now she told Rooney, "Find CW7 and Vega."

A few days on the street was enough for Rooney to determine, "CW7's gone, left the country. She's in Bolivia."

"And Vega?" Bonnie asked.

He grinned. "She's living in Queens."

The question now became, what to do about her. They could pick her up and question her, but about what?

Investigations like this are complicated jigsaw puzzles. If you don't know where a piece fits, sometimes you can guess right, which is fine. But sometimes you can guess wrong, which risks screwing up other parts of the puzzle. Often, the best thing is to do nothing. You just keep the piece on the table in front of you until you have a better idea of where it fits.

Unsure how important Vega might be, Bonnie decided, "We'll leave her alone until we can make a case against her."

Lobo was the obvious one to focus on. But that wasn't going to be easy. When you have several witnesses, they frequently contradict each other. Even at the best of times they don't always agree. The women said that Ignacio Lobo was actively in charge of the remitters, although they weren't 100 percent certain if he owned them, or if he just managed them, or if he owned one or two and managed whatever he didn't own. In fact, from what her witnesses were telling her, the only thing Bonnie knew for sure was that Lobo was the man who told the women what to do, and that Lobo knew everything that was going on.

In sworn statements, the women said that couriers delivered bags of cash to Lobo at the stores, which he then divided into smaller amounts. They said it was Lobo who ordered them to fill out the paperwork for wires to Colombia in those smaller amounts, and that it was Lobo who supplied names and addresses of the senders that were totally made up. The women said Lobo took names and address straight out of the Spanish language telephone book that had been confiscated at Tele-Austin I.

While it was one thing to invent senders' names so he could fill in the blanks on the reporting forms, recipients' names were different. At that end of the money trail, real people had to collect real cash. Yes, the task force had collected lists with thousands of recipients' names at the end of thousands of wires, but conventional wisdom had it that most, if not all, of those names were made up. Even if some weren't, the people collecting the money were all in Colombia. Whether or not, somewhere down the line, Washington could convince the government in Bogotá to help identify the recipients was another matter entirely. But that was a problem Bonnie decided she could worry about much later.

For the moment, she was curious where those recipients were. From experience, she knew that drug money almost always went to Medellin, Cali, Bogotá, and some of the outlying cities nearby. That was the center of the cocaine industry. That's where the traffickers were. However, based on the documents seized at the storefronts, the addresses Lobo was using for the recipients were all in three small Colombian towns that neither Bonnie nor Rooney had ever heard of—Armenia, Pereira, and Manizales.

Checking a map, she and Rooney found these three cities in the middle of nowhere, in the high mountains of the Cauca Valley region, about halfway between Cali and Medellin.

Armenia sits 5,000 feet above sea level, with a population of around 325,000. The local economy depends on coffee and, to some extent, bananas. Pereira sits lower, in a small valley of the western Andes mountain range, about 4,700 feet above sea level. The population is around 580,000. In addition to having the largest zoo in Colombia, here, too, the main trade is coffee. Manizales, a university town, is known as the "world capital of coffee." Higher than the others, at just over 7,000 feet, the population is about 415,000. None of the three cities were known cocaine centers. None of them showed up on any of the databases that Rooney checked in relation to any cases at all.

Sending so much money to these towns didn't make sense to Bonnie or Rooney, or to anybody else at El Dorado. It was, they all agreed, "curiouser and curiouser."

Except that this wasn't something they could spend a lot of time worrying about because they had too many other things to do.

Among those other things, Bonnie would need to prove in court that the names and addresses Lobo was listing as senders of the wires were false. So Rooney went through the Spanish language phone book and matched dozen of names that had been circled in the book with specific wires. They then recruited two IRS agents, Ed Sorocki and Bob Wanderer, to help. They'd done most of the financial background work on the money-laundering side of the case, crunching all the numbers to prove that the three storefronts were clearly structuring their wires to fall below the GTO's limits. So Rooney, Toby, Sorocki, and Wanderer started banging on doors to find out who was living at those addresses. They were looking for the people who'd been named as Lobo's clients.

To no one's surprise, there wasn't a single valid sender.

"We were able to establish a pattern," Rooney says.

To that Bonnie adds, "We're like sharks. We follow every lead right down to the end. Even when other people would have walked away long ago, as long as we keep moving, we're okay."

Based on sworn statements from the young women who'd taken Bonnie's deal and were now cooperating, plus the paperwork found at the three storefronts, plus Rooney's sworn statement that Lobo had falsified names and addresses, Bonnie got a warrant for Lobo's arrest.

With that in hand, Rooney and a team of agents went back onto the streets to look for him. They hit all the addresses he was known to frequent. But Lobo was nowhere to be found. Word was that he'd escaped to Colombia.

Rooney assured Bonnie, "He's never coming back."

The group had only seized around $40,000 from the three locations—it wasn't much to brag about—but in their minds they'd put an end to a major operation that had washed $70 million. Everyone patted themselves on the back and moved on to the next job.

The El Dorado Task Force was on a roll and there wasn't time to gloat.

3

Whenever his beeper went off, Rooney automatically assumed something was wrong.

Logically, he reckoned, anybody he knew who needed to find him had his cell phone number. The beeper was for people who didn't have his cell phone number. Which meant, anyone who rang his beeper was someone he didn't know or who didn't know him. And people he didn't know, or people who didn't know him, only got in touch because they needed something. Which meant, therefore, something was wrong.

It was seven months after the Tele-Austin raids and as far as he was concerned, those raids were ancient history. The El Dorado team was neck deep in the ongoing remitter raids. For each storefront they took down, there was a mountain of evidence to sort through and weeks of witnesses to interview.

Rooney was working on affidavits in the federal building in Garden City that morning in August 1997—just down the hall from where Bonnie was using a small office to prepare for a trial—when his beeper went off. He pulled it off his belt to see that the message "please call" was coming from a 305 area code. That's the Miami area. He and Bonnie worked closely with agents and prosecutors down there, but he didn't recognize this number. So he took his phone and made the call.

A Customs agent at Miami International Airport answered.

The two men went through the usual routine of identifying themselves—they both had to know for sure who they were talking to—after which Rooney said, "What's wrong?"

The agent in Miami said, "It's about your guy."

Rooney didn't know what he was talking about. "What guy? Who?"

The agent explained, "I'm running passenger manifests for flights inbound from Colombia . . ."—checking to see who's flying into the country from South and Central American gateways is standard procedure for Customs and Immigration—". . . and we got a hit on one of the names. The tag in the system said to notify you. That's what I'm doing."

"Notify me about who?" Rooney wanted to know.

The agent said, "Last name Lobo, first name Ignacio."

"Holy shit," Rooney said. "Arrest him."

The agent in Miami explained that Lobo had just boarded a flight in Bogota, but in order to nab him when he landed, Miami needed to have a copy of the warrant.

Rooney hung up and hurried to find Bonnie. "You'll never guess." But then, he never gave her a chance to. "Lobo."

She immediately dropped what she was doing to dig up the paperwork, which Rooney faxed to Florida.

Three and a half hours later, as Lobo stepped off the flight, agents handcuffed him. They took him into secondary holding and started to interview him. But Lobo wasn't talking. That's when the agent in Miami called Rooney to announce, "He's in custody."

Rooney asked, "Was he surprised?"

The agent said, "Not really."

Which, in an odd way, kind of made sense to Rooney. After all, Lobo definitely knew that the feds had taken down the three storefronts. That's why, Rooney and Bonnie had both assumed, he'd fled the country. Lobo also knew what the feds would find at the three locations. Lobo would know they'd be looking for him, and that there would be an arrest warrant out on him. So, Rooney reasoned, why should he be surprised? But then, Rooney also had to wonder, why would he come back? Lobo had a wife named Doris, but she'd already dumped him for a man half her age.

"Maybe," Rooney told Bonnie, "it was for the kid."

"Or maybe it wasn't," Bonnie said, acute skepticism being part of the job description for a federal prosecutor. "He knew there was a risk. Maybe he needed to come back. Maybe he's just stupid. Or maybe he's so arrogant he thought we'd forgotten."

It doesn't take people working in law enforcement long to see that being stupid and arrogant enough to take a risk like that is part of the job description of many criminals.

If Lobo had stayed in Colombia for the rest of his life, he would have been safe. But he didn't. And now he wasn't.

Eight days later, after Lobo waived his rights to an identity hearing in Florida, U.S. Marshals escorted him, handcuffed, on a commercial flight to New York. From Kennedy Airport, they delivered him to the Metropolitan Detention Center (MDC)—a massive eight-story warehouse of a prison on 29th Street in south Park Slope, Brooklyn—where he would wear a fluorescent orange jumpsuit and live in a tiny cell while the long legal process ran its course.

Bonnie met Lobo for the first time several days later, in an interview room in the federal courthouse on Cadman Plaza East in Brooklyn.

Lobo was there with his public defender, a woman named Randy Chavis. She and Bonnie had faced each other many times over the years, and during that time the two women had become friends.

The way Bonnie worked, she liked to put her cards on the table as soon as possible, believing that when defendants know how strong the case against them is, they're more likely to plead guilty and co-operate. Also, Bonnie knew she could count on Chavis to understand the difficult position her client was in, and hoped that Chavis would not have any trouble convincing Lobo to work out a deal.

But the moment Bonnie spotted Chavis waiting for her in the hallway outside the interview room, pacing the floor, looking anxious, she realized this wasn't going to be quite so easy.

Chavis told her, "This guy is terrified. He won't talk to me. He won't say anything. He needs a deal."

Bonnie asked, "What's he got to offer?"

"I don't know," Chavis explained. "He won't tell me anything. I've tried to talk him into cooperating. I'm still trying. But he's afraid. You've got to do something."

"What's he afraid of?"

"I don't know." She paused, then opened the door to the interview room. "See for yourself."

Bonnie stepped inside and the instant she laid eyes on Lobo, she realized, "This man is scared shitless."

Lobo was short, innocuous-looking and, as Rooney put it later, "kind of goofy."

It was hard for Bonnie to believe that this was the man who'd been running one of the most important drug money Laundromats in New York. He didn't look the part. He didn't strike the pose. But he was obviously terrified.

After introducing herself, Bonnie described to Lobo what the government had against him.

Lobo refused to say anything. He just sat there in abject fear, his eyes darting from Bonnie to Chavis and back to Bonnie again, shaking his head.

Bonnie tried to convince him that the best thing he could do for himself was to cooperate.

Chavis tried, too.

But Lobo wasn't talking.

After nearly an hour, it was obvious to Bonnie that Lobo wasn't going to talk, so she ended the interview and Lobo was sent back to his cell.

Over the next two months, Bonnie reached out to Lobo several more times. Rooney did, also. The two of them met with Chavis, and the three of them met with Lobo. But he still wasn't having it.

Pressed by her own superiors to move the case along, Bonnie had no option but to indict Lobo on drug money-laundering charges. Bail was denied because he was a flight risk.

Now that he was fully logged into the system, Bonnie was in no hurry to speed up the process. She let Lobo sit in the MDC for six months.

That was a lot of time to spend alone in a cell, thinking about life, constantly surrounded by the sound of metal on metal and men screaming throughout the night, the smell of disinfectant, the mind-numbing daily routine and the lack of daylight.

Eventually, he couldn't stand it anymore.

Which is exactly what Bonnie had been counting on.

Lobo decided he had to do something to help himself. He called for Chavis, discussed it with her, and she phoned Bonnie to say that Lobo might, finally, be willing to work out a deal.

Bonnie knew, however, that prisoners are always playing mind games with prosecutors, and if that's what Lobo was doing, she couldn't afford to let him win any points. "Not interested. Why should I bother? I already gave him his chance. I'm not going to schlep all the way to Brooklyn to see him again. He can tell it to the jury."

Chavis persisted, "He wants to speak to you. You've got to talk to him. He says he's ready. Please."

She thought about it. "No . . . why should I . . . not worth it . . ." But after Chavis asked her to do it as a personal favor, she finally agreed. "Tell him, okay, I'll talk to him, but he better have something to say."

Chavis passed along Bonnie's message, and without any hesitation, Lobo agreed.

The marshals drove him the couple of hours to Suffolk County, in handcuffs, from Brooklyn to the old federal courthouse on Rabro Drive in Hauppauge, and sat him down in an interview room with Chavis.

Bonnie stepped through the door and right away said to Lobo, "If you have something to say, you better say it now because I'm not going to spend any time listening to your lawyer telling me that you're too scared to talk."

"I am scared," Lobo blurted out in English. "He will kill me. I don't want to get deported. I'm afraid for my family."

Bonnie promised, "If you cooperate, you can stay in the United States. We can protect your family and they can stay, too. But you have to tell me the truth."

"I will." He nodded several times. "I will."

She wanted to know, "Who will kill you?"

Shaking his head and breathing very deeply, as if he was trying to psyche himself up to tell her, there was a long pause before he blurted out, "Monsalve."

"Who?" The name meant nothing to her.

"Monsalve," he said. "Juan Albeiro Monsalve. He owned Tele-Austin."

This was news to Bonnie. "No, no, no . . ." She had too much experience with suspects lying. "You owned Tele-Austin. The businesses were yours."

"It's not me," he insisted. "The businesses . . . they're not mine. It's him." Lobo insisted, "The paperwork says me but I was only the manager. I was the front. I worked for him. It's really Monsalve."

Bonnie stared at him for a few moments, said, "Okay, I want to hear more," and sat down.

Lobo told her this story:

Juan Albeiro Monsalve, a Colombian national, had been running a cocaine distribution operation in Queens, moving six hundred to eight hundred kilos into New York every month. That added up to be between seven and ten tons a year. And he'd been doing it for nearly six years. The drugs were shipped from Colombia to Mexico, then smuggled into the United States across the California border. Once a shipment arrived in Los Angeles, a team of couriers would bring it to New York.

In some cases, couriers would fly with the drugs in their checked-in luggage. But Monsalve's preferred method of transport was to have older women drive the drugs across the country, packed into RVs, because older women in cars like that attracted less attention.

With so much money coming off the streets, Monsalve needed a way to wash his dirty money and get it to Colombia, which is why he opened the storefront agencies. They were Tele-Austin I, Tele-Austin II, and Around the World Travel—the three that Lobo managed—and a fourth, called Telefolklor.

On the day of the Tele-Austin raid, Lobo came back from lunch, found the shutters closed, banged on them, and heard a man inside tell him that he couldn't come in. He demanded to know why and the man said because there were federal agents inside and that the office was closed. So he ran away to Colombia, to see Monsalve, who was living in Bogotá. Lobo told Monsalve about the raid, but Monsalve had already heard that the police had shut down all three premises.

"He was very unhappy about that," Lobo said to Bonnie. "And when he is unhappy about anything, he kills people. His nickname is El Loco." The crazy one.

Bonnie asked, "Who did he kill?"

Lobo said there had been two murders in Queens, and another somewhere else in the States, possibly out west. He said he'd also heard rumors of several more murders in Colombia.

For the first time, Bonnie believed she might be able to work Lobo. He could hand her a lot of big players, especially Monsalve.

"As long as you keep talking," she promised Lobo, "you can do yourself a lot of good."

He responded quietly, "I know."

"Tell me about the murders in the United States."

He said he really only knew about the two in Queens, but couldn't remember the exact dates. He recalled that one of the victims was a drug dealer named Munoz, who was buying cocaine from Monsalve, twenty to thirty kilos at a time, and not paying for it. He said that after Monsalve warned Munoz and still didn't get his money, he hired an assassin to murder him. "It was in a pool hall."

The other victim was named Rojas. He, too, owed Monsalve money for a cocaine deal. But, Lobo said, Rojas knew how violent Monsalve was whenever someone betrayed him, so Rojas tried to kill Monsalve first. When Monsalve heard that there was a contract out on him, he hired someone to murder Rojas. Lobo said that Monsalve and a girlfriend were both standing on the sidewalk outside a nightclub in Queens when the assassin went inside, because Monsalve wanted to be certain the job got done.

Bonnie wanted to know, "Who's the girlfriend?"

Lobo answered, "Her name is Maria Vega."

4

As soon as she walked out of the interview room, Bonnie phoned Rooney. And as soon as he hung up with her, Rooney started working to find Juan Albeiro Monsalve.

There was no way Bonnie could indict or, eventually, prosecute Monsalve just on Lobo's story. To get Monsalve for trafficking and money laundering, they needed solid evidence. What's more, murder in the commission of drug trafficking is a federal offense—and a capital offense—which meant they also needed enough evidence for two counts of that charge. One for the murder of Rojas. One for the murder of Munoz.

If they could pull this off, Rooney figured, it would be the single biggest feather in El Dorado's cap.

He began by running Monsalve's name through every database he had at his disposal. But law enforcement agencies are competitive, which means that databases aren't automatically linked together, which means that he had to go through them one by one.

He searched TECS, the "Technical Enforcement Communications" database that Customs maintained. And he searched NADDIS, the DEA's "Narcotics and Dangerous Drugs Information System." In principle, if something was in TECS there should have been a note saying that there is also something in NADDIS. But he didn't find anything in either.

Next, he wondered what the FBI knew. But access to their main database is closed to anyone outside the bureau. It's even closed to the U.S. Attorney's office. So Rooney asked a friendly FBI agent to see what the bureau had on Monsalve, and the friendly FBI agent came back with, "Nothing."

Now he started all over again, this time spelling Monsalve's name every way he could think of. Then he searched by the names of the two murder victims, again, going through all the various possible spellings. He tried the Immigration database. Then he tried all the state and local databases. Finally, as a last resort, he fed the Tele-Austin addresses into DECS.

The "Drug Enforcement Clearing System" was a database that the DEA used to warn other law enforcement agencies of addresses of interest. DECS did not provide strategic information about a specific case, it simply gave a heads-up so that if one group was sitting on an address and a second group happened along, they wouldn't confuse each other for bad guys and start shooting.

Much to Rooney's surprise, DECS flagged a hit on both Tele-Austin addresses, noting that "Redrum" had an interest.

Redrum, which comes from the word "murder" spelled backwards, is a joint task force of the DEA, NYPD, and New York State Troopers, set up specifically to investigate violent drug-related homicides.

During the 1990s, Redrum did a lot of work on a particularly vicious drug gang out of Queens called Los Tuzos. These were Colombian kids—some as young as thirteen—who bragged openly about murder. At one point, in the mid-1990s, Los Tuzos went to war against a rival gang known as Mono's Crew, a band of thugs named for their drug-dealing leader. Bodies were dropping on a daily basis. One day the NYPD would find two bodies, the next day they'd find three, the day after that they'd find two more. Word on the street was that the leader of Los Tuzos had worked for Mono until the two had a falling-out, which sparked the war that promised to go on until one side eliminated the other.

In fact, it went on for months. And although there were some people left standing at the end, one person who kept popping up in that investigation was a Colombian hit man named Johnson Guzman, aka Franklin Lopez.

The NYPD had already arrested him and convicted him in connection with contract killings for Los Tuzos. Guzman, who ultimately confessed to ten murders, was facing life in prison without any possibility of parole. However, hoping that a judge might eventually strike off the clause, "without possibility of parole" Guzman had already negotiated a deal to cooperate with his Redrum handlers to help them dismantle Los Tuzos.

The name Guzman didn't mean anything to Rooney, but Redrum had Los Tuzos tied into the murders of Rojas and Munoz. Also, Monsalve's name had come up in connection with the two dead guys, which is how the Tele-Austin addresses wound up in DECS.

In the very early morning hours of Sunday, March 20, 1994, officially the first day of spring, employees of the La Petrigal Nightclub in Jackson Heights were just closing up. Later they told police that they were all in the backroom when they heard the shots. A low-level cocaine dealer named Manuel Rojas had been hanging out at the club that night, and was supposedly alone at the bar, when a man came in off the street—no one could say when—walked up behind Rojas, pulled out a gun and shot him in the head and the arm. By the time the employees rushed out to find Rojas bleeding to death on the floor, the shooter was gone. Two of the employees drove Rojas to the hospital, but he was pronounced dead on arrival.

Armed with that information, Rooney went back to the NYPD detectives who'd investigated the case, and reinterviewed some of the original witnesses. He found that after Monsalve threatened to kill Rojas if he didn't pay for the cocaine, Rojas got in touch with his two brothers back in Colombia and the three of them plotted to murder Monsalve. But Monsalve found out about it, killed the Rojas brothers first, ordered the killing of all of the male members of the Rojas family—including a retarded brother—then came after Manuel in New York.

So far, Lobo's version of events was holding up.

Six months later, on Friday night November 4, Alvaro Munoz was with some friends at a basement hangout called Abel's Pool Hall. Munoz turned out to be a part owner of the place and, supposedly, had paid for his share with cocaine money that he owed to Monsalve. A man came down the stairs, walked right up to Munoz who was standing near a table, shoved a gun in his head and pulled the trigger. In the confusion that followed, the shooter disappeared up the stairs and out onto the street. Someone called for an ambulance and Munoz was still alive when it arrived. But by the time they got him to the hospital, he was also DOA.

Again, Rooney went back to the original investigators, spoke with some of the witnesses, and substantiated Lobo's claim that Monsalve had ordered that murder, as well.

The NYPD hadn't originally linked the crimes. They treated the two murders as separate and unrelated, at least until they identified the triggermen in both murders as a couple of Los Tuzos members. That's what brought Redrum into it.

One of the triggermen was a teenager named Juan Zapata, aka Juancho. He was supposedly the man who'd killed Rojas. But before the police could put him on trial, he died. The second man was supposedly Juan Dairon Marin Henoa, aka Chino, a twenty-year-old whose claim to fame on the street was being a crack shot. Legend had it that Chino was so good with a 9mm semiautomatic pistol, he could put a bullet through someone's head from fifty feet. Chino also liked to brag that, as a teenager, he'd killed people on assignment for the Medellin cocaine cartel boss, Pablo Escobar.

As it turned out, by the time Redrum got to Chino, he was already in jail on separate murder charges. In December 1993, he'd taken a contract on a two-bit player in the Russian Maffiya named Vladimir Beigelman. The Russian had been helping some Colombians move white powder into New York and, at the same time, help-ing himself to some of their white powder. When the NYPD caught up to Chino—who was clearly not the brightest child God ever created—he immediately, and without encouragement from the police, confessed to eleven other hits.

Chino was so willing to brag about his success as a killer to any-body, that he also admitted to being involved with the murders of both Rojas and Munoz. But he swore he didn't pull the trigger in either case.

At one point, Chino had agreed to cooperate with the police, but he soon breached his deal with them. Still, he was the one who led the police to the man who'd hired Los Tuzos to fulfill the Rojas and Munoz contracts.

That was Guzman.

Like Lobo, Guzman was also being held in the MDC—it turned out the two men did know each other—so Bonnie and Rooney ar-ranged to interview him.

A light-skinned, mild-mannered, soft-spoken man in his thirties, Guzman stood five foot nine and was hardly a Hollywood version of a professional hit man. In fact, he might easily have been mistaken for a milquetoast accountant, except that he shaved his head. Bonnie also decided that Guzman had beautiful blue eyes.

Surprisingly forthcoming, Guzman seemed happy to talk about his life, almost as if he welcomed their company. He said that back home in Colombia, his father had worked on a coffee plantation, but abandoned his family when Guzman was just seven years old. Two years later, his mother—who'd been taking in laundry to pay for food—left for the States where she hoped to be able to earn enough money to send something home. He was raised by his uncle and his older brother until he was twelve, when his mother brought him to New York.

He said that because he didn't do well in school, he spent most of his teenage years on the streets. He fathered a child when he was eighteen but never set up a home with the child's mother because her parents didn't want their daughter to have anything to do with Guzman. A few years later he fathered a second child with a second woman, and after that, he had a third child with a third woman. He worked as a dishwasher, an office cleaner, and a mechanic. He said he got into contract killing because it was an easier way to make money.

But, then, Guzman wanted Bonnie and Rooney to understand, "I would never just kill anyone."

Bonnie asked, "What do you mean?"

He said, "I have a code of ethics."

"Code of ethics?" Bonnie found that bizarre for a professional killer to say. "How can you have a code of ethics when you murder people for money?"

"Why not?" He maintained, "There are certain lines I won't cross."

She looked at him, then at Rooney, then back at Guzman. "Certain lines you won't cross? Like what?"

"For some of the contracts I accepted," he said, "I pulled the trigger myself. But for others, I couldn't. Those are the ones I sub-contracted to Los Tuzos."

That didn't make sense to her. "If you kill someone face-to-face, that's one thing. But why would you pay a fee to Los Tuzos to do the job?"

"It's not difficult to understand," he said. "The ones I killed face-to-face were trying to kill me. That was easy. But I can't just shoot someone I don't know. If I have nothing against that person . . . why would I kill them? Those are the ones I paid someone else to do."

That still sticks in Bonnie's mind as one of the strangest admissions she'd ever heard. Rooney found it hard to accept as well. Still, Guzman maintained several times that it was true.

Bonnie now began questioning him about the Rojas and Munoz murders.

Guzman freely admitted, "Yes, I took those contracts." He said that he'd been paid fifty thousand dollars per contract, but subcontracted the killings to Los Tuzos for twenty thousand dollars each.

She asked, "Who paid you?"

Without any hesitation he answered, "A man named Monsalve."

Looking to substantiate the information they'd obtained from Guzman and Lobo, Bonnie, Rooney, and Toby reinterviewed the women who'd worked at Tele-Austin.

Especially Isabel.

She now admitted, with tears running down her face, that she'd lied about Lobo owning the storefronts because she was terrified of Monsalve. She said she was much too afraid to talk about him. She said, "When people talk about him, he kills them."

One of the people he killed was a woman named Berta—last name unknown—a twenty-three-year-old who'd worked at Tele-Austin I. Isabel confirmed that Monsalve believed Berta had stolen twelve thousand dollars from him. Berta always denied she'd taken any money and Lobo said he never thought Berta stole anything. But Lobo was unable to convince Monsalve who seemed determined to teach Berta, and all the other young women working there, a lesson.

Lobo told Rooney he'd overheard Monsalve on the phone with one of his henchman—a fellow who cannot be identified except by the alias Hector Rivera—giving the order to kill Berta. Lobo claimed that he'd pleaded with Hector to tell Monsalve to spare this woman's life, but Monsalve didn't care.

In early 1996, Berta returned to Colombia, although it's not entirely clear why she left New York. One version has it that she feared for her life and thought she'd be safe back home. Another is that Monsalve cooked up some sort of ruse to get her there. Whichever, Hector and two other men found her, rode up to her on motorcycles, and shot her six times in the head. Then, to hide the bullet wounds, the killers commandeered a truck and ran over Berta's skull several times, literally flattening it on the highway.

Rooney suspected that Guzman was there that day, but when he interviewed Guzman about Berta, Guzman would not admit to that killing.

In any case, Hector Rivera, also sometimes referred to by his associates either as "El Negro," because of his dark skin, or "El Chimp," because he looked like an ape, was added to the list of suspects that Bonnie wanted arrested.

Next, Rooney uncovered information about the murder of Umberto Abad Moreno. He'd worked for Monsalve as a drug courier, bodyguard, and sometime assassin. Monsalve decided he was becoming too arrogant and, apparently based on nothing more than that, ordered his death. He gave the contract to two Mexicans, but sent one of his own men to oversee the shooting, which took place in an auto body repair shop in Los Angeles.

This was the killing that Lobo had referred to as happening somewhere else in the country, probably out west.

Once Abad was dead, the three assassins cut off his hands so that no one could fingerprint the body. They put the fingers in an ice cooler and filled it with cement. Abad's remains were then dumped in a lake.

After that one, there was the murder of a trusted Monsalve associate called El Meme. According to at least one witness, El Meme—who was in his mid-twenties—had marked up the price of cocaine he'd obtained from Monsalve and kept the extra money for himself. There was also a story that one night in early 1995, El Meme got drunk and tried to make out with Monsalve's wife, Liliana. Monsalve wasn't there at the time, but heard about it. On his orders, El Meme's hands and feet were torched, and then he was shot.

Around the same time, Monsalve suspected that a trafficker in Colombia, Henry Gutierrez, was skimming money from him and ordered him killed.

The same fate was dealt to a man named José Daniel Barrihueta

Laguna when he took up with one of Monsalve's girlfriends, identified in the Colombian media as Nancy Cadavid.

A nice-looking woman with dark hair—a long way from the usual Botoxed, boob-jobbed bimbo that seem in fashion with so many Colombian traffickers—Nancy met Monsalve when she was just thirteen. Already the mother of a baby girl with some guy in Colombia who'd refused to assume his responsibilities, she came to the States where Monsalve wined her, dined her and, at least in the beginning, treated her well. But she was uneducated and far too immature to realize that the more money he spent on her, the more he decided she owed him. Although he already had other wives and several other girlfriends, for a time, Nancy became his number one. When she bore him a son, he set her up in a fourth-floor apartment at 3825 Parsons Boulevard, in Flushing, Queens.

The Lobos lived upstairs, so to help build her case against Monsalve, Bonnie reached out to Lobo's estranged wife.

A sturdy woman in her thirties with dark hair who rarely smiled, Doris Lobo told Bonnie that she was furious with Monsalve for abandoning her husband when he was arrested. She said he refused to come up with any money to help pay for an attorney, and also refused to give her any money to tide her over while Lobo was in jail. She told Bonnie that she knew a lot about Monsalve and promised that she could be a very useful source.

Bonnie felt that was a promising start. But the longer the two women talked—and over the course of several weeks, Rooney spent time talking to Doris, too—the more obvious it became that Doris was simply looking to play both ends against the middle. She complained that Lobo wasn't being treated well in jail and made vague promises of being able to help in other investigations, that is, if Bonnie would make life easier for Lobo. Doris asked, several times, if the government paid fees to informants.

According to Doris, couriers had occasionally delivered Monsalve's drugs to her apartment when they couldn't find Nancy at home to leave them with her. But when Rooney pressed Doris for the dates of those deliveries, she was much too vague. He and Bonnie were soon worrying that Doris might be unreliable. She ran off at the mouth too much, without actually saying a lot. And after a while, they concluded that Doris wasn't going to be as helpful as Doris pretended she could be.

Although she still had stories to tell. Doris claimed that Monsalve was obsessively jealous and that when he wasn't home, he demanded Nancy not leave the apartment. He didn't want her going out and, possibly, meeting someone else. He would even phone her there, randomly throughout the day, to make sure she was staying put. He didn't seem to understand that as a mother, she had certain commitments to their son, made all the more difficult by the fact that the child suffered from epilepsy. On those rare occasions when she didn't answer the phone—either because she couldn't get to it in time or, perhaps, because she'd taken the child to the doctor—he'd threatened to kill her family members back in Colombia.

After a while, Doris said, Nancy got so fed up with his mental and physical abuse, she ran back to Colombia. That's when Monsalve located her living with Barrihueta and warned that he would kill her sister and Barrihueta if she didn't return to New York.

Fearing for their lives, and her own, she complied.

It turned out that Monsalve killed Barrihueta anyway. He left Nancy's sister alone, but he murdered her cousin, Angela Hincapie, because he thought she was the one who'd encouraged Nancy to leave him.

"It's time," Rooney said, dropping a very thick file onto Bonnie's desk in Hauppauge.

There was no doubt in either of their minds that Monsalve was a major target.

But Bonnie seemed a bit hesitant. "I don't know."

"I do." Rooney had just stumbled across a pair of open homicides on Redrum's books—one on Long Island and one in Houston—which might also be attributable to Monsalve. "It's time to charge the fucker with drugs, money laundering, and at least two counts of capital murder."

She looked at him with trepidation, then confessed, "I've never done a murder case."

"Who cares?" He said, "Let's just charge him."

She wasn't sure that she really wanted to be running headfirst like that into her liberal radical law-school mind-set. "It's a capital case."

"Indict him."

"Romedio . . . it's a death penalty case."

He shrugged. "So?"

She shook her head. "So . . . I need more than just two people saying he killed someone."

Of course, Rooney understood where she was coming from, but he also knew who they were dealing with. "We'll get Lobo and Guzman to testify in front of a grand jury. Just get Monsalve's name into the system."

Bonnie was genuinely uneasy going down this path. "Is there any DNA? Are there fingerprints? I mean, come on, it's a death case."

"It doesn't matter." He assured her, "We're never going to catch the fucker, anyway. Just charge him."

She took a deep breath. "We're not going to catch him?"

"No way," he said, maybe even believing it himself. "He knows Lobo is in jail. He knows Guzman is in jail. He knows he's safe in Colombia. Would you come back?"

Bonnie stared at the huge file in front of her and finally said, "Okay."

A week or so later, she presented her case to a federal grand jury, put Guzman on the stand to testify, and indicted Monsalve on all of the charges, including two counts of federal murder.

"Done," she said to Rooney as soon as the judge issued the warrant against Monsalve. "We've indicted him. We've charged him. We've even got a piece of paper that says we can arrest him."

"Done," Rooney said.

Then she added, "Except, we can't extradite him."

Even though there's no statute of limitation on murder, all the crimes in the Monsalve warrant predated the 1997 extradition treaty which the U.S. had signed with Colombia.

"Guess not," Rooney conceded.

"So . . ." Bonnie asked, "Now what?"

"Now . . . we've got him in the system." He could see she was still apprehensive. "Don't worry about him. He's not that stupid. I'm telling you, the fucker's never coming back."

"You're sure?"

"I'm positive," he said.

Still not totally convinced, Bonnie and Rooney went to see Lobo, hoping the indictment against Monsalve would reassure him.

She said, "You can stop worrying."

Lobo wasn't totally convinced, either. "He kills anyone who betrays him. He always extracts revenge. Look what he did to people who stole from him."

"He's not coming back here," Rooney said.

Bonnie added, "Not now. Now with this warrant hanging over his head."

"He doesn't have to be here," Lobo wanted them to understand. "He has people here. He can kill my family in Colombia. What do you think he'll do to anyone who testifies against him? If he doesn't extract revenge, he loses face with his bosses and they will kill him."

"His bosses?" Rooney was surprised because he and Bonnie had just assumed that Monsalve was the boss. They'd both been under the impression that he ran his own operation. "Who are his bosses?"

"The people he works for." Lobo answered

"Who does he work for?" Bonnie asked.

Lobo said, "The ones in Cartago."

She stared at him. "Who are the ones in Cartago?"

Rooney wanted to know, "Where's that?"

Lobo showed them on a map that Cartago was about halfway between Cali and Medellin, in the high mountains of the Valle del Cauca.

The instant that Bonnie and Rooney saw Cartago on the map, they also saw the three cities surrounding Cartago—Armenia, Pereira, and Manizales. And the penny dropped.

"That's where you were sending the money," Rooney said.

"Yes," Lobo confirmed. "For Monsalve's bosses in Cartago."

"So," Bonnie decided, almost jokingly, "this is the Armenia, Pereira, and Manizales Cartel?"

"No," Lobo answered very seriously. "It's the *Norte Valle* Cartel."

It was the first time that Bonnie, Rooney, or anyone at El Dorado had ever heard the name.

There was no mention of it in the DEA database.

The biggest cartel in Colombia, and it was as if it didn't exist.

5

Wherever you look, you are constantly reminded that Colombia today is a dangerous place to be.

Drug money has done this.

The narco-economy turned a once backward, peaceful Third World agrarian nation into a corrupt and violent society.

In the capital, Bogotá, a sweepingly large city of 6.2 million people that sits 8,000 feet high in the northern Andes—a place where you should find all that South America's oldest democracy once was and could be again—a constant undertone of insecurity gnaws at you, like some irritating, only-just-audible, background noise. You sense it wherever you go. And, wherever you go, there is no way to avoid it.

Wherever you look there are armed police and SWAT teams, especially in the more affluent parts of the city where residents have political muscle. They demand protection from all the usual threats, but especially from the very real threats of home invasions, kidnappings, and contract murders.

And there are armed uniformed police officers on a motorbike—that's not a typo with a missing plural—it's two policemen riding piggyback on one motorbike, because the local cops can't afford enough motorbikes.

And there are private guards with guns and dogs who stand sentry in front of businesses.

And there are Colombian soldiers in battle dress with machine guns, stationed at airports, train stations, government offices, police stations, and courthouses.

And there are private police forces, armed with substantial weapons, patrolling those more affluent neighborhoods where residents have learned the hard way that they cannot necessarily trust the government, which in the past has been infested with politicians and bureaucrats who are in the pockets of traffickers.

Drug money funds the right wing paramilitary group Autodefensas Unidas de Colombia (AUC) in the north and the left wing terrorist organization Fuerzas Armadas Revolucionarias de Colombia (FARC) throughout the rest of the country. A third group, the National Liberation Army, known by the Spanish acronym ELN, is a leftist guerrilla organization with spurious ties to the FARC. Sometimes they cooperate, sometimes they kill each other. Mostly the ELN does whatever drug deals it can to stay in business. While its power has been greatly reduced in recent years and the ELN has, at times, been critical of the drug trade, it still protects, regulates, and taxes production in the diminishing areas it controls.

Drug money corrupts the political system, the judiciary, and law enforcement. Honest cops, like honest judges, all too often, die young. Those who live long enough to retire, all too often, have bullet wounds to show for their efforts, and harrowing stories of having just escaped assassination.

Drug money fuels crime and gratuitous brutality, and throughout Colombia today, gratuitous brutality is a regular occurrence.

Tourists in Bogotá are warned, for example, not to hail a taxi on the street, especially late at night. To protect yourself, you have to know that there are two types of taxis, yellow and white. The white taxis work off hotel ranks and the drivers are registered with the hotel. They are regarded as being relatively safe. Although, in Colombia, there are never any guarantees. The yellow taxis are the ones that roam the streets. And, while many drivers are honest, some are decidedly not. Every week or so a tourist gets into a yellow taxi and is merely driven around the block where other men jump in, with guns, and drag him to the nearest ATM machine where he is ordered to empty his bank account.

Every week or so, another dead body is found in some street not far from an ATM machine.

The profound influence of drug money on life throughout the entire country cannot be overstated. And, in the past twenty-five years, it has spilled over to neighboring countries. Venezuela is now totally polluted, as evidenced by trafficking, drug transshipment, political corruption, and violence. The black economies of Ecuador and Peru are deeply dependent for foreign income on coca paste exports. Brazil has become the largest cocaine market in South America and deteriorated into a violent, crime-ridden state. Panama is the region's primary staging point for drugs and bulk cash, while the Colon Free Trade Zone is the world's largest market for counterfeit goods, illegal arms, and other contraband, most of it paid for with Colombian-sourced drug money.

And there certainly is a lot to be spread around. According to the World Health Organization, worldwide, more money is spent on illicit substances than on food. Much of that is cocaine. Where cocaine is concerned, Colombia rules. And where Colombia is concerned, the narco-economy distorts absolutely every aspect of daily life.

Illegal markets disguised as modern shopping malls are filled with contraband—computers, televisions, cameras, stereos, designer goods—all bought abroad with narco-dollars and smuggled into the country. Known as "*sanandrecitos*," they're named for the Colombian island off the coast of Nicaragua, San Andres, that is used as a transshipment point for drugs moving into the Caribbean, Panama, and Mexico, and goods and contraband coming back to Colombia. Everybody in the country knows about the *sanandrecitos,* that buying there indirectly supports the drug trade and directly robs the state of import duties. But the goods are new and top of the line and the prices are cheaper than in regular retail outlets. The people in power also know about the *sanandrecitos* and could do something about them, but don't because many of the *sanandrecitos* are owned by the people in power.

The country may be famous for coffee, but unlike the coffee business, where exports are paid for legitimately through global financial markets, the narco-economy is cash based. Shrink-wrapped pallets of cash arrive in the country, matching the drugs that have created this wealth, pretty much, pound for pound. One hundred kilos of cocaine sent out usually nets back one hundred kilos of cash. A ton of cocaine equals a ton of cash.

Gargantuan volumes of cash arrive on ships by the containerful from Boston, New York, Philadelphia, and Miami. It's hidden inside machinery on planes from Chicago, Detroit, St. Louis, and Denver. And it's secreted into the wall linings of trucks from California, Arizona, New Mexico, and Texas, shipped through Mexico and Panama.

Cash arrives from everywhere, even brought in by ordinary people doing ordinary things, like traveling as a family.

Landing in Bogotá on the midday flight from Miami, a handsomely dressed Colombian couple with two young children were met in the corridor between the air-bridge and Customs, by a man wearing an airport security access badge. He greeted them quickly, took the woman's well-packed, over-the-shoulder carry-on, then hurried away. The whole scene lasted ten seconds.

No one minded that an American was walking right behind them and witnessed it.

This is life in Colombia.

If the story of Colombia yesterday begins with Simón Bolívar, the man who created a region of nations, then the story of Colombia today starts with Pablo Emilio Escobar Gaviria, the man who put the country at the epicenter of a global empire.

By the time he celebrated his fortieth birthday in 1989, the most famous man in South America controlled 80 percent of the world's cocaine and was the seventh richest billionaire on the planet.

As long as the Colombian government turned a blind eye—which it did because so many important people were on his payroll—Escobar ran his business with impunity from his various properties around Medellin, but especially from Hacienda Napoles, one hundred miles east of the city, in Puerto Triunfo.

On his eight-square-mile property, complete with fourteen lakes, he built himself a zoo stocked with elephants, buffalo, giraffes, ostriches, elephants, antelopes, camels, zebras, lions, and hippopotamuses. He employed seven hundred farmhands, had his own airfield, had stables for dozens of horses, had his own five hundred-seat bull ring, and built himself a large classic car collection with garages to maintain and show off the cars. Life-sized models of dinosaurs locked in combat with other prehistoric beasts were scattered across his countryside. Hanging over the cement entrance to the estate was a Piper Super Cub airplane which, legend had it, was the one Escobar used to make his first drug run. A few years ago, someone turned the hacienda into an Escobal theme park.

There were other properties, corporate jets, young women in bling and, for a while, there was even political office. But nothing was enough for Escobar's ego, and he soon became so intent on self-aggrandizement, so driven to generate international publicity for himself, that he turned himself into a huge embarrassment to Bogotá. The then Colombian president, César Gaviria, had no choice but to give in to pressure, mostly from the Americans, and order Escobar's arrest.

Everyone knew where to find Escobar, but Gaviria also knew that, if he sent troops to capture him, there'd be a bloodbath. So the government opened talks with him, hoping to make a deal. They said he had to come in. Everything else was negotiable.

For Escobar, surrender opened the possibility of extradition to the United States, which was the absolute last thing that he wanted or would ever accept. He couldn't buy judges there and, he knew, if the Americans locked him up he would die in prison. Instead, he supposedly made this counteroffer: Let me stay here, at home in Colombia, and I will single-handedly pay off the national debt.

True or not, the Colombian government agreed to let him stay.

With extradition off the table, Escobar was willing to serve a few years, because that would wipe his slate clean, but he refused to go to the dreaded Combita Prison.

A maximum-security jail high in the mountains of Boyaca Province, eighty miles northeast of Bogotá, Combita is where all "*los extraditablos*" are held until they're shipped out of the country. Notorious for being horribly cold—there is no heat and there is no hot water—everyone who has ever been locked up there complains about the freezing conditions and ice-cold showers. The place is falling apart and prisoners are given no more than two dollars' worth of food a day. If there is anything just about bearable at Combita, it is that every forty-five days, prisoners are allowed a conjugal visit. But even that is pretty awful, as the tiny room they each use in turn is barren except for a filthy, old, single-sized cot.

If it wasn't going to be Combita, the government didn't seem to know where else to send him. So Escobar offered this alternative: Let me build my own prison, at my expense, and you can keep me there.

Officially called La Catedral—but more often referred to as Club Medellin or Hotel Escobar—he constructed a comfortable suite of several rooms which would serve as his cell, in a modern farmhouse on a hill overlooking Medellin. The place came complete with a soccer field, a well-stocked bar, a Jacuzzi, a waterfall, fax machines, phones, his personally selected prison guards, live-in girlfriends, and his own chef.

Astonishingly, the Colombians actually bragged to the world, we've locked up Escobar.

Except that he continued running his business from there, as if nothing had changed. That is, until a year or so later when he got fed up with prison life and let himself out. He returned to Hacienda Napoles to traffic drugs, declare war on upstart competitors, and murder everyone who got in his way.

The government objected, so he declared war on the government.

At one point, over the course of an especially bloody two months, he was killing twenty people a day. He was responsible for the assassination of 30 judges, 457 policemen, and 110 innocent passengers on an Avianca Airlines jet that he ordered bombed out of the air.

As pressure mounted and the government upped the stakes by raising the price on his head, tossing money at his fate like chips in a poker game, an increasingly paranoid Escobar fought back. He killed those whom he couldn't bribe, and bribed those who knew that Escobar would kill them. It was said in Colombia that while half of the country was hunting for him, the other half was protecting him.

But Escobar was now fighting too many wars on too many fronts.

Some 205 miles and one mountain range to the south, in Cali, Gilberto Rodríguez Orejuela and his brother Miguel, along with their best friend José Santacruz Londoño, were fast becoming the heirs to Escobar's throne.

Cali is a city of two million people, and the cartel's influence on every aspect of life there is deeply entrenched. The Orejuelas merged trafficking with legitimate businesses, and one estimate has it that their drug money was running through 80 percent of all the commerce and industry in Cali. At their height, the Orejuelas' oversaw what has been called "the most powerful international organized crime group in history." They employed perhaps as many as 10,000 to 12,500 people in Colombia, and thousands more outside the country. They also ran a huge fleet of aircraft—including Boeing 727s—to ferry drugs to Mexico. At one point, the DEA estimated that the Orejuelas' personal wealth exceeded $2 billion.

They challenged Escobar's supremacy, but competition in the drug trade does not make for better product. It simply lowers prices which, in turn, increases violence.

Now Escobar declared war on them, too.

Gilberto was a university-educated businessman, ten years older than Escobar, who ran a successful chain of pharmacies. His younger brother, Miguel, was a lawyer. Londoño had a degree in engineering, but became a student of the complex logistics of world trade and developed a real expertise in smuggling. At one point, Londoño was considered by many governments to be the most dangerous man in Latin America.

These three men had been trafficking together since 1970 and although they could be ferociously violent, their first instinct was the pragmatic approach. Whereas Escobar murdered anyone who got in his way or otherwise refused to cooperate—or did nothing at all and he just felt like killing them—the Orejuelas were comparatively more restrained. Their first choice was to send in armies of lawyers, inundating the courts with writs and motions. Option two was to hand out envelopes stuffed with cash. They spent tens of millions of dollars bribing judges and policemen. The assassins were demoted to option three.

The Cali mob rose in stature as the government chased Escobar off his ranches and from hiding place to hiding place. They watched as his old chums turned their backs on him, stealing what businesses they could, and as his grip on the cocaine trade slipped into chaos.

In the mid-1980s, Escobar and his cronies had formed a militia, recruiting teenagers out of the Medellin slums and coercing them to commit a reported eight thousand assassinations. Fighting fire with fire in the early 1990s, the Orejuelas and their cronies formed "Los Pepes"—People Persecuted by Pablo Escobar—to protect their labs, their ranches, their transportation networks, and to seek out and destroy Escobar's militiamen.

The end came for Escobar on December 2, 1993.

A special force of Colombian police commandos located him, cornered him, then killed him, on a rooftop in a middle-class Medellin barrio. Hardly anyone seemed surprised to learn, later, that they were acting on a tip-off from the Orejuelas.

The Medellin organization was called a cartel but wasn't. Instead, it was a classic corporate pyramid, closely resembling the structure of General Motors, with Escobar as chairman of the board and chief executive.

The Orejuelas looked on the cocaine business as just that, a business—like cattle ranching, pharmacies, even hamburgers—and accordingly based their corporate model on McDonald's. A main holding company oversaw manufacturing and the sale of product but, like the famous hamburger chain, they franchised much of their distribution.

Anyone who aspired to become a Cali franchisee was invited to fill out a detailed form which listed all his relatives so that the brothers had a Rolodex filled with people to kill if someone tried to betray them. Franchisees paid cash up front, or put up suitable collateral and, at that point, transport, marketing, sales, and money laundering were no longer the Orejuelas' problems. If cargoes were intercepted, it wasn't the Orejuelas' cocaine. If cash was confiscated, it wasn't the Orejuelas' money.

Such was the success of the Orejuelas' business model that by 1994, the Cali mob was racking up annual profits of around $7 billion, more than three times that of General Motors.

Such is the power of narco-dollars that as many as three hundred "minicartels" rushed into business with them.

One of these minicartels was, in fact, a cartel in the strictest sense. A group of uneducated degenerates who were brought up in the mountain villages around Cartago—at the northern tip of the Cauca Valley Department—banded together to raise money and buy product from the Orejuelas. They were soon joined by friends and family who'd been working for and with the Orejuelas. Through peasant cunning and vicious force, it wasn't long before the Orejuelas' most successful franchisee became their staunchest competitors.

Then the Orejuelas' kingdom crumbled.

Less than two years after Escobar's death, in June and July of 1995, six of the seven men who ran the day-to-day affairs of the Cali mob—including both brothers and Londoño—were arrested. Londoño managed to escape but, within months, he was killed in a shoot-out.

The Orejuelas tried to run their business from jail, got out for a time, and hoped to put Humpty back together again. But the government had learned its lesson with Escobar, so the Orejuelas were extradited to the United States where they are currently serving thirty years in federal prison without the possibility of parole.

Immediately, the gangs from Cartago moved into the commercial void left by the Cali cartel. They took over some smaller rivals, murdered competitors, forced other rivals out of business and assumed the Orejuelas' mantle. Even then, their names had not yet appeared as major blips on the radar of U.S. law enforcement. Some agencies, like the DEA, knew who these men were. But no American law enforcement agency had begun to make a serious case against any one from Cartago.

Bonnie and Rooney didn't yet know it, but the field was wide open for them.

Essentially, this was a mob of independent brokers who ran their own organizations, united into a cooperative for mutual benefit, much like the syndicate of the five Mafia families who once ran crime in New York. An army of too many generals with nearly eight thousand foot soldiers, they coinvested in loads, competed against each other, shared shipments, coinvested in labs, shared labs, stole from each other, joined forces when it suited them, and cheated each other when it suited them. Most of the major players had grown up in and around Cartago. Some were founding members, some assumed command over a faction when one of the others was captured or killed. Some branched out on their own. Many had no more than a third-grade education.

Individually and collectively, they forged personal relationships with members of the FARC and the AUC. They purchased coca from the FARC and processed it in labs deep inside AUC territory.

Their cocaine sailed from several ports along the Caribbean coast in small, fast boats, which could handle one-and-a-half-ton loads. Their shipments from the Pacific coast left from Buenaventura in tankers, shrimp boats, and large fishing vessels, with loads averaging three to five tons per boat. From there, Mexican gangs were commissioned to smuggle the drugs into California, where couriers would fly or drive them to New York.

To be king of the hill and stay there in the trafficking world, this bunch murdered whoever and whenever it took their fancy and constantly held the threat of unprovoked violence over the heads of everyone who worked for them or did business with them.

Individually and collectively, they were extraordinarily violent.

Some ran private armies of six hundred to eight hundred men, and kept a large squad of professional hit men on their payrolls. Between 1990 and 2004, they killed several thousand people, including each other, their relatives and their associates, while importing more than 1.2 million pounds of cocaine—545 metric tons—into the United States. They controlled nearly 60 percent of all the cocaine in the country for more than ten years, and for their efforts they would earn more than $10 billion.

When they were friendly, which meant when they were doing deals together and not killing each other, they decided they ruled the world.

They declared themselves the rightful owners of the Medellin and Cali legacies, avoided publicity, and convinced themselves that this would go on forever.

They took pride in calling themselves, *"los intocables"*—the untouchables.

Los Intocables.

All this was new to the El Dorado Task Force.

And the more Bonnie and Rooney looked into this bunch, the more fascinated both of them became. Lobo led them to Monsalve. Now Bonnie and Rooney wondered, could Monsalve lead them into the heart of the Norte Valle Cartel?

And, if they could get inside this group, could they systematically take it apart?

Around WTC6, and around the U.S. Attorney's office in Brooklyn, too, a lot of people were fast to write off Bonnie and Rooney as dreamers. Some of El Dorado's managers believed there were enough drug traffickers in New York, and enough storefront ren... Queens, to keep everyone busy for a long time.

In offices in Washington—at the Department of Justice and the Department of the Treasury and later at the Department of Homeland Security—the idea of taking on the world's most important drug cartel from a tiny outpost in Hauppauge, Long Island, was pure fantasy.

But Bonnie wasn't so sure.

And Rooney didn't give a damn what anybody thought.

6

Capital murder cases on the federal level are handled under the terms of the very strictly written "Death Penalty Protocol," which requires prosecutors to put their evidence and arguments through a series of hoops before the government will agree to the death penalty. Everything ends up on the attorney general's desk for him to take the final decision.

Long before anyone steps into a courtroom to face a jury, prosecutors must outline the facts and evidence of their case, explain any aggravating or mitigating factors, include whatever other relevant information they deem necessary and make a recommendation for the attorney general to rule on. That recommendation is also reviewed by a special committee which then makes its own independent recommendation to the attorney general.

In states like Texas, prosecutors tend to recommend for the death penalty. In states like New York, they tend to recommend against. In Bonnie's "Eastern District of New York" office, there have been only a few death-penalty prosecutions, none of which have ended with an execution. Those defendants who were found guilty wound up doing life without the possibility of parole.

While Bonnie has never been sure she wanted one of her cases to go that route, she says she absolutely understands that there are some people who have committed crimes so horrific that other people believe they deserve to die for them. And the more she looked at Monsalve and his crimes, the more she saw how some people could surmise that he qualified for the ultimate punishment. But staying true to herself, she says, she's never wanted to be the one to make that judgment call.

The Justice Department recognizes that many prosecutors have strong beliefs about such a serious matter and allows them an opt-out for the death-penalty part of the case. Prosecutors work the case they've been assigned and go right to the verdict. At that point, if they want to step away, another prosecutor is brought in to try the penalty phase.

Thinking that far in advance made Bonnie slightly uneasy. But worrying about that now, she told herself, was putting the cart before the horse. First things first meant building a watertight case against Monsalve.

It didn't matter that Monsalve himself probably had no intention of ever stepping foot in the States again, he was simply too important to leave on a back burner. Men like him always slip up and Bonnie wanted to make absolutely certain that everything was ready for him when he did. The new extradition treaty with Colombia meant that he could run, but he could not hide forever.

She would set out to prove that from approximately January 1993 through January 1997, Monsalve ran a cocaine distribution operation that imported thousands of kilos of cocaine from Colombia; that he smuggled the drugs through Mexico to Los Angeles or Texas and then transported them to New York by car or airplane; that he laundered the proceeds of his cocaine operation through the four money remitter storefronts in New York—Tele-Austin I, Tele-Austin II, Around the World Travel and Telefolklor—which were run by Ignacio Lobo, the manager of Monsalve's money-laundering operation.

To support that last claim, she intended to produce records from those businesses, which would prove that Monsalve laundered at least $70 million during the four years that they were in operation.

Furthermore, she would contend, Monsalve was notorious for exacting the ultimate penalty against those who betrayed him. And with the help of cooperating witnesses like Lobo and Johnson Guzman, she would prove that Monsalve ordered the murders of Manuel Rojas and Alvaro Munoz.

In addition to those murders, she would also present proof that he was responsible for numerous other killings.

The only problem was that just about everyone she spoke with about Monsalve was utterly petrified of him.

Maria Vega was still high on Bonnie's list as a possible cooperating witness. She was the former Monsalve girlfriend who'd been running his Telefolklor remitter and was supposedly with Monsalve on the sidewalk in front of the pool hall the night Munoz was killed. According to Guzman, Maria was also a drug courier for Monsalve. So Bonnie put together a complaint on Maria. Rooney and Toby arrested her, but ultimately Bonnie didn't prosecute her. Maria was too low down the pecking order and the only information she had to offer was that Monsalve was moving money. Obviously, Bonnie already knew that. She let Maria go, much to Toby's chagrin, because he kept telling Rooney, "She's hot."

Another person at the top of her cooperating witness list was CW7. She'd managed the Tele-Austin stores for a short time in 1993, when Monsalve replaced her with Lobo because Lobo is Colombian and CW7 is Bolivian. CW7 then opened two money remitters of her own, Tele-Lapaz and Universal. Bonnie had witnesses who told her that Monsalve sent excess money to CW7 when there was too much coming through his own four storefronts.

But CW7, who had one prior conviction as a drug courier, had since left New York for Bolivia. Bonnie assumed she'd fled to avoid being arrested again.

Rooney's attitude was, let's find out. He came up with a phone number for her down there and rang her.

At first, CW7 was very suspicious and wouldn't go near the subject of Monsalve. She wouldn't even say his name over the phone. She told Rooney that she was much too afraid to speak about that particular subject.

It was obvious to Rooney that CW7 feared their conversation was being recorded and that Monsalve would one day find out she'd ratted on him. So he changed the subject. He made small talk, speaking to her about her life in Bolivia and her life in New York and, after a while, he said he'd call back another time. He did. And again, the name Monsalve wasn't mentioned.

Over the course of six months, Rooney phoned CW7 every week or so. During those many phone calls—two people just chatting about the world—CW7 explained that she hadn't run away to avoid being arrested, that she'd gone home to help her daughter prepare for her wedding.

In the meantime, Bonnie indicted her on money-laundering charges. Some people in the office wondered, what are you wasting your time on her for? But Bonnie was counting on Rooney to work his charm, convinced that given time, they could flip her.

Eventually Rooney asked CW7 if and when she planned to come back. Her parents were living in New York, and she had other family here, too. He reminded her that she had a green card and that if she didn't come back, U.S. Immigration might take it away from her. If that happened, he said, she'd never be able to come back.

CW7 said she was worried that if she came back she'd be arrested.

Rooney told her the truth that, yes, she will be arrested. But he explained that if she came back voluntarily, and pleaded guilty, Bonnie would consider her a self-surrender and see that she was allowed out on bail.

CW7 said it was something she'd have to think about.

Understanding her predicament, Rooney didn't push her. And slowly but surely, CW7 seemed to be more and more amenable to surrendering.

He was totally up front with her, explaining that when she came back she'd have to spend her first night in New York in jail. He said he wanted her to be prepared for that. But then he assured her that she'd be arraigned early the next morning and at the hearing, Bonnie would not oppose bail. He gave her his word on that, and said that Bonnie did, too.

For CW7, coming back not only meant putting her past behind her and getting on with her life, it meant seeing her parents again. But before she made her decision, her daughter flew up, obviously, to test the waters. She met with Bonnie and Rooney—they went over the whole process and explained exactly what would happen—and she went home with reassurances from both of them that her mother would be permitted out on bail.

Shortly after CW7's daughter returned to Bolivia, CW7 phoned Rooney to say, okay.

He then flew to Bolivia with a U.S. Marshal to arrest her—it's standard operating procedure that the marshals accompany all fugitives—and the three of them flew back together.

Arriving late at night in New York, Rooney put CW7 in his car and headed for the MDC in Brooklyn. On the way, he phoned the jail to give them a heads-up that he was bringing in a prisoner. But the man on the other end of the phone said, "There's no room at the inn, pal, you have to take her to Manhattan."

So Rooney and CW7 headed for Manhattan and, along the way, Rooney phoned the Metropolitan Correctional Center (MCC) to tell them he had a prisoner.

But a fellow there said the same thing, "Sorry, we're full."

Rooney blurted out, "What the hell's going on? How can everybody be full? Who's just arrested seven hundred people?"

He never got an answer.

Third choice was the Nassau County jail in East Meadow—federal prisoners were sometimes temporarily housed there—but that was twenty-five or thirty miles back in the wrong direction. And by now it was 2 A.M.

Rooney was exhausted and he could see that CW7 was as well.

"I'm too tired to drive all the way out there to put you up for the night. It's been a long day and a long flight and anyway, the place is a shit hole." So he said to CW7, "I'll make you a deal. I'm going to take you to your mother and father. You can sleep there tonight, in your own bed."

She couldn't believe it. "I'm not going to jail? Really?"

"Really," he said. "But please . . . please don't run away. It would not be good. You've got to be there tomorrow morning at nine when I come to pick you up. This would be very bad for me if you disappeared."

She told him, "I've come all the way from Bolivia, I'm not going to run away."

The next morning when he went to her parents' home to fetch her, she was right there waiting for him, true to her word.

True to Bonnie's word, CW7 was arraigned and released on bail.

By now she was willing to talk about Monsalve's business, explaining for example how Maria Vega would bring in money for Monsalve. But she stopped short when it came to talking about him personally because, she said, she feared for the lives of her family.

Rooney and Toby reinterviewed as many of the young women who'd worked at Tele-Austin as they could find. Some had disappeared. Some refused to talk. The half a dozen or so who would talk were reminded that, by not mentioning Monsalve the first time around, they'd lied. These young women were warned that they had to tell the truth this time, or face the consequences. But they were still very afraid of Monsalve.

Bonnie also tried to bring Lobo's wife Doris into the case. She was now living with a twenty-four-year-old Ecuadorian boy, while still blaming Monsalve for abandoning her husband when he was arrested. She said Monsalve refused to give them any money for an attorney, and wouldn't give her any money for food or rent while her husband was sitting in jail.

Later Bonnie would learn that Monsalve believed Doris was the cause of all of his troubles because she had a big mouth.

There were other people who lived in the same building as

Monsalve and Nancy that Rooney and Toby went to speak with. Bonnie came to believe that gossip had actually been invented there, as the place seemed to be filled with women who spent every afternoon going from apartment to apartment, talking about the other people in the building.

One of them in particular seemed uniquely placed to testify to the fact that Monsalve maintained other apartments in the building which were used by couriers or as a stash location. Bonnie could prove that this person had, in fact, been paid by Monsalve to guard drugs and money. But apparently he'd stolen $1.2 million in drug money from Monsalve's apartment and was smart enough to get out of town before Monsalve found out.

Also on the list of people Bonnie, Rooney, and Toby interviewed were two women who regularly carried drugs from Los Angeles to New York for Monsalve. And several women Monsalve was sleeping with. There were also a few Mrs. Monsalves running around whom they interviewed. Apparently he liked to stay close to those women, especially if they'd borne him a child. One of those women had married him as a sham simply so that he could get a green card. Some of those women did have bits and pieces of information that was useful. But most of them said they were too frightened to talk.

One woman clearly at the center of their radar was Nancy Cadavid. The problem with her was that, as long as Monsalve was a free man, she'd never talk. And even if they somehow captured him, Nancy might still be too scared that he'd do serious harm to her and her family, even from inside prison. Of all the people who knew Monsalve, Nancy was best placed to see firsthand just how barbaric he was.

The question became, how do we approach her? And when a golden opportunity presented itself, Bonnie decided the answer was, not now.

Doris was always looking for Bonnie's help in making life a little more comfortable for her husband, and possibly turning it into a handout for herself. She'd phone Rooney every now and then with some useless piece of gossip, or some rumor she'd heard in the building. Most of the time, nothing came of it. But now she phoned to say that she'd heard Nancy was about to make a money run back to Colombia. She wanted to know, if money is seized, is there a reward?

This sounded a lot more promising than most of her calls—especially with Bonnie's interest in Nancy—so Rooney told her that there could be a reward, and pressed her for details. Doris even supplied a flight number.

It was a Sunday night. Rooney and Toby tailed Nancy to Kennedy Airport, watched her check in for her flight to Bogotá, followed her through security and right up to the jet bridge, where they stopped her.

They said they knew she was carrying a large amount of cash.

She denied it.

They searched her carry-on and found forty thousand dollars stuffed in shampoo bottles.

She insisted she didn't know anything about it.

They seized the money and detained her at the airport long enough to miss her flight. Then, as prearranged with Bonnie, they did not arrest her. Bonnie didn't want her locked up.

"Getting her on a money case," she said, "who cares? We could always hold it over her."

They allowed her to go home that night and then allowed her to fly out the next day, but without any money. She was presumably on her way to meet Monsalve and somehow had to explain to him why she didn't have his forty grand.

That same day, Bonnie indicted her on money-laundering charges, but asked that the indictment and arrest warrant be sealed. Her plan was to keep Nancy on the street, in case she might lead them to Monsalve.

7

President's Day 2000 fell on Monday, February 21, and George Washington's Birthday was the next day.

For Bonnie, it was a short week, with just enough time to clean up paperwork before she left on the family's annual winter ski break. Given the chance to spend quality time with both her sons—especially the older one—Bonnie and her husband were anxious to get away.

Her older boy, born ten years before, had been a very difficult baby. He wasn't easy to console. She couldn't put him in a stroller for very long. He always seemed to need constant attention. And yet the child seemed to be brilliant. He was already speaking in full sentences by the time he was just sixteen months. But the older he got, the more unmanageable he became.

When he reached thirty months, an age where other kids could play together, her son didn't seem interested in being with other children. And his temper tantrums were increasingly severe. Concerned that something clearly wasn't right, Bonnie started reading books about the difficult child, and the explosive child, and what parents needed to know to cope with severe mood swings.

Nothing helped and, within a year, things became so troublesome that she and her husband consulted a psychiatric social worker who had a practice specializing in difficult children. He met the child and made some suggestions. When the child didn't respond to treatment, he told Bonnie and her husband that they had to consider that he was suffering from a severe attention deficit problem.

In a way, that came as a relief to Bonnie because she believed that she and her husband were doing everything right. They did whatever any book said, whatever any doctor said. They were consistent. They had rules. They didn't enable the child. And yet, nothing worked. So now they began taking him to a psychologist who specialized in adolescent attention deficit problems. At the same time, they also started seeing a psychiatrist who began to medicate the boy.

That was the beginning of a five-year journey into one medicine after another. The child would be on one drug, and it would work for a while, but then his condition would get worse. They'd change the medicine and he'd appear to get better, but his mood would get worse. They'd start on antidepressants and he'd get agitated. Some eighteen different drugs later, they finally switched doctors.

This physician prescribed a drug that caused severe mania. The child became so violent that he tried to jump out a window. Understandably, that scared the hell out of Bonnie and her husband, and as a result, they changed doctors again, this time consulting one in New England who'd been diagnosing bipolar disorder.

Around the same time, Bonnie discovered the Web site http://www .bpkids.org and found some solace in knowing that she and her husband were not alone on this journey into the son's childhood.

"Back then," she says, "there really was nobody to talk to. Nobody knew what we were going through. People would think we were exaggerating. Or that we were just lousy parents. And then we found an entire social support community on the Internet. The bipolar diagnosis was brand-new."

Although the doctor in New England confirmed the bipolar

diagnosis and suggested some medication, unfortunately, there's a very small category of bipolar kids who can't tolerate the usual class of drugs which are used to control the problem. Bonnie's son fell into that class. And the boy got worse.

That's when they heard about a doctor who was doing cutting-edge research into the problem, and worked with him for several years. The child made some progress, but for every few steps forward, there were some steps back. He'd have three good days, then put his fist through a wall. He'd be calm for two weeks, then start fighting with everyone.

The manifestation of the problem is described as a "perservation," coming from the word "persevere." A child may ask for something ten times but when the parent says no ten times, the child will eventually stop. But children suffering from the same ailment as Bonnie's son never stop. They go on insisting and demanding and tantrumming for five and six and seven hours.

Needless to say, parenting two young sons took up a lot of Bonnie's energy.

In those days, she was only working part time as a prosecutor, which meant she was only being paid to spend three days in the office. But the workload required more, so after her three days on pay, she'd spend the other two days at home working on her cases for the government, pro bono.

"I had to work," she says. "My son's illness was all consuming and if I didn't work, all I would have done was think about him. Work for me was a blessing. It was like therapy. No matter how hard I tried I couldn't fix him so I had to have something else to think about."

Not everyone in the office was supportive. Some people didn't hide their opinion that a mother with a child like that shouldn't have this job. Even members of her own family kept saying that her son was the way he was because he had a working mother.

But some people were wonderfully supportive. And at the top of that list was Rooney. He was always there for Bonnie when it came to work, and always there for her family when it came to friendship.

They'd be in the middle of a meeting and Bonnie would get a call that her son was too agitated and that she needed to take him home from school, so right away, Rooney would say, "I'll come along," and the meeting would continue in the car. She'd get her son home, give him something to eat and settle him down, and Rooney would stay with her, working, until her husband got home.

"Not everybody would do that," she says.

With Bonnie on her way out of town, Rooney was counting on having a quiet week. And he almost made it.

On Thursday morning, February 24, out of the blue, he received a call from Doris Lobo. He hadn't spoken to her since before Christmas and wondered what this was all about.

She said, "He's coming back."

Rooney asked, "Who's coming back?"

She answered, "Monsalve."

Rooney didn't hide his surprise. "Holy fuck."

When he told Bonnie the news, she was just as shocked. "You were the one who said there's nothing to worry about if we indict him because he's not stupid enough to come back. You said he's never coming back. Now you say he is coming back?"

He reminded her, "That's what Doris says. You want to believe her?"

They agreed that Doris was hardly the most reliable source.

"But . . ." Bonnie said, "what if he does come back?"

Rooney told her, "Just go skiing and don't worry about it."

He pressed Doris for whatever information she had—"When is he coming back? Is he flying in? Is he driving in? Where's he going? What's he going to do when he gets here?"—but all Doris could say was, "I don't know anything. I don't know how he's getting here or when. I'm just hearing he's coming back."

Rooney reassured Bonnie, "Doris has been wrong before. I'm telling you, go skiing, have a good time. I'll worry about Monsalve."

"How can I not worry?"

"Listen . . . Monsalve knows we're looking for him, and he knows what will happen to him if we capture him, so why would he risk it?"

"Call me right away if you hear anything."

He promised he would.

Bonnie left with her family as planned on Saturday, but not before chiding Rooney, "Every time I go away with my family, you pull a stunt like this."

She knew that the 1997 warrant Rooney had begged her to file meant that, if Monsalve flew in, he'd be arrested immediately. His name was on everybody's radar. That is, as long as he was using his own passport and his own name. So she assured herself, "Maybe Romedio's right . . . maybe Doris is wrong . . . maybe Monsalve is too smart."

It was only much later that Rooney and Bonnie would find out how Monsalve actually got into the country.

Nancy flew to Mexico City with the child that she and Monsalve had together. She had a green card, and so did Monsalve, but their son was born in the States, making him a citizen, which meant they had a U.S. passport to flash.

From Mexico City, the three made their way 680 miles north to Matamoros, on the Texas border with Brownsville, waiting there until three of Monsalve's friends arrived. Those friends had flown down from New York, rented a van at the airport, and driven across the border, ostensibly to go shopping. That same day, Monsalve, Nancy, their baby and three friends drove back into Texas.

The Gateway Bridge, which crosses a narrow and surprisingly shallow Rio Grande River, is always chaotic, a never-ending exhaust fume–filled stream of trucks trying to get in from Mexico, and families in overpacked cars moving at a snail's pace to get through inspection, and literally thousands of people walking across into the United States, all of whom must be checked, at least to some extent.

Because the six people in the van appeared to be two families, and because they told the U.S. Immigration inspectors that they'd only driven down for the day to go shopping, and because they had

Texas plates on the van, and because everyone in the van seemed to have valid paperwork—especially the baby's U.S. passport—and because there were just too many cars backed up for miles behind them waiting to be inspected, they were waved through.

No one bothered to put any of their names in the computer.

From Brownsville, they drove four hundred miles to Houston, where Monsalve, Nancy, and their child caught a commercial flight back to New York.

The El Dorado Task Force was busy making plans to try to capture him.

A round-the-clock stakeout of Nancy's apartment building was made ready. Three teams were designated with ten agents each. Preliminary surveillance was done and everyone was reminded that Monsalve was considered highly dangerous. Accordingly, various routines were discussed to capture him, all of them taking into consideration that weapons might be used and that the general public had to be kept safe.

Then, on Sunday, February 27, 2000, three days after her first call to Rooney, Doris was on the phone again, this time in a panic. "He's here."

Rooney demanded, "Where?"

She said, "Parsons Boulevard. With Nancy."

Rooney pushed the panic button, alerting the team, and within two hours the first group was set up on the building.

A surveillance van was parked right across the street from the entrance, just in front of a small construction site which was being used as a parking lot. One agent would man for eight hours, watching the front door for Monsalve, while other agents in unmarked cars were spread around several blocks to grab him when he was spotted.

The building sits on the northeast corner of Parsons Boulevard and Roosevelt Avenue and takes up almost a third of the block. The main entrance is a few steps down from the sidewalk. There are recessed balconies on each floor above the entrance and fire escapes all the way up next to the balconies.

Rooney and his team—with New York State Trooper George Soto in the surveillance van—took the first shift. Monsalve never showed.

The second shift came on to spend Monday night. Still nothing.

On Monday morning, Doris phoned Rooney to say that Monsalve was not feeling well. Because Doris didn't live in that building anymore, Rooney wanted to know how she knew. Doris said she was hearing it from one of her old neighbors.

In fact, her information turned out to be wrong. Monsalve wasn't even in the building. Only later did Rooney and the others find out that when Monsalve arrived in New York, he went with Nancy to the apartment, left his clothes there, then headed off to New Jersey to be with friends.

Later still, they would find out his plans were to live in Miami.

But no one on the task force knew that then, and no one on any of the surveillance teams waiting for Monsalve had any reason to doubt what Doris was telling Rooney. So they stayed in place all day Monday and throughout Monday night. Still nothing.

They stayed in place all day Tuesday and through Tuesday night. And all day Wednesday and through Wednesday night.

On Thursday morning, March 2, George Soto was back in the surveillance van and saw Nancy and her son leaving the building. He radioed Rooney. As Nancy and the boy walked down the block, eventually on their way to the Flushing Hospital Medical Center, about nine streets away, Rooney had two agents follow them.

Now, radio traffic between the surveillance van and the agents in cars picked up—if she's out, maybe he's coming out.

Radio traffic between Rooney on the ground and the task force managers back at WTC picked up too—if she and the kid are out, maybe we can go in.

It was nearly ninety-six hours since the team had set up on the address, and everyone was, to say the least, getting very ansty. Spotting Nancy only heightened the tension.

Doris didn't help matters by phoning Rooney several times to insist, "He's there, inside the apartment."

Until Nancy and her kid left, there could be no talk of slamming down the door. Everyone understood they were dealing with an extremely violent man, and the little boy was Monsalve's obvious trump card. If Monsalve was forced into a corner, it was not inconceivable that he would use his own child as a hostage. The agents could never risk the child's life by storming the apartment with him inside. But now, Nancy and the boy were gone and the agents tailing them could make certain they did not return unexpectedly.

So Rooney decided to raise the stakes.

He went to the van to speak with George, discussed the plan with him, then radioed the others, "I'm going up to the apartment. I'll listen at the door. And if I hear someone scurrying around inside, then we're going to slam the door down."

The managers at WTC6 agreed and agents scattered around the block made ready to scramble.

Rooney stepped out of the van, walked across the street, went down the few steps to the entrance, and started ringing bells to get someone to unlock the door and let him inside.

"Who is it," someone asked over the intercom, and just as Rooney said, "Delivery," a man walked out the door, past him and up the steps onto the street.

The door slammed shut before Rooney could catch it. He didn't see the man's face, but when the door closed, he turned to look.

The man was on the sidewalk, gazing up and down Parsons Boulevard as if he was trying to find a taxi or a lift. He was around forty, a stocky five foot six, with no neck.

Rooney could now see the side of his flat, thuggish face.

It was Monsalve.

He signaled to George in the van, not knowing that George had already radioed to the others.

Unsuspecting, Monsalve walked right past the van and climbed into a car waiting in the parking lot.

As he did, George jumped out of the van. Rooney screamed in his radio, "He's out on the fucking street. He's out. He's on the fucking street." Cars converged on the parking lot, blocking Monsalve's exit. Rooney raced across the street. Agents jumped out of their cars, guns drawn. George got to Monsalve first.

At six foot three, the solidly built, goateed state trooper was menacing enough. But now, with his huge semiautomatic pistol pointing at the head of the man sitting, stunned, in the passenger's seat, George left no doubt that if Monsalve did something stupid, he'd be dead in an instant.

"Get out of the car," George ordered.

Other agents surrounded the car with their weapons drawn. "Federal agents. Get out of the car. Keep your hands in sight. Federal agents."

George yanked open the door and Monsalve stepped out. The driver was taken out the other door. Both men were spun around, pressed flat against the car, and their hands were cuffed behind them. Before Monsalve could even ask what the hell was going on, the agents had bundled him into a car and were speeding off to WTC6.

First, Rooney called the agents tailing Nancy. Now that they had Monsalve, they could execute the warrant that Bonnie had held back on Nancy after she tried to smuggle forty thousand dollars onto a flight to Colombia.

He told the agents, "When she's finished at the hospital arrest her."

After that, he began questioning the man who'd been with Monsalve.

He gave his name as Daniel Giraldo, which matched his driver's license. He said that he didn't know the man who was with him. He said he was just a driver who'd been told to pick him up and take him to somewhere in New Jersey. One of the agents ran Giraldo's name and date of birth through the NCIC—the computerized index of criminal justice information—and it came back blank.

With no way of knowing that this particular man's license had been acquired with a fake Social Security card, the decision was eventually made to cut him loose. Later, Rooney would admit, "It was a huge mistake. We should have brought him back to the WTC and broken his balls. But there was no paper on him."

Except there was. Immigration had lodged an outstanding warrant for him, which showed up on their database but not on NCIC's. Had the agents found it in time, they could have arrested this man who, in fact, was not Daniel Giraldo. Instead, Rooney, Toby, and George spent three weeks looking for Giraldo, never found him, and wouldn't know why for several more months.

It was because Giraldo was really Jaime Rojas Franco.

Making the situation even more bizarre, NCIS did not show any outstanding warrants for Rojas, who turned out to be a Norte Valle henchman and alleged murderer. Had he been using his own name, at that point, he would have walked, no problem. Instead, he had paperwork for a man who was wanted, and only walked because someone had screwed up and not put his phony name into the system.

Later, Rooney would learn that when Rojas made it back to Colombia, he started telling people, "Those stupid agents in New York, they let me go."

Once Monsalve was locked up, Rooney phoned Bonnie.

She and her family had just come in from the slopes and because she could see who was calling, she answered, "Hi, Romedio."

He said, "You're never going to believe who we caught."

She knew immediately. "Holy shit . . . Romedio . . . it's a capital murder case. . . . you promised me he wasn't coming back."

8

Within two hours of Monsalve's arrest, a lawyer was on the phone to announce that he was representing Monsalve. But Monsalve hadn't yet phoned for a lawyer. Rooney could only conclude that the driver, Daniel Giraldo, alerted someone who then called for an attorney. After all, Giraldo was the only other person who knew that Monsalve had been arrested. That only heightened Rooney's interest in the man he still thought was Giraldo.

The first time Bonnie actually saw Monsalve was a week or so after she got back from the family ski trip, when they faced each other in court for a hearing. And now he had a new lawyer.

She knew that Monsalve had a lot of money and could afford heavyweight representation but what she didn't know was that Monsalve was a serious cheapskate and hated to spend money. So he wound up with this fellow, who struck Bonnie as someone who specialized in drunk driving cases. It turned out that he didn't even have an office, that he worked out of his car, using his cell phone.

It was so pathetic, and Bonnie felt so sorry for him, that on at least one occasion before they went into court she actually coached him and told him what he needed to say.

Monsalve didn't express any interest in speaking to Bonnie, and Bonnie didn't show any interest in cooperating with him.

By that point in their careers, she and Rooney had dealt with hundreds of people who had distributed hundreds of thousands of kilos of cocaine. And as hard as it was to admit, she didn't automatically think of them as evil people. They were drug traffickers. That's what they did for a living. Not all of them were murderers. Not all of them were violent. Not all of them were nasty, vile, and despicable.

Monsalve was all of the above.

Bonnie reminded Rooney that they'd seen many devils over the years, but he was the worst. He was a control freak who took delight in hurting people. Everything about him repulsed her. And from his body language in court, she could see that Monsalve was a man who would be defiant to the end, never showing any remorse, never showing any shame.

He'd been remanded to the MCC in Manhattan, and she was more than happy to let him stay there, in the general population, until he came to trial.

Because prisoners are always looking for ways of reducing their sentences, the MCC—like all jails—is filled with people who will rat on anyone if it's going to help their own case. Which is why Bonnie wasn't surprised when a prisoner there asked to see her and said that he had it on good authority, Monsalve was planning an escape.

He told Bonnie it would happen during a hospital visit or an attorney visit.

The fact that it is near-impossible to escape from the MCC didn't stop Bonnie from passing the information along to the proper authorities.

Some days later, a guard on an evening round discovered Monsalve's laundry bag inside his bed. From outside his cell, the laundry bag made it appear as if he was sleeping. Monsalve, at the time, happened to be in the dayroom watching television. But the warden took this to be an escape attempt and, as a result, Monsalve was immediately transferred to the MDC in Brooklyn, and housed in the SHU.

The top-floor "special housing unit"—every prison has a SHU—is referred to by the inmates as "El Hueco," or "the Hole." It's where the most hardened, most dangerous, most high-risk criminals are kept. It's where they house terrorists. It's where they house the really violent prisoners. It is inescapable. And it is horrible.

Prisoners are totally isolated and locked down twenty-three hours a day. They live in an eight-by-six-foot cell, with a cement bed covered by a thin mattress in the middle of the room so they cannot lay sleeping against the wall. There's a toilet and a sink and a cement table, and nothing else. The ceiling light is always on. There is heat, but not a lot and most prisoners complain that, during winter months, they are constantly freezing. They can requisition long underwear and if they're lucky, they may even get it. They are permitted attorney visits and very limited family visits. They are granted fifteen minutes of phone calls every month. They eat all their meals in their cell. The one hour a day they're allowed out of their cell is for exercise, which they do alone, in a small empty space where there is a tiny strip of daylight coming through a narrow window running along the edge of the ceiling. They cannot see out and the light that comes in is not enough to tell what the weather is like.

To put it mildly, life in the SHU is a disconsolate, lonely, and dreadful existence. Most men start showing signs of madness very quickly. They become despondent, then clinically depressed. They can't sleep. They stop eating. They start screaming out in the middle of the night.

Monsalve sat alone in the SHU for fourteen months, and never showed any of these signs. The isolation didn't seem to affect him whatsoever.

If Bonnie and Rooney thought he was evil before he was housed in the SHU, his ability to survive under such extreme and adverse conditions made them realize that here was a man more depraved than they'd ever imagined.

Bonnie charged Monsalve with two murders—the killing of Rojas and Munoz—and wrote her death-penalty memo. In theory, murder is murder but in practice the assassination of traffickers by other traffickers is not necessarily considered to be in the same category as the murder of "civilians." She couldn't prosecute any of the non–drug trafficking related killings that Monsalve had committed for jurisdictional reasons. So she recommended no death. That's mostly because New York is not what prosecutors refer to as "a knee-jerk death jurisdiction." When you're talking about the murder of drug dealers, New York is not Texas.

With Monsalve in "the hole" and the case against him pretty clear-cut, there was no reason to sit down with him. Bonnie would see him in court and make a point, every time, of reminding the judge that this was a death-penalty case. But the death-penalty protocol was delayed for months as it wound its way through the system, causing the judge to put off setting a trial date.

By now, John Ashcroft was the attorney general, and he tended to take a much more draconian approach to the death penalty than his predecessor, Janet Reno. Still, in the matter of the *United States versus Juan Albeiro Monsalve*, Ashcroft agreed with Bonnie's recommendation and ruled no death.

Monsalve was facing two life sentences without the possibility of parole for the murders, plus whatever time the judge gave him for various drug-trafficking and money-laundering offenses. Bonnie felt confident in her case—Monsalve was going to spend the rest of his life in prison—and saw no reason to negotiate with him. Anyway, with the death penalty taken off the table, there wasn't anything to negotiate.

Yet after more than a year of waiting for the case to come to court, Monsalve's lawyer said he wanted to meet with Bonnie. She couldn't understand it, but agreed to sit down with him. But within a matter of minutes, it was clear to her that Monsalve was lying.

"I'm not a narcotics guy," he insisted. "I'm not some criminal,

I'm a veterinarian. I lived in the United States until 1997, and maybe while I was here I did a little bit of trafficking. But nothing major. When I went home to Colombia, I never did any trafficking. I worked as a veterinarian and a rancher."

"Forget it." She stood up. "You're not telling the truth and it's not worth my time, I'm ending the interview now."

And she walked out.

Shortly after that, Monsalve changed lawyers and asked to see Bonnie again, to negotiate a plea.

The new lawyer told Bonnie, "We want to work something out."

She reminded him, "There's nothing to negotiate. There is no plea in this case."

"There's always a plea," he contended. "We can always work out something."

Had the death penalty not been ruled out, maybe she would have considered trading down to life in exchange for Monsalve's cooperation. But not now. "It's a life-sentence case. We have nothing to trade."

"He wants to cooperate," the lawyer said,

"We're not interested," Bonnie responded.

"Come on." The lawyer wouldn't let go. "At least sit down and talk to him."

She said, "Fine . . . as long as he understands that there is no deal."

So Bonnie met with Monsalve a second time. But this time, for some reason, the meeting was in Manhattan, in an interview room at the office of the U.S. Attorney for the Southern District.

And again, Monsalve began with lies.

Bonnie was ready to walk out when the Southern District prosecutor exploded at Monsalve. "You're a fucking lying son of a bitch," he screamed at the top of his lungs. "Fuck you, this is over."

The two lawyers walked out together.

Monsalve's lawyer was on the phone that same afternoon, begging Bonnie to hear out his client. And after playing hardball, putting him off for weeks, she gave in. But now she insisted, that this third session would be held in the courthouse cell block.

Bonnie told the lawyer that, given Monsalve's previous performances, it wasn't worth her time or effort to make other arrangements. "We'll come downstairs and talk to him there for a few minutes."

The lawyer agreed. Except that by the time that session was to take place, Monsalve had fired him and hired lawyer number four.

The marshals brought Monsalve out of his cell in the SHU and took him into their basement cell block at the courthouse. Bonnie met them there, with Rooney and Toby, and they were shocked to see who his new lawyer was.

Monsalve had hired a guy who basically does immigration work, and advertises his services on Hispanic TV at two o'clock in the morning. As far as she knew, he had limited federal experience.

"I'm warning you," she said to lawyer number four before they walked in to see Monsalve, "His first lie is his last. I'll walk out. That's it. Over. No more."

"Trust me," the lawyer said, "he will tell the truth."

So Bonnie, Rooney, and Toby, together with the new lawyer, plus an FBI agent working for the prosecutors in the Southern District and an interpreter, stepped into this tiny space where Monsalve was sitting on the other side of a grating.

It was a steaming hot July day, made all the more uncomfortable by being crammed into this little room with so many people.

That's when Bonnie smelled something awful. "What's that?"

The others smelled it, too.

They all looked to the floor and the new lawyer bent down a little to check his shoes and everyone realized what he'd stepped in.

"Dog shit," someone said.

It was so hot and smelled so bad that Bonnie thought she might pass out. "The pool hall . . ." She turned to Monsalve. "Able's Pool Hall, when Alvaro Munoz was shot . . . did you have anything to do with it?"

Monsalve started shaking his head. "No. I don't know anything about that."

He was still lying, so she ended the interview and left the cell block, desperate for some fresh air.

Once Monsalve was in custody and on his way to WTC6, Rooney turned his attention to Nancy. He waited with Toby for her to return from the hospital with her son, then he went upstairs and knocked on the door to get what's called "a consent search." Because he didn't have a warrant to go inside her apartment he needed her permission.

He told her that Monsalve had been arrested, and her initial reaction was as if a huge weight had been lifted from her shoulders. He then told her that she was under arrest, too. It was that old money charge—the forty thousand dollars in the shampoo bottles—which didn't seem to surprise her. Deep down, she must have been expecting it would happen, someday.

Rooney Mirandized her—you have the right to remain silent—then asked if she would consent to let them search her apartment. She agreed. After the agents looked around, Rooney asked her if she wanted to talk. She said yes. When he asked about Monsalve, Nancy admitted that he was a major cocaine dealer.

She answered every one of Rooney's questions truthfully and seemed more than willing to cooperate. She told Rooney that Monsalve wasn't staying with her in the apartment. Which meant that for all the days and nights the agents had sat in the van and in cars waiting for Monsalve to appear, he wasn't even there. The reason Rooney found him that day, Nancy said, was because he was coming back to fetch some clothes.

According to Nancy, Monsalve must have gone upstairs and knocked on the door, expecting her to be there. He didn't have keys and had no way of knowing that she'd taken her son to see the doctor. Obviously, when she didn't open the door, he left. And that's when he passed Rooney downstairs at the front entrance.

That night, they escorted Nancy to court, along with Monsalve, to be arraigned.

Nancy appeared to want to cooperate and said that she knew Monsalve sold drugs.

Monsalve had hired a lawyer for Nancy, who immediately advised her to stop talking to the feds. The magistrate denied bail to Monsalve, but released Nancy. She was back at her apartment that night, around midnight, when Doris phoned. Nancy couldn't understand what Doris knew about this, assumed that Rooney was telling her everything—it wasn't true—and got angry.

By the time Bonnie was back in New York, Nancy had clammed up and wouldn't talk to her about anything.

It's a shame, Bonnie thought, because she really wanted Nancy's help. Without it, she built a strong drug case against Nancy and indicted her. Lobo was willing to testify that Nancy stored drugs and money for Monsalve, and Doris was willing to corroborate that. But Nancy was listening to her lawyer, and he was being paid by Monsalve.

If Nancy had been helpful, Bonnie says, she would have used her as a witness. Instead, Bonnie built a small drug case against Nancy. She got arrested again and wound up in jail.

Bizarrely, Nancy Cadavid is the only person in this matter to have been arrested twice.

She spent a few months behind bars, and during that time, Bonnie and Rooney visited several times. During those visits, Bonnie and Nancy sort of bonded. Their sons were the same age and on similar medications. Bonnie could relate to Nancy as a mother.

Eventually, Bonnie decided that keeping Nancy in jail really didn't serve much purpose. She knew Nancy wouldn't flee, not with an epileptic child under care in New York. Anyway, running back to Colombia would only put her and the little boy in jeopardy. So Bonnie made arrangements to free Nancy. A lot of people warned Bonnie that Nancy would run. But Bonnie believed that Nancy was of more use as a cooperator outside rather than in. So Bonnie got her sprung from jail, Nancy promised she would stay in New York, and for the next several years, she kept her promise.

Her level of cooperation, however, wavered back and forth. At first she was too scared to be helpful. At one point, she decided she wanted to get even with Doris for all the trouble she'd caused. She was also out to find any other witnesses who would testify against Monsalve, doing everything in her power to help him.

As time wore on, Nancy came to understand that Monsalve was never getting out of prison, and that his power to do her harm was waning. Monsalve had abused her mentally and physically and treated her like his slave. Over time she began to realize that it was Bonnie and Rooney who'd free her from a life of horror.

Before long, she was worshipping Rooney, saying that he saved her life, that the best thing that ever happened to her was that they'd arrested Monsalve.

Then she decided that what she needed to do, to protect herself and her son, was move from Parsons Avenue. The entire building was filled with gossips, and all of them seemed to be talking daily to Doris. Nancy didn't want to live there anymore, and told Romedio. He and Bonnie agreed that it would be a good idea to relocate her.

In situations like that, when the government relocates someone for their own safety, the move is usually thousands of miles away. But Nancy said she needed to keep her son in the same school, so this relocation was three blocks.

Bonnie filled out the paperwork for "emergency witness assistance" money. She was told it would take at least two weeks, and maybe even longer. She had to remind the people with the purse strings, "It's an emergency. That's why it's called emergency assistance."

But the government moves at its own snail's pace.

Later Rooney would complain, "It's a miracle we don't have more dead witnesses."

When the money was finally approved, nearly two months later, it was only a few thousand dollars, hardly enough to put a deposit down for the rent on another apartment and also pay a moving company. So Rooney decided that he and Toby and a few of the other guys could do the job. They got a government station wagon, filled it with her stuff, put her couch on the roof and moved her quickly and efficiently.

Later, word came from Washington that Internal Affairs was concerned with Rooney's "misuse of a government vehicle for non-government purposes."

Fortunately, nothing ever came of it.

9

In one of their many conversations, Nancy mentioned to Bonnie that Monsalve's right-hand man, the fellow who must be called Hector Rivera, was on his way back to New York from Colombia. His wife's sister just had a baby and he wanted to be at the christening, which was scheduled for the coming weekend in Union City, New Jersey.

Rooney ran a criminal history check and found that, in 1994, Hector had been arrested in Costa Mesa, California, for possession of 130 kilograms of cocaine. It was Monsalve who posted bail for him.

Hector jumped bail, returned to New York briefly, then fled to Colombia. Accordingly, there was a fugitive arrest warrant from California already in the system. In fact, there was also an outstanding 1994 warrant on him from New York State for driving while intoxicated.

To corroborate Nancy's story, Rooney turned to Lobo, who confirmed Hector's stature in the organization, and then to some confidential informants. One of them said that Hector was responsible for Monsalve's distribution network, and that when Monsalve was out of the country, it was Hector who was in charge. A second informant not only said he knew the church where the christening was going to be but was, himself, an invited guest. He said he, too, had heard that Hector was planning to attend.

The only problem with the second CI was that, in the past, he'd consistently gotten stories wrong or had just downright lied.

Because they couldn't trust anything he said, Rooney and Toby drove out to Union City, to the address he'd given them. And it was a church. However, when they asked the priest what time the christening was on Sunday, he said there was no christening on Sunday.

Rooney shook his head, thinking to himself, "This knucklehead informant's a pain in the ass."

The two agents thanked the priest and were about to leave when the priest wondered if the christening might not be at another church, a few blocks away. So they drove to the second church and sure enough, the christening was on the calendar for Sunday morning, August 5.

Bonnie decided they could arrest Hector on the outstanding fugitive warrant from California, then work up their own charges once they had him in custody. Rooney pulled a mugshot off a database, but it was so old that he worried he wouldn't be able to identify Hector from it. So he convinced Nancy to come along to make a positive ID. And on that Sunday morning, Rooney and Toby— with Nancy in the backseat of their car—and four other agents in two other cars, including George Soto, set up on the church.

From different vantage points around the block, they watched people arrive. Then, a few hours later, they watched people leave. None of those people was Hector.

After the service, the agents followed the family and their guests to a house where a party was happening.

And still no Hector.

Nancy kept pressing Rooney and Toby, "How much longer are we going to sit here like this?"

They assured her, "Not much longer."

Except, they sat there, watching the house, waiting for Hector, for the rest of the afternoon.

Every time a new person showed up, Rooney or Toby would ask, "Is that him?" and Nancy would say, "No, that's not Hector."

They were still sitting in their cars at seven o'clock, and by then it was getting dark.

Rooney was starting to think that Hector was never going to show, and that he had to stop torturing Nancy by keeping her there like that. He was probably only fifteen minutes away from calling the whole thing off, when the knucklehead CI phoned to say he was inside the house, at the party, and, "By the way, Hector is here."

In fact, after that call, the CI phoned Rooney every fifteen or twenty minutes, to say, "Hector is still here," and after a while Rooney began thinking, maybe this time the knucklehead's got it right.

With women and children inside the house, there could be no question of raiding the party to arrest Hector. Sitting there, waiting for Hector to come out, was the only thing they could do. So Rooney left everyone in place.

It was after eleven when Hector finally appeared.

A beefed up, musclebound man, five foot ten, wearing tight clothes and carrying a small black backpack, walked out of the house with a few other guys and some women.

Nancy suddenly got very excited. "That's him. That's Hector."

Rooney alerted the others, and watched as the group climbed into a white van. When the van pulled away, the agents followed.

The best time to take Hector would be when he was outside the van, separated from everyone else. They wanted him alone. They didn't want to have to worry about interference from anyone else in the van, or the possibility that he might use one of the women with him as a hostage or human shield. They also had to worry that the people in the van with Hector, and Hector himself, could have guns. They would only get one chance to grab him, so they needed to take control over the situation quickly and forcefully.

The last thing they wanted was to find themselves in a situation where there was any possibility of a firefight on the street.

They continued following the van, which made a few stops to let people out—among them, Hector's wife—always ready for that single optimum moment when they could grab him.

It came when the van pulled up to an apartment house and Hector stepped out alone.

Rooney waited, anxiously, to see who else would get out of the van. And then, just like that, the van pulled away.

Hector was alone.

Rooney shouted on his radio, "Let's go now."

Six agents jumped out of their cars, guns drawn, screaming, "Federal agents, get down on the ground . . . get down . . . federal agents . . ."

It all happened very fast. George Soto tackled Hector. Three agents surrounded him. George and Hector fought on the ground. Hector twisted and turned, making it as difficult as possible for Rooney and Toby to cuff him.

To be 100 percent sure that they had the right man, they kept Hector on the ground while Toby drove by with Nancy. She confirmed, "Yes, it's really him."

When Toby called him to say they had a positive ID, Rooney said, "Bundle him up and let's go."

They strapped Hector into the front seat of George's car, and just to make sure he would stay put, they kept him handcuffed behind his back, and hog-tied his feet so he couldn't start kicking.

By the time Rooney got an exhausted Nancy back home, it was after 1 A.M.

An equally exhausted Rooney then drove to WTC6, where he found that Hector was being very aggressive.

Rooney assumed Hector was high—"He was flying"—but Hector insisted he hadn't taken any drugs. He said he'd been drinking. Whichever, Rooney decided, Hector was in no shape to be processed or even to be read his rights.

The backpack he'd been carrying contained two cell phones. They'd need a warrant to get into those, so Rooney locked up the backpack, then decided the best thing to do with Hector was to let him sober up in one of the small holding cells.

A concrete eight-by-four-foot space—with a heavy steel door that had a tiny but very thick bulletproof window so that agents could check on their prisoner—there was a cement bench bolted to the floor, and a pipe running next to it from the ceiling to the floor. Prisoners would be handcuffed to the pipe while they sat on the bench. There was also an office chair in the cell, one of those short-backed, no-arm chairs with wheels.

To make Hector comfortable—Rooney and George were hoping that he would just go to sleep—they took the thin mattress off the bench, put it on the floor and, because the pipe was then too far away, handcuffed one of his arms to the foot of the bench.

Hector kept asking, "Why are you kidnapping me?"

"We're not kidnapping you," George said, "just lie down and go to sleep."

"You're kidnapping me," Hector went on and on. "Why are you kidnapping me?"

George said, "You're too drunk. I'll tell you in the morning."

Because it was so hot in the cell, George felt he couldn't leave Hector like that, so he fetched a bottle of water for him, and put a fan in there with him.

"You're kidnapping me," Hector wouldn't stop. "I'm not drunk. I'm not. Tell me why you are kidnapping me."

Now George said, "Okay," and told Hector about the arrest warrant.

But Hector was far too drunk. "I don't understand."

"See what I mean?" said George.

"See what?" asked Hector. "Why are you kidnapping me."

"Never mind." George pushed him back in the cell, "I'll tell you later," and locked the door.

Rooney announced, "We can worry about him in the morning." Keeping Hector in the cell overnight meant that at least two agents had to babysit him. But Rooney, George, Toby, and the others had been working on this since nine the previous morning. Still, Toby and George volunteered to stay until replacements arrived. So Rooney made some calls, found some guys willing to come in, then headed home.

That's when Hector started throwing the bottle of water at the fan and screaming, "Why are you kidnapping me?"

George rushed back to the cell, opened the door again, said, "No more fan," took it out and kicked out the now destroyed water bottle.

"Why are you kidnapping me?" Hector grabbed the chair.

George realized that Hector was going to throw it at him, so he tried to take it away from Hector. The two men struggled with it, yanking and pulling, until George managed to shove Hector back into the cell, throw the chair out, and slam the door shut.

Now Hector started screaming and yelling, all the time banging something against the door.

Toby and George looked through the four-inch reinforced glass window to see Hector, kicking at the door, and with each kick, getting closer to ripping the bench out of its bolts and off of the floor.

At that point, Toby's replacement arrived downstairs. However, the replacement didn't have his elevator pass with him, which meant he couldn't get upstairs—you needed to put a card into the elevator's reader if you wanted to stop on that floor—so George went downstairs to let him in.

That left Toby alone with Hector, which would have been fine, except that Hector was going berserk. And, suddenly, there was a tremendously loud cracking noise. Toby ran to the cell and saw through the window that Hector had ripped the cement bench off its bolts and was using it like a battering ram, trying to smash through the window.

Toby said out loud, "Holy shit," raced to his locker and reached for his gun. But Toby was an IRS agent, a mild-mannered guy who'd been doing tax cases all his life.

He stared at it, reminded himself, if I shoot this guy, I'll be filling out forms for the rest of my life, put it down, picked up a can of mace and ran back to the cell.

The glass window was totally shattered and the door had taken a severe beating. Toby could see that Hector was suffering, too. He appeared to be near-exhausted.

Worried that Hector might make one final attempt and actually break out, Toby reached for his cell phone.

Some seven miles away in Queens, Rooney was just getting out of the shower when his pager went off.

"Oh fuck," he said out loud, and grabbed it, astonished to see the display showing Toby's phone number, followed by the message, "911." In all the years they worked together, Rooney had never received a beeper from Toby.

Immediately, he phoned Toby who announced, in a slight panic, "Hector's going fucking crazy. He's battering the door."

"This cannot be happening," Rooney said. "Where's George?"

Toby explained, "He went down to let the replacement in and he's not back yet."

Rooney said, "I'll be right there."

As he jumped into his clothes, he decided that what he really needed to do was send for the cavalry. So he dialed the NYPD's Emergency Services Unit (ESU), and told them they had an emergency at WTC6.

The ESU is a specialized tactical group, sort of a SWAT team on steroids, who work in tandem with the EMSO, Emergency Medical Services Officers. As a group they're equipped to respond to anything from a mass-hostage situation or a heavy weapons standoff to a wild tiger loose on the streets.

With them on the way, Rooney drove like a madman back to WTC6. He arrived in under fifteen minutes, to find a half dozen ESU guys in full battle dress—including the sergeant in charge, a big-bellied, ruddy-faced Irish cop—unable to get inside because they didn't have a card for the elevator.

"The others are already there," the sergeant said, so Rooney brought this bunch up to the fifth floor, where they found twenty more ESU guys, in full battle dress, standing with Toby and George, in front of the cell, peering through the broken glass window at Hector.

He was still handcuffed to the bench, which was lying on its side next to him on the floor, but he seemed to be fast asleep.

The sergeant announced, "We're going in there," then asked, "What's this guy's name?"

Rooney told him, "Hector."

"Hector?" The sergeant barked to the prisoner, "Hector, listen to me. Listen to what I'm about to tell you."

A groggy Hector grunted, "Huh?"

"We're coming in there to get you," the sergeant growled. "And if you make a fucking move, I'm going to light up your ass like it's never been lit up in your life. Don't fucking move. You understand what I'm telling you?"

Hector grunted again.

They unlocked the door, the sergeant went in with some of his team, uncuffed Hector from the bench and handcuffed him again.

Rooney, Toby, and George stood there watching, incredulously, as Hector behaved like a docile baby.

A paramedic looked at Hector and said it didn't matter whether he was drunk or stoned. "You can't keep him here without worrying that he'll go crazy again. You've got to get him to a hospital."

After thanking the ESU guys and watching them leave, Rooney decided that the best place to take Hector was Bellevue because they have a small lockup for prisoners. So they chained Hector and brought him downstairs, got him into a car, and drove to the Bellevue emergency room at Twenty-seventh Street and First Avenue.

Rooney told the receiving nurse that the prisoner was drunk, had some superficial wounds from his battle with the cell door and cement bench, and needed to stay there for the night.

The receiving nurse called for the doctor in charge.

She took one look at Hector, in handcuffs and chains, and announced, "You can't bring him in here like that."

Rooney asked, "What do you mean we can't?"

"I mean, you can't bring him in here like that," the doctor said, "The handcuffs and chains come off."

"No way," Rooney said. "This guy is violent."

George added, "He's got to stay in cuffs because he's too drunk."

"In that case," the doctor said, "we don't want him."

It was now coming up on four in the morning. "You have to take him," Rooney insisted.

"I really don't have time to argue about it," the doctor said.

Rooney stood his ground. "We have nowhere else to go."

"You can't stay there," she said. "You're in the way."

Rooney, George, and Toby simply refused to leave.

The standoff at Bellevue didn't last long.

The doctor blinked first. "He can stay, but only if he's handcuffed to a gurney with all three of you sitting right there, in case he goes ballistic."

So Rooney, Toby, and George chained the groggy Hector to a gurney, then pulled up chairs and sat surrounding the bed, while Hector slept off his drunken stupor.

Around seven, they transferred him to one of the holding cells, and read him his rights. Rooney then showed Hector a picture of Monsalve and demanded to know if Hector recognized the man.

Awake, but now in a state of denial, Hector started protesting that they had the wrong man. He refused to identify Monsalve. He continued to insist that they'd kidnapped him, that he was innocent and that he didn't know anything at all about why he was there.

He also said he didn't remember his battle with the cement bench and cell door.

Too exhausted to argue about it, Rooney and the others checked him out of Bellevue and drove him—still in chains—all the way out to Long Island, where he was checked into jail to await a hearing.

The guards there took Hector's old clothes from him, including his Prada suede shoes, and dressed him in a prisoner's orange jumpsuit. Bonnie then arraigned him and the judge ordered Hector to be held.

Again, Rooney tried to question him about Monsalve, and again Hector refused to say anything, except, "You've got the wrong man. Why have you kidnapped me?"

So Rooney and the others made plans to drive him back to the MDC in Brooklyn. But before they left, Rooney went to get Hector's shoes because he wanted to show them to Bonnie.

"Ever see anything like this?" He asked, "Who the hell wears shoes like this? Guy must be half a homo."

Bonnie didn't seem terribly amused. "My husband has the same shoes."

Without saying anything more, Rooney tossed Hector's shoes into the trunk of his car.

That was August 2001.

With other things on his mind, Rooney simply forgot that they were there and the shoes never made it into the evidence locker at WTC6.

A month later, the World Trade Center was destroyed.

It would be almost seven years before Rooney remembered the shoes and Hector would earn them back.

10

They woke Hector from his stupor at around seven that morning. He was exhausted and groggy but no longer aggressive. They moved him from the emergency room at Bellevue to one of the hospital's holding cells, where he slept off the rest of the day until they took him to be arraigned.

Charged with drug trafficking and resisting arrest, Hector was ordered held without bail and delivered to the Nassau County jail. Federal prisoners are often stored there, for convenience's sake, when their case is being dealt with on Long Island.

At the time of his arrest, Hector had been carrying a black backpack. Inside was a silver pay-as-you-go Panasonic cell phone and a Palm Pilot personal digital assistant (PDA).

Pay-as-you-go phones are tools of the trade for criminals because they create anonymity. Sellers are supposed to register buyers' names and check IDs, but many don't. Anyway, under-the-counter markets are rife with pay-as-you-go phones and top-up cards. All you have to do is change your prepaid phone every time your $50 or $100 credit runs out, which gives you a new phone number. It means the good guys are always chasing warrants for abandoned phones.

It's a different matter, however, when the cops can take a phone off a trafficker. They're hoping to mine his speed-dial list of friends and clients, plus the lists of calls made, received, and missed. PDAs can be even more valuable because traffickers typically use them to keep detailed records of drug transactions. Unfortunately, the information they found on Hector's phone and PDA did not add much to what they already knew—Hector was Monsalve's right-hand man.

Not surprisingly, that relationship was on the top of Bonnie's list to discuss with Hector when the two met for the first time, a week or so after his arrest. Hector had been telling Rooney that he couldn't remember being so violent on the night they nabbed him. But Rooney remembered and delivered Hector to Central Islip in hand-cuffs, chains, and leg shackles.

Bonnie didn't like that and said, right away, "Please take those shackles off him."

"No." Rooney waved her off. "Absolutely not."

"Romedio?" She insisted, "I'm not talking to him while he's in chains."

"Tough," Rooney said.

She said, "We can't interview him like this. It isn't humane."

Rooney stood his ground. "I don't give a fuck, humane or not, he almost killed us."

"He's not going to do anything," Bonnie said to Rooney, then looked at Hector. "Are you?"

"He's too dangerous." Rooney wasn't having it. "He's too strong. This guy can break me in half. You want the chains off, I'll give you the key."

Hector stayed in chains and shackles. But the meeting didn't last long because Hector decided they had nothing to talk about.

The second time Bonnie met with Hector, Rooney again delivered him in chains and shackles. But this time he took them off during the interview to show Hector that if he cooperated, they could make life more comfortable for him.

Except that Hector still wasn't cooperating.

So Bonnie went ahead and put together her case against him. Lobo would testify that Hector operated the money-laundering side of Monsalve's organization, that Hector worked directly for Monsalve from 1993 to 1997, and that Hector had personally distributed cocaine to Monsalve's customers. Lobo would also claim that Monsalve used Hector to arrange for murders in New York. Johnson Guzman would testify that Hector had personally given him fifteen to twenty-five kilos of cocaine on several occasions. A confidential witness would add that, between 1988 and 1997, Hector was Monsalve's right-hand man and responsible for overseeing the shipment of cocaine from Los Angeles and Miami. Another confidential witness would swear that he saw Hector frequently deliver money and drugs to Monsalve's stash houses.

Once that was done, she moved on to other matters.

After sitting in his cell for four months, Hector was finally willing to admit that, unless he did something to help himself, he was looking at a very long time behind bars. Stuck in the Nassau County jail and faced with the strength of Bonnie's case, he now wondered if there was some way to work out a deal. So he hired a lawyer and agreed to be proffered. But when he and his lawyer showed up for that first proffer, Bonnie decided the lawyer was clueless. The man just sat there, didn't seem to understand what was going on and, afterwards, said to Bonnie, "I don't want to attend any of these again."

The lawyer never came back.

With Hector left to fend for himself, Bonnie decided to show him that this didn't have to be an adversarial relationship. That she could, and would, do things to make his existence in prison a little more comfortable.

First, she had him moved from the appalling conditions of the Nassau County jail to the slightly more accommodating MDC in Brooklyn. The gesture did not go unnoticed.

Other considerations followed, including food. Many prosecutors meet with prisoners in the morning so that they can be done with them by noon. The lawyers go their way for lunch and the prisoners are returned to jail where the food is borderline edible. Bonnie took a different approach. She kept cooperating prisoners in the proffer room during lunch. She'd send out for Colombian food—Rooney would pay for it out of his own pocket—to show them that they weren't the enemy, that they could talk together, break bread together, work out a deal together.

The prisoners liked that. Some of them even got homemade cookies. Taking pride in her ability to bake, Bonnie would show up with cookies she'd made the night before, saying that this was a little reward for telling the truth. On one occasion, a certain prisoner demanded to know why someone else got cookies and he didn't. Bonnie explained, "Because he tells me the truth and you keep lying. And when you start telling me the truth, you will get cookies, too."

It doesn't sound like much, but when you're spending every day in an orange jumpsuit, confined to a very tiny space, without any control over your daily life, suffering mind-numbing boredom, and looking at the prospect of ten or twenty or thirty years of the same, even a little act of human kindness can go a long way.

The more they met, and the more they talked, and the more Bonnie and Rooney treated Hector like a human being, the more he was willing to confide in them. He talked about Monsalve. He also spoke about Cartago, where he'd grown up, and how the cartel flat-out owned the city. The place was tightly controlled, he said, with lookouts on every street corner and on the bridges, keeping everyone aware of what was happening by walkie-talkie, twenty-four hours a day.

The lookouts saw every car coming into Cartago and every car leaving Cartago, and took a particular interest in cars with out-of-town plates, especially from Bogotá. Every stranger who showed up was checked out, too.

"Sometimes," Hector said, "people who shouldn't be in Cartago get beat up. Sometimes they get killed."

After rambling on about Cartago, he started talking about his old pal, "Rasguño."

He told Bonnie and Rooney, "We grew up together there. We used to go running together. We used to exercise together. We went to football together. Monsalve worked for him. I did, too. I laundered money for him in Jersey."

Bonnie wanted to know. "Who's Rasguño?"

"Gomez Bustamante," Hector said. "Luis Hernando Gomez Bustamante. We call him Rasguño."

The nickname means "scratch" and supposedly comes from a childhood incident when someone took a shot at him, the bullet grazed the left side of face and he told his friends, "It's just a scratch."

Hector went on, "Nothing happens in Cartago without Rasguño knowing about it."

Rooney asked, "And this Rasguño . . . this Bustamante guy is . . . ?"

"El Señor," Hector answered. The man. Then he shrugged, as if it should be obvious, "The head of the Norte Valle Cartel."

The story of Bustamante's rise to power in the Norte Valle began in the waning days of the Cali Cartel with the man known as "the last Cali kingpin"—Francisco Helmer "Pacho" Herrera-Buitrago.

The Orejuelas and Santacruz Londoño were gone and Pacho, desperate to maintain his hold on what was left of the cartel's business, was on the run.

Born in Palmira, a suburb of Cali, in 1951, Pacho was the oldest of five boys and one girl. But he was homosexual, which can be a problem in the ultramacho world of rural Colombia, and that may account for why he left the country at the age of twenty to seek his fortune in New York.

It was a time when cocaine was a wide-open game, and entry-level players could get in with a very small stake. Pacho put together a crew to deal white powder in Queens and Brooklyn but very quickly got busted. After a year in jail, he figured he'd learned from his lessons and went back to the streets. He brought one of his brothers into business with him and, better organized, the partnership expanded. At least, it did until he and his brother got busted together. This time Pacho spent four years in prison.

Returning to Colombia in 1983 determined to succeed, he looked for ways to run a New York operation by remote control. He brokered a supply agreement with the Orejuelas, redesigned his distribution network, and sent two of his brothers to New York to oversee the operation on the ground.

Socially polite and ordinarily soft-spoken—apparently he did not use profanities and objected when other people did—Pacho was, nevertheless, an unforgiving taskmaster who ruled with an iron fist. He was generous to a fault with his family and friends, but never hesitated to deliver severe punishments to anyone who crossed him. He established new sources for cocaine in Peru and Bolivia and set up numerous conversion labs in jungles controlled by the FARC. He shipped multiton loads from private airfields or ports along the North Coast to staging points in the Caribbean or directly into the U.S.

By 1990, he'd built himself a near monopoly on the New York market and was considered the fourth most powerful man in Cali, just behind the Orejuelas and Londoño.

But a man who fancied men—particularly in the traffickers' world where "real" men paraded women around like prized cattle—was always going to make some people uneasy. And along the way, Pacho had a serious run-in with Pablo Escobar.

Ostensibly, they argued about Pacho's stranglehold on New York, but any excuse would have been good enough for the ultramacho Escobar and his colossal ego. Tempers flared, Pacho refused to back down and Escobar threatened to wipe out Pacho's entire family.

The Orejuelas sided with Pacho. In 1988, a bomb exploded in a Medellin apartment building nearly killing some of Escobar's immediate family. Everyone suspected Pacho. Two years later, Escobar sent a team of assassins, disguised as policemen and soldiers, to one of Pacho's many ranches where his family was gathered for a soccer game. The murder squad machine-gunned nineteen people. Pacho himself only just barely escaped. Two years after that, Pacho and the Orejuela brothers exacted the ultimate revenge by tipping the national police to Escobar's hiding place in Medellin, where he was, unceremoniously, gunned down.

In those days, the Orejuelas had a former Colombian police sergeant on their payroll named Wilber Alirio Varela-Jarado. He was an enforcer whose nickname "Jabón" (soap) was a tribute to his ability to "clean up" problems by murdering people.

An oval-faced man with black hair, brown eyes, and a very thick black moustache, he was born in 1954, in the jungle village of Roldanillo, about thirty miles from Cartago. His relationship with the Orejuelas was tenuous, at best, and when it soured he drifted into Pacho's employ. But the two of them were never going to get along.

Varela was an extremely ambitious man who did not hide his jealousies. The Orejuelas had always suspected that Varela was untrustworthy, and Pacho could never afford to be too trusting of anyone. Creating additional tension between the two, Varela collected women as trophies. At one point, he started inventing beauty pageants around the country just so that he could meet aspiring young models and actresses, arrange to have them named Miss Something-or-Other, then show them off in his bed, victoriously, to his envious mates. On another occasion, when one of his beauty queen girlfriends spent too much time talking to another man, he had her shot. He was definitely not the sort of man who was comfortable paying respect to a gay boss.

The relationship didn't last very long. A year after the Orejuelas got busted, so did Pacho. Like the Orejuela brothers, Pacho was also sentenced to six years, although the government appealed and that was extended to fourteen. Unlike the Orejuelas, Pacho would never be extradited to the U.S. Varela and his new friends would see to that.

Under the regime of President César Gaviria, who served from 1990–1994, the Colombian government had instituted the "reduced prison sentence surrender program" intended to put the traffickers out of business.

Call it amnesty-light masquerading as retirement.

In exchange for turning himself in, a trafficker could wipe the slate clean. He would have to plead guilty to drug trafficking, but he would be sentenced to no more than five years. He would have to forfeit some of his money and some of his properties, but not everything. He could hold on to a healthy chunk. The idea was that, once he got out, he would be free to live his life as he saw fit—with whatever monies and properties he'd managed to keep—as long as he did not go back into the drug business.

For the traffickers, being able to come out the other end still rich was a real incentive. Also, by taking the deal before the Colombian constitution was changed to allow extradition to the United States, they were putting themselves beyond the reach of the Americans.

In Washington, the Clinton administration grew more and more frustrated with the leniency of the deal, with the fact that the traffickers could keep their illicitly acquired assets and, most important, with the Colombians refusal to hand over these criminals. The State Department decertified the country twice, cutting off financial support and trade relations.

The Colombian congress responded by changing the constitution to permit extradition. But one clause specified that the new law would not operate retroactively. No one would be extradited for crimes committed prior to the ratification date, December 17, 1997. President Ernesto Samper objected. His government even filed a suit to remove the nonretroactivity clause. After all, he'd been bragging that his track record was noteworthy, having put all of the Cali leadership behind bars. But then allegations surfaced that the Cali cartel had contributed $6 million to Samper's campaign. In response, Samper denied knowledge of any such contributions.

Beside any obvious corruption implications, the U.S. voiced real concern that the nonretroactive clause could be applied to non-Colombian nationals, which meant that foreign fugitives would be protected as well. But here the Constitutional Court ruled that non-Colombian nationals could be extradited for offenses, even if they occurred before the December 17 deadline.

When Andrés Pastrana succeeded Samper, the new president made an effort to restore Colombia's soured relations with Washington. Although extradition of Colombians remained dormant for another few years.

By the time Pacho was marched into Palmira Prison, Varela had taken up company, back home in the Norte Valle, with another former police officer, Orlando Henao.

Pacho decided that was treason because Orlando was a mortal enemy of the Orejuelas.

Two clans had emerged from the shadows of the Cali cartel, having once been their biggest "minicartel" clients to becoming their most important competitors to, eventually, becoming their successors.

The Urdinola Grajales faction was run by brothers Ivan and Julio. The Henao-Montoya clan was run by Orlando and his two younger brothers, Arcangel and Fernando. Nicely enough, the two groups were related by marriage, as Ivan was married to Orlando's sister, Lorena.

Ivan and Julio were born in Cali and, for a while, worked as hired assassins for the Orejuelas. By the time they'd moved to Cartago, they'd been credited with having personally participated in more than one hundred murders. Ivan was also linked to a pair of massacres in Trujillo, a nearby village, when dozens of peasants were hacked to death by machetes for, supposedly, cooperating with the authorities. Ivan was also known for killing homeless men and street vagabonds that he happened to find by chance, believing that this brought him good luck.

Much of the Urdinola cocaine was destined for Chicago, Houston, and Los Angeles, but Ivan's claim to fame is that he took the Colombians into the heroin business. He was the first to do a joint venture with the Sicilian Mafia to expand the European cocaine market. He sent them white powder and they paid him in heroin. He then moved that heroin alongside his cocaine, through Mexico and into the States. Recognizing that he could make a fortune with this sideline, he was also the first Colombian cocaine trafficker to process his own heroin.

In 1993, a mere one hundred days after Pablo Escobar's death, the Colombian national police arrested Ivan. Julio surrendered two years later. Neither was ever charged with any killings. They were sent to Modelo Prison in Bogota for drug trafficking, and continued running their business from there. Ivan actually ordered some of his associates to rent houses next door to the prison, then had walkie-talkies smuggled in so that he could talk to them.

Interestingly enough, one of the rising stars in the Urdinola faction was a young hoodlum from Trujillo—site of the massacres—named Diego León Montoya Sánchez. A cousin of the Henao brothers on his mother's side, before long, he would assume command and surpass the Urdinolas in everything they'd ever done, including violence.

Meanwhile, Orlando Henao was just as ambitious as the Urdinolas, and just as ruthless. But he was taken out of the game in the mid-1990s. Baby brother Fernando, who oversaw the family's American operations, was smart enough to become the heir apparent, except that he was captured in the late 1990s and extradited to the States. The burden to keep the family in business fell onto the middle brother, Arcangel, known as "El Mocho," (the amputee), a Thalidomide child, he had a withered left arm.

What made the Henaos important was the family's close ties to Carlos Castaño, the paramilitary leader of the AUC. It was alongside Castaño that the Henaos developed jungle labs and secured shipping arrangements.

And one of the rising stars in the Henao faction was Luis Hernando Gomez Bustamante. But unlike Don Diego, he wouldn't take over anyone else's interests, he'd go out on his own and, with Castaño's help, build an even bigger empire.

Orlando Henao was a worried man.

Pacho was in jail but he had friends who were not in jail, so his threats were just as real.

At the same time, the amnesty program was picking apart the bones of the Cali cartel. Orlando feared that, as the government worked its way down from the generals to the field-grade officers, many of them would agree to cooperate. It hardly mattered that he was heading a rival gang. Colombia is a small enough country, and the drug business is so highly incestuous—so many people are related to each other—that everybody knows everybody else's business. Orlando was an obvious target, having earned the right to be near the top of the list of the government's most wanted criminals, and needed to protect his family, his business, and himself.

In turn, he systematically ordered the murders of any Cali guys whom he thought might talk. Included among them was Miguel Orejuela's son.

Orlando ordered Varela to send assassins to a popular Brazilian steak house in Cali, where they stormed in with guns blazing at a table where the son was having dinner with several cartel associates. Four other people were killed, although Orejuela junior survived, badly wounded.

But the Cali mob wasn't his only worry. For the man whose sartorial preference had earned him the nickname *"el hombre del overol"*—the man in the overalls—time was running out. He didn't know when or if the government in Bogota would actually begin extraditing, but he knew that day would come. If the final bell sounded before he arranged something, he could be shipped off to America. And there, he'd be "dead man walking."

Spending five years in a Colombian jail wasn't a happy prospect, but it was much better than a one-way ticket to the States. Anyway, he knew he could continue running his business from prison—they were all doing it—so that, no matter what, five years later he'd be even richer than he was now.

The more he thought about it, the more he saw it as a no-brainer.

In the fall of 1997, with Fernando already out of the picture, Orlando handed over the day-to-day control of the business to Arcangel. Orlando was also counting on Varela's loyalty.

That was his first mistake.

By now, Don Diego—a 230-pound former truck driver—had risen through the ranks of the Urdinola gang, forged his own ties with the AUC, developed new shipping routes through Mexico, and strengthened his own alliance with the Arellano Felix Cartel in Tijuana. It made him and his brothers a force to reckon with. Because they'd known each other as kids, Orlando felt that Don Diego would just go about his own business and not worry about the Henaos's. He didn't see Don Diego as a direct threat.

That was his second mistake.

And then there was Orlando's old friend Bustamante. He, too, had taken advantage of the disarray created by the Cali cartel's undoing and created joint ventures with Mexico's Juarez Cartel. Orlando recognized Bustamante as a very smart trafficker. But because they had history, Orlando felt that he and Bustamante shared a natural bond.

Mistake number three.

Understandably, the jailed Orejuela brothers were outraged at the attack in Cali on Miguel's son. They wanted Orlando dead.

Pacho, who was already furious with Varela, became even more incensed as Varela and the Hanao family vultured-in on the carcass of Pacho's business. Locked in his cell with a lot of time to think about these things, Pacho ordered Varela's murder.

One night in late August 1997, a dozen men attacked Varela's convoy of cars and armed guards as they sped along a mountain road. Varela's men fought back. Some of the failed assassins escaped and some were killed, but two were captured. Varela personally tortured them until they confessed that they'd been paid by Pacho. Then he killed both of them.

A month later, on September 29, after pleading guilty to illicit enrichment and money-laundering charges—but not to drug trafficking or murder—Orlando took up residence at Modelo Prison in Bogotá. Coincidentally, Pacho's younger half brother Juan Manuel—a cripple in a wheelchair—was also there. So was Pacho's cousin Pedro.

Two weeks after that, on October 13, Juan Manuel wheeled his chair up to Orlando, pulled out a 38-caliber revolver, and shot him in the back six times.

In response, Orlando's friends stabbed Juan Manuel, although he survived the knife attack.

On November 5, just three weeks after Orlando's death, a thirty-two-year-old man named Rafael Angel Uribe came to the front gates of Palmira Prison. He announced that he was a lawyer and was there on a legal visit.

Inside the high walls of this maximum-security jail, there are five inner courtyards, with guards in open towers armed with machine guns. Pacho was in one of the courtyards, standing with other prisoners, watching a soccer game when Uribe walked up and embraced him. Clearly, the two men knew each other. Uribe then pulled out a 9mm pistol—no one ever found out if he'd smuggled the weapon into the penitentiary or whether it was already inside—and shot Pacho five times in the head.

The men with Pacho turned on Uribe and beat him unconscious. He survived, but Pacho didn't.

Back in Cartago, as the Henao clan rallied around Arcangel, Varela had ideas of his own. He began taking over shipping routes to move whatever product he could buy, or steal, with the help of the FARC.

He grew fast and ruthlessly.

Before long, Varela declared open war on anyone who dared to get in his way, challenging Arcangel and setting his sights on Don Diego. In the posturing that signaled the first stage of what would become a bloody civil war, a void appeared in the cartel's leadership. And Bustamante stepped up to assume it.

11

He was born in March 1958 in El Aguila, an "eagle's nest" in the mountainous northernmost corner of the Cauca Valley, about twelve miles outside Cartago. His father was a shoemaker. And while stories vary, he is said to be one of at least twelve children.

He stood a stocky five foot nine, and weighed 190 pounds. He had brown hair, brown eyes, and a deceptively harmless-looking face. He had no formal education but of all the ones from Cartago, he is said to have had the best-honed gut instincts.

For most of his life, Bustamante worked as a farmhand, a gas station attendant, and a hoodlum. Records in Bogota note that in 1986, while employed at a gas station, he did not own any property and, in fact, had a bad credit rating as a delinquent debtor. A year later, a report says, he was worth $200 million.

Even with Orlando Henao's help, there's no way Bustamante could have built up that kind of fortune that quickly. But there's no doubt that, by 1990, he had acquired great wealth, acquired several companies, and owned a lot of property throughout the Cartago area.

Bustamante pretended to be a rancher and cattleman, while all the time moving tons of cocaine into the U.S. At the height of his power he owned as many as eight planes and maintained private airstrips on several ranches. He owned a number of "go-fast" speedboats and even a few oceangoing cargo vessels. He employed six hundred to eight hundred men just to protect him.

With Orlando dead and Varela taking aim at both Arcangel and Diego Montoya, Bustamante proclaimed himself neutral. He refused to take sides. Instead, while the others were posturing for war, Bustamante took advantage of their distraction to increase his business in the States, at their expense.

Because Hector grew up in Cartago, he knew all these stories, and knew all of the people, and was very good at describing the inner mechanics of the cartel.

He told Bonnie and Rooney that Bustamante liked really young girls. He would either seduce them with money, jewelry, and cars or use whatever means to get them into his bed. Hector said that if you were in Cartago and saw a teenaged girl driving a BMW, that meant Bustamante had sex with her.

Over the course of several months, Hector told Bonnie and Rooney what each person in the cartel did and what their relationships were with the others. He said that Bustamante moved around a lot, going from place to place, rarely sleeping in the same place two nights in a row. He said that many people in town knew where his farms and ranches were, and that a few knew where he preferred to live, but hardly anyone knew where he was at any given time. He said that no one ever knew when he was going to appear at the office.

"Office?" Rooney asked. "Like he's some sort of guy who sits behind a desk from nine to five?"

Hector said that Bustamante's office was in a shopping mall in Cartago, above a parking garage. It didn't have "Norte Valle Cartel" written on the door, but he went there to meet with people and to run his business and those people who needed to get in touch with him knew where the office was.

"They go there to work," he said. "It is a big business and there is much to do. There is bookkeeping and there are salaries, and there are bribes to pay and there is transportation and logistics and protection and there is money to collect. They go to an office, just like you."

Not only did Bustamante have an office, but his lieutenants had their own offices, too.

The first was Orlando Sabogal Zuluaga.

A thuggish, oval-faced character from Toro in the mountains southwest of Cartago, he was known as "Alberto" and "El Mono" (the hand) and sometimes also as "Caraqueso" (cheese face). Clearly intelligent, Sabogal had been Bustamante's right-hand man from the early 1990s when he was still in his mid-twenties; Bustamante entrusted him with nitty-gritty logistics—quantities, routes, and arrival times—so that the drugs got out and the money came back in.

But in 1998, Sabogal and Bustamante had a falling-out. According to what Sabogal later told Bonnie and Rooney, he was not only working for Bustamante, he was also moving fifty-kilo shipments for his own account. On several occasions, to save money, he combined shipments. Bustamante found out about it and fired him.

Lucky to still be alive, Sabogal went back to work for Bustamante a few years later. By then, Bustamante had divided his logistical operations. Not wanting to be so dependent on one person, he'd promoted Jaime Maya Duran to run one office, and split the second office between Jhonny Cano and Gabriel Villanueva.

Jaime Maya, who was three years older than Sabogal and born in Cartago, dressed in button-down shirts, a tie and jacket, and looked at drug trafficking as he would any multinational enterprise. Instinctively, he understood that violence gets in the way of doing business and making money and did whatever he could to stay away from the violent side of the trade.

On the other hand, José Gabriel Ramirez Villanueva did not shy away from violence, and built a reputation for himself as a dependable player on Bustamante's team. Nicknamed "Truchi," one of the many jobs he handled for Bustamante was to launder cash through the acquisition of large properties and livestock in the Antioquia and Cordoba regions.

But the real star was Eildelber Jhon Cano-Correa, known as Jhonny or "Flechas" (arrow). He was Bustamante's chief enforcer.

Five years younger than Bustamante but born in the same village, he'd known Rasguño all his life. A couple of inches shorter and twenty pounds lighter, Jhonny was a lot of things that Bustamante wasn't. Known for his love of fishing, which he used to do not with a pole but with dynamite, he had long dark hair, a cool way about him, and soap opera bad-boy looks. Where Bustamante gave off a genuine sense of amorality, Jhonny was more thoughtful, straighter, a more direct kind of character with a sense of vulnerability—decidedly an odd quality for a professional killer—but one that women picked up on. He'd joined Bustamante's gang as a low-level teenaged "sicario"—a hit man—whose specialty was shooting people from a motorcycle, and quickly rose through the ranks.

After firing Sabogal that first time, Bustamante compartmentalized his operation. At the top of the chain of command, he made sure that no one knew as much as he did. Further down, a man might be a local butcher during the day and sit on a bridge as a lookout at night. He had a walkie-talkie and a contact to call if he saw something suspicious. But he didn't know the people who counted the money, and the people who counted the money didn't know the people who transported the drugs.

The same went for the men who worked directly for Sabogal, Villanueva, and Cano. They only knew what—and who—they needed to know.

Bustamante's office had satellite phones, cell phones, faxes, computers and walkie-talkies. Bustamante even had a laptop. Under normal circumstances, that can be dangerous because offices, phones, faxes, and computers can be bugged.

But not in Cartago. This was home. This is where Bustamante

took care of his friends. This is where he and his cronies were protected.

Hearing about Bustamante and the others firsthand from Hector was very helpful, but Bonnie knew if she was ever going to use anything he said in court, she needed a lot of corroboration. So Rooney began hunting through every database he could find to see if there was any mention, anywhere, of Luis Hernando Gomez Bustamante and his stature as head of the NVC.

The only thing he came up with was a drug importation indictment out of Roanoke, Virginia, dated 1990–1991. It was a small kilo deal. Bustamante wasn't in the country at the time and seemed to be named almost as an afterthought, appearing on the indictment as the twentieth defendant. Anyway, it was pre-extradition.

Still, Bonnie contacted the prosecutor. He told her he didn't believe anybody was still around, although he thought there might be a witness who could talk about the case, but the last he'd heard, the witness was living in Florida.

A few days later, Bonnie and Rooney—with the prosecutor from Virginia in tow—flew to Miami. They met with the witness and Bonnie put him through a six-hour interrogation. She came home with a lot of good background material, but nowhere near enough to make her own case.

The technical term is, "historical drug case."

The reality is, it's probably the most difficult type of drug case to prosecute.

In an ordinary, run-of-the-mill drug case, you rely on a seizure or a wiretap. You have the drugs and the cash and other hard evidence to tie the suspect to the drugs.

In a historical case, there are no drugs, there is no cash, there are no CCTV tapes of the suspect committing a criminal act.

Instead, the historical case almost always relies on direct testimony from witnesses who, at best, are just as suspect, just as sleazy, and sometimes just as guilty as the defendant. Most of the time they're other traffickers. They take the stand as part of a plea bargain, in exchange for a more lenient sentence or reduced jail time. The prosecutor must always worry, is the jury going to believe these guys? Everybody in the courtroom knows that the witnesses have a motive to lie.

But you can't make a historical case without cooperators and you can't have cooperators without plea bargains.

Cumulative weight is the key. You go hunting for witnesses and talk to as many of them as you can find, and pile in everything—make it really heavy—until you reach that tipping point. Two or three sleazebag witnesses is okay. Six or seven is much better.

The indictment itself is stock language. It's boilerplate. Fill in the blanks. In those days, because it was a lot less rigid than it is today, Bonnie didn't have to write "prosecution memos" to convince someone that she had a thorough case. All she had to do was go into a boss and say, I've got enough evidence.

Most prosecutors couldn't be bothered. It was too much hard work for results that are never guaranteed. Not with those sorts of witnesses. They're sitting ducks for defense attorneys to cast reasonable doubt about their testimony simply by reminding the jury of their motive for testifying.

What's more, historical cases hardly ever produce the kinds of headlines with pictures that prosecutors like best—suspects being dragged away, bags of white powder alongside weapons and stacks of cash. With historical cases, there may be a small mention of a verdict. More often than not, when a deal is struck with the defendant—meaning there's been a plea bargain to avoid a trial—a prosecutor doesn't even get that small mention.

At the Central Islip outpost, there were about a dozen other prosecutors. They worked white-collar crime, mortgage fraud, and gang violence. If there was a drug case, it was usually a one kilo buy-bust: An undercover DEA agent would purchase a kilo on a street corner, his friends would jump out of unmarked cars and arrest the seller who'd get done in court.

The Brooklyn office wasn't much different, except that they were doing things on a larger scale, like three hundred to five hundred kilo busts.

In Miami, because South Florida is so flooded with cocaine, they were working on a gigantic scale, hunting for guys moving powder by the ton.

Historical cases weren't anybody else's thing. Especially when the DEA was involved. With them, everything was reactive, geared up for slam-dunk cases. They'd grab someone off the street, flip him, and go on to the next bust. Their style suited prosecutors, too, because everyone was being judged on how many kilos they'd taken off the streets and how much money they'd seized.

That said, Bonnie was more than happy to stay under the radar for as long as possible. She needed to be on Long Island because of her oldest son. It suited her that no one in Central Islip or Brooklyn or even at Main Justice in Washington, D.C., seemed to care how many warrants she'd written for wires. No one seemed to care how many suspects she'd turned into cooperators, which in turn brought in more suspects to turn into cooperators, which in turn brought in all those drugs piled high next to stacks of money.

No one seemed to care about historical work.

Those few people who knew what Bonnie and Rooney were doing simply thought the two of them were crazy.

At one point, she actually had a supervisor in Long Island say to her, "You're wasting government time and money trying to arrest people in Colombia. Why don't you just leave them there where they belong?"

That was the level of the lack of understanding around her office.

At El Dorado, they were still busy hitting remitters. Rooney was part of a money-laundering group, and bringing in the numbers, so his supervisors left him alone, too. When John Forbes was running things at WTC6, he understood that you got the best out of Rooney by trusting him and leaving him alone. When Forbes retired and Diane Hanson took over, she understood that, too. Both of them were outstanding investigators before they became bosses. Which made them unique. The people over them didn't necessarily comprehend what was going on or how these things develop. Many of the people higher up, above Forbes and Hanson, didn't know how the streets really worked, and didn't have the time to care. They were too busy protecting their own asses.

So Bonnie and Rooney kept doing their thing.

And now their thing was Luis Hernandez Gomez Bustamante.

At the same time, a major DEA operation against Colombian traffickers was underway out of the U.S. Attorney's office in Miami.

Operation Millennium was a long-term, highly complex investigation into the inner workings of what remained of the Medellin and Cali cartels and their partners in Mexico. It would result in the arrest of 31 traffickers, plus the seizure of 13.7 tons of cocaine and $2.25 million in cash.

It was all about suspects in handcuffs, drugs and cash, exactly the kinds of headlines and photos that the DEA and the prosecutors love.

Specifically, Operation Millennium secured the arrest, extradition, prosecution, and thirty-year sentences of two main targets: Alejandro Bernal-Madrigal, the blue-eyed forty-year-old known as "El Juvenal"—the young one—and his friend, forty-four-year-old Fabio Ochoa-Vasquez, a trafficker with a pedigree. Both men were original members of Escobar's crew, had assumed positions of leadership and, during 1997–1998, were smuggling thirty tons of cocaine through Mexico and into the United States every month.

Bernal was interesting because he was the man who began modernizing the business by adapting to the times. For example, he was the first to set up private Internet chat rooms, secured with sophisticated firewalls, to communicate with members of his organization. He perfected the use of pay-as-you-go phones for texting. He also created a highly lucrative niche for himself as the clearinghouse for other traffickers. He brokered deals with the Mexicans and the paramilitary forces, moving drugs and illegal weapons between them.

But Fabio was a major catch. He was the youngest of three famous trafficking brothers. The one in the middle, Jorge, was a founding member of the Medellin Cartel, along with Escobar, Carlos Lehder, and José Gonzalo Rodríguez Gacha. Older brother, Juan David, the least involved of the family, ran a restaurant in Bogotá but invested heavily in shipments.

When Fabio was twenty-one, Jorge sent him to Florida to be the main contact with his close friend and business partner, Barry Seal, an American pilot who flew drug runs for the Medellin mob. Some years later, when it came to the Ochoas' attention that Seal was cooperating with the DEA, and that the CIA had installed cameras in his planes, the Ochoas took it personally. Jorge, especially, had considered Seal like a brother. And he might well have done something about Seal's betrayal, except that in 1984 Jorge was arrested in Spain and held there.

The U.S. applied for his extradition, and one of the witnesses they scheduled to testify against him was Seal.

But on February 19, 1986, while Seal was sitting in his car in a parking lot in Baton Rouge, Louisiana, several men approached him and one of them had a machine gun. Apparently Fabio wanted to be the man who pulled the trigger, but three other men were convicted of Seal's murder and sentenced to life imprisonment.

Without Seal as the main witness, the U.S. extradition request faltered and Jorge was sent home.

In 1991, all three Ochoas surrendered to the Colombians under the amnesty program. And all three were back on the streets before the extradition law passed. It meant that the U.S. could not ask for their deportation for any previous crimes, including the murder of Seal.

Of course, the brothers remained on American radar but they were smart enough to stay out of American reach. Juan David and Jorge announced that they were going straight and became horse ranchers. Trafficking had made them very rich and it is just possible that they actually retired. But Fabio stayed in the business.

Unfortunately for him, Operation Millennium uncovered crimes post-1997, which put Fabio in chains and brought him to the States.

He was convicted on drug-trafficking charges and sentenced to thirty years.

On the surface, Operation Millennium seemed straightforward. But running beneath the surface of the case against Fabio, and several others, was a clandestine DEA sting intended to lure traffickers into surrendering. The fellow at the center of this top secret Operation Cali-Man, was an informant in Miami who was being paid by the DEA to arrange phony cooperation deals. Unbeknownst to Bonnie, Rooney, or anyone else outside the DEA, one of Cali-Man's top targets was Luis Hernando Gomez Bustamante.

In December 1999, an assistant U.S. attorney from the Miami office, along with two DEA agents, met secretly with Bustamante in the Cartagena Hilton on Colombia's Caribbean coast. The Americans broached the subject of a possible surrender deal. Bustamante, who was beginning to feel the heat generated by Varela, suggested he might be amenable to something, as long as it did not involve him giving up information about his associates or testifying against them. The Americans said they weren't interested.

A second meeting, scheduled to last two days, was arranged for January 13–14, 2000, in Panama City. During that meeting, Bustamante revealed to the agents that serious corruption was going on inside the DEA's Bogotá office. He named a very senior official working there and insisted that he was on the payroll of the former Colombian National Police (DAS) Colonel, Danilo Gonzalez.

A lawyer at the Department of Justice looked into the allegations and discovered that some agents in Bogotá did have suspect ties with traffickers. The dossier was passed along to the Office of Professional Responsibility Affairs—the DEA's version of Internal Affairs—to discover the extent of the relationships between Danilo and their own agents.

That investigation turned up an even more complete picture of the clandestine sting operation run with the informant in Miami.

In turn, the FBI was called in to investigate the allegations of corruption in Bogotá, unaware that the bureau was also working the same informant in Miami. It then came to light that the informant was allegedly extorting money from traffickers in exchange for promises of lenient jail sentences. In other words, he was apparently brokering deals with the traffickers behind the DEA's back. But then, there was reason to suspect that it was the FBI, not the DEA, which might have authorized the informant's alleged freelance extortion scheme. It was later revealed that the informant in Miami was working not just for the DEA and, behind their backs, the FBI. He was also working behind both their backs for the CIA, as well.

The more these two investigations unraveled, exposing Danilo's involvement in both, the messier they got. One week after meeting Bustamante in Panama City, the DEA launched another top secret operation, this one called Rainmaker, to target Danilo.

Bonnie had no way of knowing that the DEA was already on to Bustamante. Had she known, it would have made a lot of things much easier for her.

And for Danilo, too.

Linking him to Bustamante would get him murdered.

Oscar Rodriguez is a larger-than-life character, straight out of central casting. A hulking bear of a man, his charm and intelligence is just as big.

He was born in Cuba, but his family managed to get out very early on. Castro had just come to power when they moved to Miami. He grew up there, bounced around several schools but eventually got his law degree there. Everybody in Miami's Latino community knows him. Everybody wants to shake his hand. And there are some people who honestly believe that if "Big O"—as he is affectionately called by friends and strangers alike—ever decided to run for mayor, he'd be elected hands down.

But Oscar insists he isn't interested in that. Now in his sixties, and a grandfather, he says he's more than happy to be just another lawyer.

Except he isn't just another lawyer.

He is, perhaps, the most famous criminal defense lawyer in the

Latino community. And his reputation stretches all the way to Colombia.

Sometime after Bustamante's Panama City meeting with the DEA, Oscar received a call from a man he'd known for nearly fifteen years, to say that a friend of his might need some help.

"You need to come meet him," the man said. "Come alone. If he likes you, we'll see where we go from there."

So Oscar flew to Bogotá and was driven to Cartago. He stayed there overnight and early the next morning, was taken to Bustamante's Hacienda El Vergel—Bustamante's 1,150-acre farm, five miles south of Cartago on the way to Obando, where he raised and bred 2,000 head of cattle.

Bustamante had several other farms in the area, and one nearly twice as large in Monteria, but this was his favorite, and when he arrived, Oscar could understand why.

"It was," he recalls, "the most impressive ranch I have ever seen. It was enormous. Spectacular."

He admits that when meetings like this happen, he is always a little nervous at first, but only because he wants to get the case. The man who brought him to the ranch was a gentleman and, accordingly, was guaranteeing Oscar's safety. Their relationship was built on mutual confidence and Oscar trusted the man. Still, he recognized the fact that this could be a dangerous place to be.

They arrived at a big gate, which was unlocked and opened by a single guard who let them through. They then drove quite a while to the stables, where hands were tending to a lot of horses.

Oscar says, "If there were guns, I didn't see any. If there were people watching me and protecting the person I was meeting, I didn't see them either. If we were being observed, the people watching us were never visible or close by."

One of the buildings that made up the large stable complex was an office. And that's where he met Bustamante for the first time.

"He was very pleasant with me," Oscar says. "And I found him very smart. I saw the scar on his left cheek, the one that gave him the nickname Rasguño. I called him señor and he called me señor.

He wanted me to negotiate a settlement. He said he wanted to co-operate, but he said he also wanted some protection for his organization."

Oscar tried to encourage him that a settlement was almost always the best course. He told Bustamante that, in principle, if someone like him wanted to go to trial, there was a chance that a technicality could come up and he might get off. But the reality of life was that it probably would not happen.

Bustamante understood and repeated that he wanted to cooperate.

Carrying that message back to Miami, Oscar went to see the U.S. Attorney there in the hopes that he could negotiate something for his client. But no one in Miami was interested. Oscar had to inform Bustamante that the prosecutors found his terms "unworkable."

Eventually Oscar and Bustamante had to agree that this wasn't going to happen. Bustamante grew hesitant. Oscar went back to work for other clients.

Oblivious to the fact that people on the same team had been working the same target, Bonnie forged ahead with her own case, alone.

12

It's not that the DEA never learned to play in the sandbox, it's that, deep down, law enforcement agencies don't trust each other.

They all have their own agendas.

Customs runs a sting and doesn't tell the DEA because they worry that the DEA will take what evidence and witnesses they want and use them to make their own case. The DEA comes across something in the Caribbean and doesn't mention it to the FBI because they'll get better mileage for themselves by bringing in the CIA. The FBI stumbles onto drug cash that can be seized and doesn't bring in the state or local police because why divvy up those assets if you don't have to?

The El Dorado Task Force was a rare exception where agencies actually worked well together. That's because the mission was narrowly defined—go after drug money—because supervisors like John Forbes, Diane Hanson and, later, Joe Webber, were exceptionally good at team building, and most important of all, because they had a forfeiture fund.

The idea behind forfeiture funds is that when the bad guys' money is taken away from them, it should be used by the good guys to take more money away from other bad guys. It goes back to the basic philosophy, if you bankrupt the bastards you take product off the streets. So a percentage of seized assets, especially drug money, was divided up between the various task force agencies. That went a long way toward breaking down the jealousies, barriers, and tensions that invariably exist between the feds and the other feds, and the feds and the locals.

Sharing the bounty was the glue that bonded together El Dorado.

On the morning of September 11, 2001, dozens of El Dorado agents were inside WCT6. They evacuated within minutes of the first plane hitting the north side of the North Tower. Everybody eventually got out, although Joe Webber decided he'd be the last man out. He ran through the smoke-filled, burning building to see that the offices were clear, that no one was left, and wound up getting trapped inside. His heroics were matched only by the heroics of two firefighters from Ladder Company 11 who somehow located him in there and pulled him out.

Bonnie was getting ready to go to work when her mother-in-law phoned in a panic. Bonnie's husband had flown out on a business trip the day before, and when her mother-in-law said, "Have you heard the news," Bonnie's first thought was that something had happened to her husband and his plane.

When she learned it was the World Trade Center, Bonnie hung up, turned on the television—the first plane had just hit—and tried to get in touch with people. She eventually found someone at Central Islip who said the office would be closed, but she never got hold of anyone at WTC6, and couldn't reach Rooney, and spent the rest of the day at home, watching in horror, as the events of 9/11 unfolded on television, worried sick about all the people she'd spent so much time working with at El Dorado.

Rooney was in Queens that morning, with Toby, on his way to pick up an informant. He heard what had happened on the radio, and immediately went back to a special meeting point near La Guardia Airport. He and Toby sat there for the day, unable to reach anyone at WTC6.

It was two days later before the task forces regrouped at Kennedy Airport. Everyone had gotten out of the building safely.

Six days after the attack, Rooney went back into WTC6, into a small section of the building still standing at the corner of West and Vesey streets, which is where the El Dorado offices were. The crumbling towers had brought down everything else.

The streets were three- and four-stories high with rubble.

It was, he recalls, a war zone.

A team of NYPD emergency services guys escorted Rooney inside the building hoping to recover any of the computer network backup tapes that might have survived. Rooney knew where they were stored. And, in fact, he did find them and get them out.

But being in what was left of their offices, he says, was the most surreal moment of his life. Everything was burnt—the cubicles, the desks, the chairs—nothing was left except dozens of four-drawer-high file cabinets. They were flame-retardant and still standing. The files in the drawers were gone, but the cabinets themselves were still lined up in rows.

To Rooney, they looked like tombstones in a cemetery.

Two weeks later, with fires still burning belowground and crews working nonstop, desperately hoping to find survivors—finding instead limbs and body parts and horrible reminders that 2,800 people had been murdered here—Webber and two other agents, Alysa Erichs and Tina Zimmerman, went back inside.

In the main seizure vault there were 3,200 pounds of cocaine, 983 pounds of heroin, and some ecstasy. In another part of the building there were firearms, including a cache of fully automatic weapons and 1.4 million rounds of ammunition. There was cash in one safe and thousands of classified documents, confidential informant source files, and case files in other safes. They got everything out.

Within three months of the disaster, the El Dorado Task Force was back in business in new offices farther uptown.

Organized crime is the planet's biggest business and North America is its most lucrative market. Globalization has turned organized criminals into the most powerful special interest group in the world. Unfortunately, on November 25, 2002, law enforcement—at least on the federal level—lost the plot. That's when, exactly 440 days after the terrorist attacks, the Department of Homeland Security (DHS) was born.

George W. Bush's grand vision was one agency fits all. But his knee-jerk reaction in the immediate aftermath of September 11, demonstrated an unfathomable misunderstanding of how law enforcement works in the real world, how territory defines the mission both for good and bad, how agencies need to have separate identities, and how the war on crime needs to be fought.

It wasn't broken, so he fixed it.

He merged twenty-two disparate agencies into a single department, believing that by bringing them together they would miraculously function as one. But the best will in the world is not enough to mix oil and water. As a result, the president created a shrine to territorial battles by polarizing two distinct spheres of concern.

The first is terrorism.

That became the nation's priority. By presidential order, Customs, Immigration and Naturalization, the Secret Service, and the Coast Guard were melded together into Homeland Security. In Bush's model, the "big four" would homogenize with an ensemble of smaller agencies and everyone would live happily ever after. But the elements were inharmonious. As a result, traditional missions were irreparably distorted.

After defining the role of Homeland Security—"To lead the

unified national effort to secure the country and preserve our freedoms"—Bush made certain that the real power to deal with threats to the homeland was not handed to the DHS, but rather to the FBI. Which is why he deliberately left the FBI, and three other important agencies, out of the DHS mix.

Politically, the bureau has always had too much clout to be messed with. Talk about not playing well in the sandbox. It's tough to find many people in other agencies who have anything good to say about the FBI. The bureau's demeanor tends to be, our ball, our bat, our rules. They have never met a law they didn't like. And they have never shied away from taking credit for anything positive, even when they've had very little to do with it. The bureau is a bully. Bush pandered to them.

That said, prior to 9/11, the FBI worked in multiple areas. Where it did not have overall investigative control, at least it coordinated authority with federal, state, and local agencies. When Bush handed the FBI lead agency status in protecting the homeland—essentially saying that Homeland Security's mission wasn't really the security of the homeland—manpower was a concern and the bureau had to downgrade priorities in other areas.

The second agency the president didn't dare mess with was the CIA.

They play by their own rules, too. Traditionally, the CIA doesn't talk to the FBI and the FBI doesn't talk to the CIA. Except when one of them decides there's something to be gained in its own best interest. Forming the DHS to get agencies to play as one had no effect on either. So the president ordered that "desks" be set up in each other's operations room, giving the CIA a physical presence inside the FBI and vice versa. But you don't tear down decades of innate distrust by putting a desk somewhere.

The president also ordered both agencies to brief him together every morning. On paper that works. But in practice, when one agency has something to say that it doesn't want the other agency to know about—for whatever reason, top-secret security or basic territorial jealousy—it gets spoken about in private, or not at all.

Despite public pronouncements and much hail-fellow-well-met photo opportunities, these two agencies have never gotten along and there is no reason to think they ever will.

Next, the president left the DEA out of the DHS. That's because the DEA was born from the rib of the CIA and neither of them is going to stand for anyone, or any other agency, getting in the middle of their special relationship.

Finally there is the Bureau of Alcohol, Tobacco, Firearms and Explosives (ATF). Mr. Bush used the Homeland Security Bill of 2002 to move ATF's law enforcement function from the Treasury Department into Justice, but kept their tax and trade functions at Treasury.

At the same time, there was talk of reassigning ATF investigators to the FBI. But ATF agents had no interest in becoming FBI agents, and the FBI had no interest in any ATF agents. What the bureau was secretly trying to finagle was the ATF's explosives lab. In bureau-think they were whining, it's a much better, more sophisticated operation than ours, so why can't we have it? This time the president sided with the ATF. But only just. By putting the ATF and its lab under the Justice Department, where the FBI is also housed, he left the door open so that someday, if and when the Justice Department declared ATF agents redundant, the transfer of the lab to the FBI would be a simple administrative procedure.

If the Department of Homeland Security is really going to fortify the country from terrorist attacks, it's only logical that the law enforcement function of ATF needs to be there because the F in ATF is "firearms" and no agency in the world knows firearms—and absolutely everything about explosives—better than the ATF.

The second sphere of concern was street crime.

This is a conventional "reelect me" agenda, where politicians reassure voters that by putting more cops on the beat, the streets will be safer and, therefore, the politician is worthy of reelection. Except that crime has not been local for a generation. Most crime in America today is fueled by outside forces, national and international. Local is merely a symptom.

While both spheres of concern are important, by focusing assets on terror and street crime, Mr. Bush clumsily created a huge no-man's-land in the middle. As a consequence, transnational organized criminals filled the vacuum, solidifying their financial interests in drugs, arms, illegal immigrants, intellectual property theft (including software, music, and trademarks), counterfeit money, counterfeit designer goods, identity theft (including credit and bank fraud), securities' fraud, child pornography, Nigerian 419 fraud, extortion, smuggling (including cigarettes, alcohol, hazardous materials, and PCPs), plus money laundering.

For example:

As soon as U.S. Customs was ordered to shift assets away from drug-money laundering to target terror fundraising, drug-money laundering increased significantly.

As soon as U.S. Customs tried to move into the terror fundraising arena, the FBI balked and demanded overall control of all terror fundraising investigations. The battle for territory was brutal and, after sidelining many of Customs' most experienced financial investigators, the bureau promptly downgraded its own money-laundering investigations. That, in turn, created a rise in terror-related fundraising in the United States.

Within a matter of weeks of assuming the role of lead agency in all things terror related, the FBI relinquished its role as lead agency in crimes such as interstate truck hijacking. At which time, interstate truck hijackings increased significantly.

At the same time, the FBI, incentivized by its increased budget for the war on terror, downgraded drug-trafficking investigations. Except where they saw substantial assets to be forfeited. Drug investigations were shifted to the DEA. But because the DEA was outside both the Homeland Security and FBI loop, it was virtually left to its own underfunded devices. As a result, America remains cocaine saturated and is, today, nearly heroin and methamphetamine saturated.

Support for the Bush reorganization of American law enforcement was widespread, enshrined in the "protect the country from another terror attack" anthem. Some of the people singing that song where it affected law enforcement, were simply incompetent. A few were outright corrupt. Notable among the culprits is a hard-core faction of Texas politicos who have, for years, benefited from the funding largesse of the Texas banking lobby. That group, which so actively fought legislation to defeat any and all money-laundering regulations, has been a major beneficiary of cross-border Mexican drug-money laundering.

As a rule of thumb, the reward for a successful criminal conspiracy is directly proportionate to the size and complexity of the conspiracy. Just as it is in the world of legitimate business, the biggest rewards are won on the biggest playing fields. When extortion, fraud, identity theft, drug trafficking, child pornography, insider trading, arms smuggling, people smuggling, and counterfeiting stem from global conspiracies, the rewards can be colossal.

While the FBI is beating the bushes for terrorists, and cops on the street are making sure that little old ladies are not getting mugged at the mall, and the DHS pretends that it is the reason why the country might be safer, organized criminals and global terrorists remain multinational powers.

At the same time, some multinational powers have become organized criminal conspiracies. Witness the money-laundering exploits of Enron, which mirrors techniques developed by the Cali Cartel. Since 9/11, several major American businesses have moved into this no-man's-land of criminal enterprise. In addition to Enron, there is WorldCom, Parmalat, Riggs Bank, Bernie Madoff; and then there are some major tobacco companies that have allegedly been dealing directly with organized criminals and terrorists to exploit new markets.

One year before the 9/11 attacks, a special report on America's ability to deal with international terrorism was submitted to Congress.

It leveled criticism at the intelligence community: "The CIA has created a climate that is overly risk averse. This has inhibited the recruitment of essential, if sometimes unsavory, terrorist informants and forced the United States to rely too heavily on foreign intelligence services."

It leveled criticism, too, at the FBI: "Law enforcement agencies are traditionally reluctant to share information outside of their circles so as not to jeopardize any potential prosecution. The FBI does promptly share information warning about specific terrorist threats with the CIA and other agencies. But the FBI is far less likely to disseminate terrorist information that may not relate to an immediate threat even though this could be of immense long-term or cumulative value to the intelligence community. . . . The problem is particularly pronounced with respect to information collected in the FBI's field offices in the United States, most of which never reaches the FBI headquarters, let alone other U.S. government agencies or departments."

It contained a warning of things to come which, these days, reverberates: "Neither al-Qaida's extremist politico-religious beliefs nor its leader, Osama bin Laden, is unique. If al-Qaida and Osama bin Laden were to disappear tomorrow, the United States would still face potential terrorist threats from a growing number of groups opposed to perceived American hegemony. Moreover, new terrorist threats can suddenly emerge from isolated conspiracies or obscure cults with no previous history of violence."

And then there were a few paragraphs, otherwise obscured by that criticism and those warnings: "Transnational terrorist networks are difficult to predict, track, and penetrate. They rely on a variety of sources for funding and logistical support, including self-financing criminal activities such as kidnapping, narcotics, and petty crimes."

In the late 1990s, as the El Dorado Task Force was taking down wire remitters on a weekly basis, the agents stumbled across an oddity that no one seemed to understand. Records at a few of these remitters showed drug money going someplace new. Instead of it being wired to Colombia, there were several instances when cash was sent to Pakistan.

John Forbes passed that information along to his superiors, asking the question, "What the hell is going on here? Why Pakistan?"

He never got an answer because, at the time, no one upstairs seemed to give a damn.

As long as we live in a world where a seventeenth-century philosophy of sovereignty is reinforced with an eighteenth-century judicial model, defended by a nineteenth-century concept of law enforcement that is still trying to come to terms with twentieth-century technology, the twenty-first century will belong to traffickers, terrorists, and criminals in the corporate world.

And the day will come when it is impossible to tell them apart.

13

While Rooney continued building a case against Bustamante, Bonnie also had to prepare for Monsalve's trial.

Ever since his failed attempt at an escape—if, in fact, that's what he was trying to do by putting his stuffed laundry bag under the sheets on his bed at the MCC—he'd been housed in the SHU on the top floor of the MDC in Brooklyn. He hated it and did not hide his resentment at having been sent there. Defiantly, he refused to cooperate, taking Bonnie right up to the eve of trial.

The charges against him were voluminous. From January 1993 through January 1997, the government would contend, Monsalve was responsible for the importation of several tons of cocaine. The drugs were smuggled in through Mexico to either Los Angeles or Texas and then transported to New York by car or airplane. Bonnie had details of specific deals, and could document his money-laundering activities through the storefront remitters. She also had several witnesses ready to testify against Monsalve, including Lobo, Guzman, and Hector. But her ace card was Nancy Cadavid.

Rooney was talking to Nancy regularly and she was being, as he put it, "fabulously helpful." She'd been present at a lot of meetings Monsalve held with other traffickers, buyers, sellers, transporters, money launderers, and murderers. And she'd overheard a lot of conversations. She'd waived her rights when Rooney arrested her and continued to speak freely about Monsalve. She was prepared to testify under oath. She was ready to answer the question, "What does Mr. Monsalve do for a living?" with the answer, "He sells cocaine, what do you think he does!"

Much later, after it was all over, Monsalve's lawyer told Bonnie that of all the witnesses she'd lined up against him—most of whom were killers, convicts, criminals, and scumbags—the one he knew he had to fear the most was Nancy because she was unimpeachable. He said, "She was the one Monsalve could never refute."

With the case against Monsalve taking shape, something new popped up. Rooney was preparing Johnson Guzman to testify when he mentioned a July 26, 1993, murder in Queens. Rooney checked it out with Redrum, where it was still on their books as unsolved.

The victim was one of life's losers, a poor soul named Hugo Betancur. He was an illegal immigrant in his late twenties who minded a stash house run by a man named Abelardo Rojas Franco where, Bonnie believed, the cocaine belonged to Monsalve. Connecting Monsalve with that cocaine and then somehow tying him into Hugo's murder is why Rooney pursued it.

The way the Redrum officers told the story, it began when Abelardo's brother Jaime Rojas Franco—the same fellow who'd been driving Monsalve's car when Rooney grabbed him and who'd escaped arrest by claiming to be Daniel Giraldo—got it into his head that Betancur had been stealing drugs from the stash house.

The truth later came out that someone else had been stealing the drugs and that Betancur was only babysitting them. He had nothing at all to do with the thefts.

Guzman picked up the collection contract, which consisted of going to the stash house on Eleventh Street, in Astoria, Queens, and beating the shit out of Betancur until he gave back all the missing cocaine. Guzman showed up with his nephew Jairo Zapata, a heavyset nineteen-year-old who'd only just joined the gang, Jaime, and the third Rojas Franco brother, Ramon, who was known as "Loco" (crazy).

It was a very hot day, the temperature was climbing to eighty-eight, and when they got to the place, no one was home.

A typical stash house, there wasn't much furniture and there was no food in the fridge. The windows were shut and the curtains were drawn to prevent people from seeing in. The place was unbearably hot, and stank.

The four of them discussed what to do. Guzman ruled that they had to wait there until Hugo showed up. So they sat on the one couch in the living room, telling each other how hot it was, until Guzman decided it would be better if they hid, so that when Hugo arrived he wouldn't see them waiting and run away.

They hid in closets and other rooms and waited there, in the sweltering heat, until Hugo stepped through the front door. The four thugs jumped out of their hiding places and started beating the crap out of him, demanding that he give them back the drugs. Hugo protested that he didn't steal anything. The more Hugo swore he was innocent, the more the others beat him up.

Hugo cried that if there were drugs missing, it was his partner who must have stolen them. But the four men, who were ferociously punching and kicking him as he lay writhing on the floor, didn't care. They kept on punching and kicking him until he was half-conscious.

Dragging the bloodied Hugo into the bathroom, they dumped him into the tub, then handcuffed him to the faucet so that he couldn't escape.

Back in the living room, one of them asked, "What should we do now?"

Jaime told the others, "I believe him that he didn't steal the drugs. But he's seen our faces. We have to kill him."

Guzman wondered, "Who's going to do it?"

They talked about that for a while, each one suggesting it be one of the others, until Jaime offered to pay thirty thousand dollars to whoever did the killing.

Right away, Jairo raised his hand. "I've never killed anyone. I'll do it."

The others agreed, okay.

Obviously pleased with the prospect of becoming a "made" man, and also earning thirty-grand for his efforts, Jairo announced that he was going to spend the money on drugs and alcohol.

He was handed a gun. He went into the bathroom, found a towel and wrapped the gun in it. Betancur started begging for his life. Jairo said to him, "I'm sorry, I don't really want to do this," then shot him once in the side of his head and twice in the torso.

Afterward, the men cleaned the apartment. On the way out, they found a hidden kilo of cocaine and stole it. Jaime sold it for eighteen thousand dollars, only paid Jairo ten thousand dollars for his first hit—reneging on the thirty thousand dollars promise—and split the rest with the others.

Later, Rooney questioned Guzman, "Why didn't you do it? Why did you let Jairo kill Betancur when you'd already killed a whole bunch of people?"

Guzman told him, "Because I was on parole."

The logic of that has forever escaped Rooney. That Guzman could kidnap, beat up someone, and order a murder was one thing. That he didn't want to pull the trigger because it would somehow violate his parole was beyond Rooney's comprehension.

Anyway, the late July summer wore on and the heat did not subside. It stayed in the high eighties for a few days, then started climbing.

Several days after the murder, with the temperature now in the mid-nineties, one of the neighborhood kids complained to his parents that there was a horrific smell coming from the building over there. They called the police, who called the landlord. Inside, the cops found what remained of Hugo.

Bonnie and Rooney interviewed the first officers on the scene, and the Redrum officers who covered the case. One of them asked Bonnie if she wanted to see the murder photos.

Not thinking about what heat does to a dead body, she said sure.

The detective showed her a photo of Betancur, all swelled up, lying dead in the bathtub, with half his face missing.

She stared at it, then asked, "What's that white stuff on him?"

He told her, "Maggots."

She rushed to the bathroom and threw up.

Rooney gathered enough evidence for a fresh murder case against Jairo. And because this was murder in the pursuit of drug trafficking, he and Bonnie found themselves having gone from no death-penalty cases to two.

It turned out that Guzman had already pleaded guilty to this murder in a separate case, which took him out of the picture. The cops easily found Jairo, because he was serving time on an unrelated case, and right away, he confessed. As that gave the government a very solid case against the Rojas brothers, arrest warrants were issued for Jaime and Loco.

Knowing that the prosecution could never convict Jaime or Loco just on Johnson Guzman's testimony, Jairo became the main witness. Obviously, because he was cooperating, the death penalty needed to be taken off the table. Bonnie wrote the necessary memo, her front office agreed, and it went to Washington where the death-penalty committee saw no problem, either. After all, it's common sense that you don't put your cooperator to death.

Then the paperwork landed on the new attorney general's desk. John Ashcroft had just been sworn in and, out of the blue, he overrode the unanimous recommendations of everyone up the chain and decided Jairo had to die.

Bonnie was beyond shocked. This was a maniacal act, demonstrating that Ashcroft had no understanding of how prosecutors out in the real world did their job. She complained to everyone she could think of and spent the next year writing memos to explain to Ashcroft why he needed to unauthorize the death penalty.

Inevitably, common sense prevailed. Someone in his office made Ashcroft realize that putting Jairo to death was lunacy because it could irreparably undermine the entire prosecutorial plea-bargaining system. After all, why would anyone ever cooperate if he was going to die for his efforts? Ashcroft gave in, but only sort of. He ruled that if Jairo agreed to life without any possibility of parole, he would be spared.

Jairo had no choice but to take the plea. His reward for cooperating, for telling the truth and for helping the government make its case against two other reprehensible criminals, was to spend the rest of his life in prison.

Which is exactly what Bonnie would have recommended had Jairo not cooperated.

With his trial date approaching, Monsalve decided he was crazy.

He filed a motion of incompetance and forced the court to order psychiatric tests. That not only got him out of the SHU for short periods of time, but delayed the trial. When the report came back that he wasn't incompetant, the judge chastised him for wasting everybody's time and set a date.

Monsalve finally hired himself a decent attorney—he was up to number five—who showed up on Bonnie's office doorstep to ask, "What can we do at this point?"

She told him, "Not much."

He said, "Come on, there must be something."

"We've gone through this several times," she reminded him. "I'm not going to proffer him again."

"He's got a lot of information of value," the lawyer suggested.

"I'm sure he does," she agreed, "but no one's going to talk to him. You can try to ferret out the truth while you prepare for trial. I'm too busy."

This lawyer knew what he was doing and assured Bonnie, "He has information. Valuable information. Don't turn your back on him."

Bonnie thought about it and, on the spur of the moment, decided to hand him a deal that wasn't a deal. "Okay. Monsalve goes to court and pleads guilty. He has to plead to one of the two murders and all of the drug charges. If he does that, I'll agree to interview him. He pleads guilty and I will give him one more chance to cooperate."

"Huh?" The lawyer was dumbfounded. "What kind of a deal is that?"

She answered, "The only deal he's going to get."

In effect, she was asking Monsalve to turn up all his cards in exchange for absolutely nothing. The moment he pleaded guilty to one of the two murders, the judge would sentence him to life without the possibility of parole, put him behind bars and, basically, throw away the key.

And when she explained the deal that wasn't a deal to a few of the other prosecutors in her office, they all wanted to know, "Who's going to take that?"

But Bonnie was betting on the fact that Monsalve knew he was going to get convicted. That, as long as he was never coming out of jail, maybe there was a way to make sure he got sent to a prison where life was less uncomfortable than somewhere else.

She was right.

He walked into the courtroom and pled straight up.

The United States District Court for the Eastern District of New York at Central Islip is an eccentric-looking eleven-story reinforced concrete rectangle—kind of like a giant flat-screen TV—with a strange cement grain-silo entrance, that goes all the way up to the top.

Inside, there is a lot of open space and sunlight, with each floor feeding off a walkway facing large windows that look south. On a good day, at least from the top floors, you can see the ocean.

Courtroom 1030, on the tenth floor, is where Joanna Seybert rules.

It is a large, light wood–paneled windowless room, lit with an oval neon fixture on the ceiling that's designed to look something like a skylight. The judge's bench is light wood and elevated just enough to be commanding. The jury box is to the judge's left, the witness box is to the judge's right, and the lawyers' tables are in front of her. There are computer screens on various tables, and water jugs, and at the rear of the room there is a small area, with movie-house chairs, for the public.

Seybert, in black robes with her blond hair, looks a little like everybody's soccer mom. She is an attractive woman of a certain age—she graduated St. Johns Law School in 1971—and has been a sitting judge in various courts since 1987. Appointed to the federal bench in late 1993, she has a solid reputation among lawyers who appear before her as fair and thoughtful. She is also famous, among prosecutors and defense attorneys who appear before her, for rolling her eyes. Someone will say something she believes is demonstratively untrue, and eyes roll, a sure signal to everyone that she thinks the truth has taken a hike.

After some posturing by Monsalve's lawyers and some minor business that Bonnie wanted her to deal with, Judge Seybert accepted Monsalve's guilty plea and asked him if he wanted to address the court.

He read from a prepared statement. "First of all, I would like to apologize to you for the harm that I have caused to the U.S. society. I would like to tell you that I entered the drug world because I was very poor. My family was very poor. I suffered a lot of hunger in going to school. I had to tell my teacher get me food because I'm hungry. And I do not want my children to go through the same situation as I did when I was a child."

He explained that he started working to support his parents when he was ten years old. "I struggled a lot, but I couldn't get out of poverty. And life of drugs sank me into this dark world."

Monsalve begged the judge for mercy in his name, the name of his children, and especially the name of his son who'd just been diagnosed with cancer. The boy had even written a letter to the judge, asking for the right to see his father. "If someday I am free again,"

Monsalve promised, "I will be a fair person. I have thought about it and I know I did harm and I'm here for you to exercise justice."

Without any hesitation, Seybert responded, "Mr. Monsalve, you have the worst probation report I have ever, in my entire life, had the opportunity to read. I think you are, in fact, one of the most cruel human beings I've ever come across."

She told him, "I don't care how hungry you were in Colombia. Your family wasn't that bad off that you had to go out and order the murders of seven people. And, when you had them murdered you didn't do it real gently. You tortured some of the victims, cut off their hands or burned their hands and feet, ran over their heads with a truck."

She said, "I won't lose one second of sleep sentencing you to a life term in imprisonment. And, frankly, I am delighted that the guidelines require me to do so. In addition to the cruel and inhumane manner in which your victims were brutalized, and they were victims even though some of them stole money from you or insulted your wife when they were intoxicated, you went ahead and had murdered a retarded brother of someone you killed here in the States."

To that she added, "You typify the type of person that should spend the rest of their life in jail. What you accomplished here is ruining thousands of lives and corrupting everyone around you. As far as your remorse, I sure don't see it. I think the best thing would be if your son had no further contact with you."

Bonnie says it was the strongest, most direct, most chilling rebuke by a judge to a defendant that she has ever heard.

Because Monsalve had to wait several months before the Bureau of Prisons assigned him to the maximum-security federal facility at Allenwood, Pennsylvania, he continued to be housed at the MDC.

Bonnie and Rooney visited him there and, slowly, he began talking to them. It was a long process and Rooney still can't say for sure if Monsalve was telling the whole truth all the time. But in the beginning, Monsalve related this story:

He'd been trafficking in New York for most of the 1990s when, sometime in 1997, he decided that he'd made so much money—one Colombian government estimate valued his assets in that country at $50 million—that he wanted to retire.

The Tele-Austin raids shook him up. The feds were getting too close. He knew what they'd found when they raided his storefronts, and he knew that when Lobo got arrested, his life in New York would never be the same. He told himself, he was safe in Colombia and there was no reason ever to go back to the States.

But the lure of fast money can be all too seductive, and after a couple of years in Colombia, Monsalve started thinking that maybe he wanted to get back into the business.

Much of his old network was still in place and he would have no trouble finding clients. He believed he could run the new operation long-distance, never leaving the safety of Colombia. So he went to see Bustamante—they'd known each other since they were teenagers and had worked closely for a long time—gave him a personal $7 million guarantee and Bustamante shipped three hundred kilos to the States for him.

Unfortunately, the shipment got seized. That threw a monkey wrench into Monsalve's retirement plans because he now owed his friend $7 million. And in that business, money trumps friendship.

He went to Bustamante again. Even though they had history together, Monsalve knew history couldn't keep him alive if he didn't pay his bills. But he also knew that Bustamante was someone with whom he could work out a deal.

Monsalve told Bustamante that he would go back to New York and start up the operation again. That way, he could pay back the $7 million and then, together, they'd make even more.

It was a scheme that Bustamante liked because through much of the 1990s, Monsalve had been a fabulous earner. By his own admission, Monsalve had moved nearly four tons of cocaine into New York, most of it Bustamante's.

Obviously, returning to the States posed a real risk of getting caught by the feds. But, he knew, it was less risky than staying in Colombia and not paying off the debt because Bustamante would kill him. That's when he arranged with Nancy to meet him in Mexico to sneak back into the country.

A week later he was in custody, his debt to Bustamante was still outstanding, and his retirement plans were in tatters.

Some months later, while he was sitting in jail and definitely not cooperating, word was received from Colombia that his brother Arnoldo had been murdered.

It was a professional hit.

Monsalve believed this was Bustamante sending him a message— keep your mouth shut!

But now, waiting to be sent to Allenwood for the rest of his life, he decided that he didn't have to listen to Bustamante anymore.

Little by little, he gave Bonnie and Rooney enough to point them in the direction of other witnesses who, in turn, began handing them the Norte Valle Cartel, one by one.

Bustamante was first.

14

There are good grand jury rooms and there are terrible grand jury rooms and, even if it's not supposed to make a difference, it sometimes can.

Whenever Bonnie convened a grand jury at the federal courthouse in Brooklyn, it was a tough slog because the grand jury room there was a miserable hole-in-the-wall, stuck in a rundown part of the old building. Twenty-three men and women sit in that place all day, listening to a variety of cases. Some of the stories they hear are interesting enough to keep their attention, at least for a while. Some are so deadly dull that they put people to sleep. Tax cases almost always do that.

The prosecutor stands in front of them, introduces the case, then puts witnesses on the stand. But when it's hot and they put on the fan, no one can hear the witness testify. In Brooklyn, they're always fighting to convince people stuck in that airless, dark room to bring back an indictment.

In Central Islip, the grand jury room is large and airy, with auditorium seats in a semicircle for twenty jurors. The other three—the foreperson, the secretary, and the backup foreperson—sit at a dais facing the twenty. There is a witness chair facing the audience and a little podium where the prosecutor stands. Off to the side of the room, a court reporter takes the minutes, which is always sealed and kept secret.

Typically, there are some grand jurors who listen more intently than others, some who ask probing questions, some who look inconvenienced by being forced to sit there, and some who nod off. But none of the twenty-three people in that room in Central Islip had any trouble staying awake as Bonnie told them stories about cocaine and murders and "El Señor" Bustamante.

The case she presented to them was built on affidavits from four cooperating witnesses.

After returning from Florida, interviewing the witness in the Virginia case, Bonnie and Rooney embarked on a nationwide search for anyone who might know anything about Bustamante. They phoned every prosecutor they knew, mining every resource they could find for cooperators. "Have you heard of this guy Bustamante?"

Sure enough, there were people with stories to tell. But all of them were back in Miami. Bonnie and Rooney started commuting, spending at least five days a month in Florida for nearly a year.

Most of the witnesses had been arrested in conjunction with Operation Millennium, had already pleaded guilty, and were doing time. None of them were still being interviewed. Because of the nature of the drug business in South Florida, when they were initially proffered by the Operation Millennium prosecutors, they were asked about cocaine shipments coming in. Can you get me a load today? Who can you give me tomorrow? Who's still working? Nobody in Florida even knew to ask them about Bustamante and the Norte Valle bunch.

One of the men Rooney spoke to was a transporter in Mexico

for Bustamante. He provided specific dates, times, and size of shipments.

Another was Carlos Ramon, whom everyone referred to as "El Medico" (the doctor). He'd been a med student in Colombia in the early 1990s when his father was kidnapped, then killed, by Pablo Escobar. Ramon quit school and signed up with Los Pepes, the vigilante group looking to take revenge on Escobar. After Escobar's death, Ramon drifted into trafficking with Alejandro Bernal-Madrigal. He gave Rooney detailed information about Bustamante's entire organization.

Ramon clearly knew the man well enough because, in one meeting, Ramon surprised Rooney by announcing that he'd just been approached to try to work out a surrender for Bustamante. An intermediary had written a letter saying, we know you're cooperating, see what can you do for him.

Needless to say, Bonnie and Rooney were more than willing to discuss that possibility with Ramon, and they did. But nothing ever happened.

Over the course of the next few years, they would hear that same story from several people—Bustamante wants to come in—but nothing ever happened with any of those approaches, either.

After months of interviews in Florida, armed with affidavits from Ramon and three other cooperators there, plus Lobo and Hector in New York, Bonnie summoned the grand jury in Central Islip. Her only witness was Special Agent Romedio Viola, who told those twenty-three people what he'd learned from the six witnesses during the investigation into Bustamante.

Taking Bonnie's lead, he spent three hours going through each of the witness statements, one by one, carefully explaining all the facts of the case. Bonnie asked a few questions where she felt the jurors should know more, then told Rooney he was excused. He left. After giving the jurors their instructions, she left.

Bonnie and Rooney waited outside the grand jury room while the deliberations took place behind closed doors. But it didn't take long. Within an hour, the foreperson invited Bonnie back into the room and informed her, "He's indicted."

After the indictment was delivered to the on-duty magistrate who signed off on the arrest warrant, Rooney put Bustamante into the system. He added his name to the big databases, like NCIC, to make it public record, then cross-referenced it in every database he could think of. In theory, if Bustamante was stupid enough to come to the States, someone at the border would find the warrant on the computer and he'd be stopped. Or, if he somehow managed to get into the country and was pulled over for a traffic violation, the cop would run his name and arrest him.

Except, of course, that wasn't going to happen. The only way Bustamante was coming to the States, Bonnie and Rooney knew, would be on a government plane and in chains.

If ever. Indicting him was the easy part. Arresting him and extraditing him from Colombia was more problematic.

To manage that, Bonnie needed a "Provisional Arrest Warrant" (PAW) for the Colombians to serve—if they could find him—then papers requesting the Colombian courts for his extradition.

The PAW would be issued by the Colombians, at the request of the Department of Justice's Office of International Affairs, based on Bonnie's indictment in New York. That is, as long as all the proper forms were filed correctly. Bonnie arranged for that, but had no idea when a court in Bogotá would issue the PAW. These things always take time. And normally, she would have just had to wait, to let it run its course. But an informant in Colombia notified Rooney that he knew where Bustamante was.

Then, word came from Bustamante, through an intermediary, that he wanted to meet.

The rendezvous was set for a Monday morning, at the Hilton Hotel in Cartagena. The details would be worked out later, but Bustamante needed the American government's guarantee that he would not be arrested.

To put everything in place, Bonnie planned to fly to Bogotá on the Friday before meeting. But the night before, on that Thursday, a bomb went off in a bar not far from the embassy where Colombian prosecutors and law-enforcement people hung out. One of the terrorist groups was sending a message to the Colombian government. And the American ambassador understood it. He "closed" the country—temporarily stopped all visits—because he deemed it too dangerous. That effectively pulled the plug on the meeting with Bustamante.

Rooney later learned that, even if the meeting had still been on, Bustamante might not have shown because he suspected—wrongly—that he was being set up. Anyway, the information from the informant who said he knew where Bustamnante was turned out not to be true.

In the end it took nearly four months before the Colombians dealt with the PAW. When it was finally ready, a copy was sent to the embassy, where the case was assigned to a joint-venture team of American ICE agents and vetted Colombian agents.

If Bustamante was in Cartago, which he probably was, no one seemed able to locate him, even though just about everybody who lived in Cartago knew where his many farms, homes, and offices were. Especially the local police.

Still, with the PAW in place, Bonnie set about filing a formal request for Bustamante's extradition, if and when the agents ever found him.

Unlike an indictment, which is boilerplate—fill in the blanks and add some witness statements—an extradition request is particularly delicate. It needs to set out enough evidence to satisfy a Colombian judge that there is probable cause. But, because the narco-economy permeates every aspect of Colombian life, no one ever knows for sure who can be trusted. So the extradition request, which is public record in Colombia, cannot go into so much detail that it burns the cooperators and witnesses. Their identities need to stay hidden. It takes a lot of skill to get it just right. It can't be too vague, or it won't get approved. It can't be too specific or witnesses could get killed.

Bonnie based her request on an affidavit signed by Rooney, who spelled out the case with four unnamed cooperators.

Rooney explained that according to a sworn statement by Witness #1—who cannot be identified—that Bustamante had been involved in drug trafficking and money laundering at least since 1991 and the witness knew it because he'd worked for Juan Albeiro Monsalve, one of Bustamante's lieutenants, from 1991–1997, and directly for Bustamante on other occasions.

Witness #1 had also sworn that he'd handled more than twenty tons of Bustamante's cocaine and helped to launder approximately $100 million of Bustamante's money.

Rooney's affidavit went into great detail about shipments of drugs and the movement of monies, outlining various deals that clearly showed Bustamante's direct involvement. For example, in April 1998, Rooney wrote that Witness #1 had attended a meeting at Arcangel Henao's farm. Also present were Arcangel's brother Fernando and his father-in-law, José Dagoberto Florez Rios, aka "Chuma."

Oddly, Dagoberto was not only Arcangel's father-in-law, but as he was married to one of Arcangel's sisters, that also made him Arcangel's brother-in-law.

At that meeting, Dagoberto invited Lobo to work for the Henao family in Mexico. Fernando explained that they wanted him to launder the proceeds of a five-ton shipment that belonged to him, Bustamante, and a trafficker named Miguel Solano. He was one of the smaller *capos* who ran his own organization under the NVC umbrella, often working alongside Bustamante and Fernando Henao. Witness #1 took the job, only later learning that it was Bustamante himself who had chosen Witness #1 to do this.

That spring, Witness #1 said, word came that Bustamante wanted him to return to New York to help run their money Laundromat there. He was told to hire Abelardo Rojas Franco, the stash house–owning brother of Jaime and Loco.

Witness #1 put in place a system where he would receive a page from Fernando's assistant, Juan Carlos Giraldo, to tell him how much drug money to expect. Witness #1 would page Abelardo to arrange for the money pickup. Once the money was in the safe house, Abelardo would page Witness #1 to confirm the amount, and Witness #1 would page Giraldo to say that the transaction had been completed.

Cash deliveries worked the same way, with everybody paging everybody else. Over the course of nine months, from the summer of 1998 to the early spring of 1999, Witness #1 swore that he'd laundered approximately $25 million this way for Bustamante and Fernando Henao. He said he was paid 3.5 percent of whatever he washed, and out of that, he paid Abelardo 1.5 percent.

In 2000, Witness #1 went on, he and Giraldo Franco brought a drug trafficker from Medellin to Cartago to meet Bustamante. The trafficker had clients in New York who wanted to purchase Bustamante's drugs. The initial shipment for this deal was five hundred kilos. That same year, Bustamante invited Witness #1 to his ranch to offer him a two hundred-kilo shipment, which Witness #1 then sold to Monsalve.

Next, Rooney told the story of Witness #2—who cannot be identified—who'd outlined the transportation work he'd handled in Mexico for Bustamante, totaling around three and a half tons of cocaine. Witness #2 said he met with Bustamante on several occasions to work out specific transportation agreements. On one occasion, in December 1999, Witness #2 said Bustamante arrived at his office in Bogotá with a suitcase. Bustamante said he was paying him this way, "As a Christmas present." Inside was $300,000 in cash.

Witness #3—who cannot be identified—stated he'd known Bustamante since the mid-1980s and had attended many meetings with him at which the business of the Norte Valle Cartel was discussed. Witness #3 also acknowledged that he'd participated in two large cocaine shipments with Bustamante in 2000.

The first of those shipments weighed 1.3 tons. It was transported from Colombia through Guatemala to the States. The second shipment weighed 1.5 tons and was brought by truck to the coast of Venezuela. From there, it was moved by cargo vessel to Spain. But along the way, the ship sank in a storm and the cocaine was lost. Witness #3 noted that Bustamante held the owner of the ship responsible and dispatched one of his most trusted lieutenants and chief enforcer—Jhonny Cano-Correa—to collect the debt. The boat owner immediately went into hiding in Spain and the debt remains outstanding.

Finally, there was Witness #4—who cannot be identified—whose sworn statement explained how he'd brokered nearly three tons of cocaine in the United States for Bustamante and also referred to Cano, saying that he'd done multi-hundred-kilo deals with him representing Bustamante.

Bonnie submitted the extradition request, even though deep down she didn't think it was particularly strong. With most of them you don't need four witnesses, two is sufficient. She used four because she had four and felt the other two added weight. The witnesses might not have been collectively strong enough to convict Bustamante in an American court, but they were good enough to support her claim of probable cause for an extradition. Anyway, she knew, once they had Bustamante in custody witnesses would come out of the woodwork who could be used to testify against him in court.

Which is exactly what happened.

Lawyers got wind of Bonnie's case against Bustamante and started phoning her to say, my client is in jail in Miami but no one ever asked him about Bustamante.

The magic phrase became "5-K." Every prisoner and his lawyer knows that term. It refers to Chapter 5, Part K, of the sentencing guidelines, titled, "Substantial Assistance to Authorities." It says that the courts cannot sentence someone to a lesser amount of time than the statutory lower limits, or reduce the time being served, unless the prosecutor writes a letter of cooperation, advising the judge that the defendant has cooperated "substantially" and should be rewarded for that.

As Bonnie puts it, "Every guy in jail is looking for credit and they're all looking to cooperate. We go with what we have to extradite and then it snowballs."

What began with the testimony of four witnesses, snowballed

within a year to nearly forty people who were willing to talk about Bustamante, all of them looking for a 5-K.

That's when she received a call from a lawyer in Bogotá named Gerard Candamil. He phoned to say that Bustamante wanted to come in. "I've been retained by him and he wants to discuss surrendering and cooperating."

Bonnie told him point-blank, "I've heard this story before. I don't believe it." But she quickly added, "You're welcome to prove me wrong."

Candamil insisted that it was real, and set out Bustamante's terms: He didn't want to do thirty years, but he would do five; he was willing to talk about his own trafficking and would testify against some people, but he would not testify against Don Diego and Varela; and if he came in, he would bring with him most of his guys, including Orlando Sabogal Zuluaga, Jaime Maya Duran, and Jhonny Cano-Correa.

Bustamante said through Candamil, "I come in and I bring in my entire organization. They'll all come in at the same time and that will be credit for me."

By now, Bonnie and Rooney knew who these men were. They were hearing about them all the time in their ongoing interviews with cooperators. The men in Bustamante's organization were on their list and it wouldn't be long before they came after them, but there was no way the government could strike that deal.

Bonnie told Candamil to tell Bustamante, "It doesn't work like that. He pleads ten-to-life and the judge decides how much time he does. Then he testifies against anybody we want him to. And if he brings anyone in with him, that's not credit for him, that's credit for them."

Candamil relayed the message, then came back to Bonnie to say Bustamante wanted to set his own terms.

Bonnie said she would never go for that.

Rooney said, "Tell him to pound sound."

Bustamante's offer to surrender went away.

But Candamil would be back.

They plainly had Bustamante's attention, so Bonnie and Rooney started wondering how they could turn up the heat. What they needed to do, they decided, was to offer a reward.

They didn't have any money for that, but looked around to see who did and, sure enough, there was a little-used program managed by the State Department's Bureau of International Narcotics and Law Enforcement Affairs. A fund there could offer up to $5 million for information leading to the arrest and conviction of a designated narcotics trafficker.

Being a government program, there were volumes of rules and regulations explaining who could apply and how to apply. There were a lot of hoops to go through. Rooney did what he had to do and won approval to offer rewards for seven major players in the NVC. Beside Bustamante, there was Sabogal, Cano, Maya, and Bustamante's principal money launderer Aldomar Rendon, plus Arcangel and Dagoberto.

The two big names that did not make the list were Don Diego and Varela.

There was already a warrant for Don Diego out of Miami. The FBI was handling that case and in 2004 they would include him on their Ten Most Wanted list. Interestingly enough, even though Osama bin Laden was on the same list with Don Diego, the "FBI's Top Ten" are not necessarily the world's most wanted fugitives. They are merely the most wanted fugitives being dealt with by the FBI. ICE had its own list, which isn't public, but which already listed Bustamante as one of their "most wanted."

Varela was also considered a separate matter. The case against him was being developed by the DEA and prosecutors in Miami. But because Bonnie had some of the witnesses they needed, they asked if she would separately indict Varela. Toby testified before a grand jury in Central Islip, along with a DEA agent. The grand jury indicted Varela on several counts for his role in an international conspiracy to distribute cocaine and his oversight of security and enforcement for the Norte Valle Cartel. At one point, the DEA revealed that Varela's assets and properties were estimated at $71.25 million.

Once approval for the rewards came down from State, Rooney contacted someone he knew at the embassy in Bogotá and asked, "Can you do an ad campaign for us?"

He was looking for newspapers, television, and radio down there to cover the story that the Americans were putting big money on the heads of seven NVC traffickers. And in a country where traffickers are treated like Hollywood stars, that was a big story. Who the traffickers are, what they do, and, especially, how they live is an endless fascination for the tabloid and television public. So it came as no surprise that within weeks, the reward program—"La Recompensa" as they called it—was a major, ongoing story all over the Colombian media.

Unfortunately, Bonnie and Rooney soon became one, too.

A lawyer in Washington, D.C., got in touch to say that he was now representing Bustamante and that they could work out suitable terms. He came to New York and Bonnie had a long discussion with him, honestly believing that something might come of it. And something did. But not at all what she'd expected, wanted, or was happy about.

Two days after the meeting, the entire contents of their conversation appeared in the Colombian magazine *La Semana*. That was the first time the names Bonnie Klapper and Romedio Viola were released publicly.

Immediately, she ceased talking to any lawyers who said they were working for Bustamante. They kept calling, but her stock answer became, "Until you enter a notice of appearance on the public record and become his attorney of record, I cannot discuss anything with you."

None of the lawyers who subsequently called, insisting they were representing Bustamante, ever filed that notice.

Having their names published in Colombia did not, immediately, present any real danger, although it was a nuisance because now they had to be just a little more cautious when they traveled to Colombia.

The media campaign played out for weeks, and by then there were billboards up throughout the country showing the traffickers' mugshots next to their names and instructions that read, IF YOU SEE THIS MAN, CALL THIS NUMBER FOR A REWARD.

What neither Bonnie nor Rooney knew—nor did anyone else in Central Islip or Washington—was that the indictment, PAW, and extradition request for Bustamante, plus the $5 million price on the seven traffickers' heads, plus Bustamante's failed attempts to negotiate a deal for himself, had created a major amount of paranoia around Cartago.

Varela felt it and turned his sights on Arcangel and Don Diego. Don Diego looked for Bustamante to side with him against Varela. Bustamante feared that if he did, Varela would surely come after him, too.

No one knew who to trust.

That's when Don Diego gave his old friend Bustamante an ultimatum—get out of the country or I'll kill you before Varela does.

15

In December 2001, Arcangel's younger brother, Fernando Henao, was arrested in Miami.

He'd come to Miami in 1999, under the guise of cooperating, and while he was living in Miami, he was allowed to travel back and forth to Colombia. The DEA was expecting him to help them round up other people. But Fernando was too clever by half and started playing both sides, working deals with Miguel Solano.

Unfortunately for him, on one trip through Florida, he got picked up on a wiretap by the FBI. The DEA didn't know anything about the bureau's interest in him. That is, until the FBI arrested Fernando. Which they did because they didn't know anything about the DEA's relationship with him. Ultimately, Fernando pled guilty before his trial and got a solid twenty years.

Word of Fernando's arrest shook up a lot of people back in Cartago, all of whom assumed that he would cooperate with the Americans.

That same month, some men working for Don Diego got into a shoot-out in a discotheque not far from Cali with some men working for Varela. The police intervened and arrests were made. But several men from Varela's side wound up being murdered in jail.

In response, Varela sent his chief enforcer—Luis Enrique Calle Serna, known as "Comba" which means "combatant"—into the Canon de Garrapatas area, which had been the Urdinola family stronghold. Comba tore through the region with his army of killers, stealing Urdinola family land, taking over processing labs, and forcing family members to flee.

Don Diego and Arcangel feared their families could be next, and prepared to take on Varela.

In early 2002, with paranoia spreading through the Norte Valle like a highly contagious disease, Bustamante called a meeting at his El Vergel ranch. He was looking to broker a peace between Don Diego and Varela, and invited Arcangel, the AUC leader Carlos Castaño, and a few others to help him. But the meeting was tense and, as one of Castaño's senior guys put it later, "None of them trusted each other or Carlos."

Distrust raged and anyone even slightly suspected of cooperating with the authorities was seen as the enemy by everyone and had to be dealt with accordingly.

One of those on Don Diego's list was Victor Patino Fomeque.

Like many of the others, Patino was a former policeman who went to work with the Cali Cartel. When it disintegrated, he and his half brother, Luis Alfonso Ocampo Fomeque—also a former cop—went into business for themselves, developing transport routes from the Pacific port of Buenaventura to Mexico. They worked their way into a loose association with Don Diego's gang, as contract transporters.

However, in April 2002, Patino decided he'd had enough and agreed to meet some DEA agents in Bogotá. He showed up believing that they were going to negotiate his surrender. But the agents either didn't understand the terms of the meeting, or simply didn't care. They arrested him, there and then, and eight months later shipped him off to Florida.

Facing life behind bars, Patino concluded that his only hope was playing the 5-K card. Although he'd originally been sentenced to serve fifteen years—and was facing an additional fifty years in Colombia if he ever returned—Patino gave up enough information to see his sentence drastically reduced. It is widely believed that he was the man who first exposed the traffickers' alleged support for the presidential campaign of Ernesto Samper.

Today, the Bureau of Prisons officially lists Patino's release date as "unknown" and his whereabouts as "in transit." That translates to mean he's been admitted to some witness protection program and is currently living somewhere in the United States with a new identity.

But his new identity was not without a price. Don Diego is said to have handled Patino's treason "the Colombian way," reportedly ordering the murder of thirty-five members of Patino's immediate family, including pregnant women and young children. They were gunned down at a picnic. Their bodies were then stacked by the side of the road, doused with gasoline, and set ablaze.

When Varela and Bustamante heard that Patino's half brother Ocampo might also be cooperating, they supposedly took it upon themselves to murder him.

Ivan Urdinola, who'd been in prison all these years, was set for release—and there's no telling which side he would have taken—but before that day came he was found dead in his cell. He was poisoned by food paid for by his own family.

In Cartago, Bustamante called another sit-down, this time gathering as many of his own people as he could, but particularly Sabogal, Maya, and Cano. He told them, it's every man for himself. He said that he was probably going into hiding soon and advised them to think about themselves.

Cano later told Rooney that Bustamante gave them permission to, "Do what you've got to do."

With rumors spreading that Bustamante was losing control, rats began deserting the ship.

Throughout the rest of the year and well into 2003, cooperators lined up at Bonnie's office door to say, I've got information if you've got a 5-K letter. She had enough new information by summer that she superceded Bustamante's original indictment, bringing out an updated version to include Arcangel, Sabogal, Maya, Cano, and Rendon. Warrants were issued against them and, from there, she applied for the appropriate PAWs.

It didn't take long before she superceded that indictment to include Dagoberto Flores Rios, among others. In fact, over the next five years, she updated the original indictment twelve times. She added names each time, eventually obtaining warrants in the United States and PAWs in Colombia for 23 NVC traffickers, money launderers, and murderers, documenting a total 271 counts of criminal activity.

Yet again, Bustamante called for a sit-down. This time, though, the invitation came from him and his friend, Juan Carlos Ramirez Abadia, perhaps the most ruthless man in Colombia.

Everyone knew him as Chupeta.

It means "lollipop"—a nickname earned for his boyish looks.

Born in 1963 in Palmira, Colombia, not far from the prison that would one day hold so many of his friends and cohorts, Ramirez Abadia was raised in a middle-class Colombian family and trained as an industrial engineer. Apparently, though, he worked for a while as a horse trader, which is how he is said to have met the Urdinola brothers. They introduced him to the Orejuelas who employed him as a hit man. By the time he was captured, at the age of forty-four, he'd allegedly been involved, one way or the other, in around three hundred murders, at least fifteen of which took place in the United States.

But the stocky five foot six Chupeta was not just another *sicario*. He was a smart kid who, by the early 1980s was starting to think like an entrepreneur. He watched and learned from the Urdinolas' joint venture with the Mafia as it turned them into Colombia's primary heroin traffickers. He watched and learned as the Medellin Cartel began their flirtation with the Mexicans.

In 1987, the Urdinolas put Chupeta in charge of running cocaine across the U.S. in tractor trailers. To minimize suspicion, he hired Jamaicans to drive the loads, a radical departure from the golden rule which had always been, never trust anyone except another Colombian.

When a half-ton shipment was busted in Loma, Colorado, the Urdinolas insisted he pay for it. So Chupeta started a sideline wholesale business. He minimized his risk while guaranteeing much-needed cash up front by taking only a small profit from the middle. One of his first clients was the Juarez Cartel in Mexico. The strategy worked so well that he soon branched out into a similar joint venture with the Guadalajara Cartel.

Having opened the door wide enough for the Mexicans to take control of coke sales on the West Coast, they began moving east to secure strongholds from the Rockies to Chicago. As they did, Chupeta became one of the top-five most powerful cocaine traffickers in the world, ruling a minicartel with as many as two hundred franchised agents. There was no doubt that he was the best and brightest of the younger generation.

Then came the amnesty program. Fearing deportation to the States, as they all did, Chupeta gave himself up to government prosecutors in Cali. Nine months later, he was condemned to twenty-four years in prison, the stiffest sentence to date for a self-surrendered trafficker.

But in Colombia, twenty-four years doesn't mean twenty-four years. It was quickly reduced to thirteen. Charity was administered based on his surrender and an agreement to forfeit assets worth, perhaps, as little as 10 percent of the money he'd made trafficking. But in Colombia, thirteen years doesn't mean thirteen years. In 1997 he turned against his partners, outlined for the government how his Mexican franchise operation worked, and contended that it never could have happened without a thoroughly corrupt Mexican government.

The following year he turned state's evidence again, this time testifying before a Mexican judicial panel, accusing several senior officials with ties to former Mexican President Carlos Salinas de Gortari of having been on his payroll. Among them, were Mexico's former deputy attorney general for narcotics matters and a former commander of the judicial police. Chupeta even went as far as to insist that no drugs moved through Mexico without their permission.

Apparently that was good enough to cut the thirteen years down to seven or so. But in Colombia, seven or so doesn't mean seven or so. He was out in under five.

Not surprisingly, he went straight back into the business.

Cartago was where the action was now, so he drifted into a working friendship with Bustamante. They ran loads together when they could, and laundered money together when they had to, but otherwise Chupeta trafficked for his own account, mostly out of the Cali region. He had farms and properties all across Colombia, with underground storage facilities, each large enough to hide $20 to $30 million in cash and gold bars.

By the time he sat down at that meeting in July 2003 with Bustamante, Don Diego, Varela, and the others, he was worth an estimated $1 to $2 billion, which made him as rich—and therefore as important—as anybody in the room.

The meeting was held, purposely, in neutral territory, at a farm belonging to Gabriel Puerta-Parra in the Magdalena Medio region, east of Medellin.

An attorney by profession, the sixty-one-year-old Puerta-Parra was the elder statesman of the NVC. Being at least ten years older than everyone else—and more like twenty when it came to men like Chupeta and Cano—he was highly respected in his role as consigliere. For years he resolved disputes, advised on extradition matters, and greased the machine of political influence. He invested in loads and helped his friends launder their money by setting up shell companies and phony clients' accounts with them. He opened foreign exchange *cambios* in Colombia, which made laundering dollars easy, and established several investment firms for the same purpose. Thanks to him, NVC funds flowed in and out of real estate investments and through front companies in Ecuador, Mexico, the U.S., and the tiny money-laundering

Pacific Island, Vanuatu. He also helped his friends put their money, alongside his own, in a Brazilian emerald mine.

It goes without saying that everyone showed up at Puerta-Parra's place with dozens of bodyguards, armed to the teeth. All that heavy weaponry, readily available to the first person who lost his temper, didn't help dilute the tension. Don Diego and Varela reportedly stayed at the table for several hours while Bustamante, Chupeta, and Puerta-Parra searched in vain for some common ground, to relieve the pressures that were driving Don Diego and Varela toward all-out war.

They never found it.

The only way this was going to get settled was with blood.

The word *rats,* as in traitors who turn on their friends and "rat them out" to the cops, is an American gangster expression.

The Colombian term is *sapos* or frogs.

With civil war looming large in Colombia, and with Bonnie and Rooney turning up the pressure from Central Islip, the Norte Valle Cartel was fast becoming *"el cartel de los sapos."*

The "frogs" were deserting the sinking ship.

Arcangel fled to Panama.

Chupeta escaped to Brazil.

Jaime Maya stayed around Cartago for as long as he could, then fled to Mexico.

Jhonny Cano, eventually, went to hide in the jungle.

Bustamante also made ready his exit.

One of Don Diego's closest associates, Miguel Solano, understood what was about to befall them and looked for a way to save himself. He put out a feeler to the DEA, they responded accordingly, and a deal was struck for his cooperation.

Varela also decided he had to protect himself, not just from Don Diego, but from people in his own organization. So he formed a vigilante group, along the lines of the old PEPES that had gone hunting for Pablo Escobar. The press referred to them as "Colombians Persecuted by the Gringos" but they later came to be known as

"Los Rastrojos," named for Varela's chief recruiter and militia commander, Diego Perez Henao, alias Diego Rastrojo.

Henao, who was Arcangel's cousin, ran Varela's army, made up of some two hundred hardened criminals, teenaged wannabees, paramilitary soldiers, and Marxist rebels. They reported to him, and he in turn reported to Comba, who ordered Los Rastrojos to kill "*los sapos.*"

In November 2003, when Varela learned that Solano was talking, Los Rastrojos gunned down Solano outside a nightclub in Cartagena.

Don Diego's private army was known as Los Machos—a similar collection of some two hundred hardened criminals, teenaged wannabees, paramilitary soldiers, and this time, right-wing guerrillas. He didn't know that Solano was talking to the DEA about him, and because he took Solano's assassination personally, he demanded retaliation. Los Machos ambushed a group of Los Rastrojos, killed them all, then piled their corpses in a pyramid along the roadside. After that, they went to Roldanillo, Varela's hometown, and indiscriminately wiped out whoever they wanted to. In one barbarous act, they found a group of nine taxi drivers sitting in their cabs and, just like that, yanked them out, lined them up, and slaughtered them.

Then they located Varela. Los Machos shot it out with Los Rastrojos and Varela was wounded. Long before he fully recovered, he retaliated by reigning down hell upon the country.

Over the next two years, more than one thousand people across the Norte Valle region would be killed.

Varela even put out a contract on one of his most trusted lieutenants.

Because both sides were funding this war by increasing cocaine exports to the States, Varela had sent word to several independent transporters to stop offering any services to Don Diego's organization. Some did. Many didn't. Which only increased the stakes and helped to run up the death toll.

Pedro Pineda Camargo had been one of Varela's top transporters for many years. But Varela got word that Pineda was switching sides. It took Varela two years to find Pineda, and when he did, he murdered Pineda and his wife.

Long before this point, Don Diego understood that he needed to protect his family and, by the late 1990s, he'd already started moving relatives to Florida. That included his mother, sister, ex-wife, two sons, his former sister-in-law and her three children. He put younger brother Eugenio in charge and it was Eugenio who set up a bunch of shell companies in the British Virgin Islands to launder drug money to finance the family's opulence in America.

When one of Don Diego's old-time employees, Jhon Jairo Garcia Giraldo, made plans to go to Florida, Eugenio decided to send some extra money with him to the family.

Known to his friends as "Dos Mil" (two thousand), he was in charge of the mob's cell phones and pagers. He took the money, duly delivered it, and returned home, only to have Eugenio and Don Diego wonder about what else might have happened on Dos Mil's trip.

They got it into their heads that he'd gone there to meet with the DEA.

Acting on Don Diego's instructions, Eugenio's men kidnapped Dos Mil, with the intent of torturing him until he confessed that he'd turned coat. They told him that they needed some new cell phones, which he agreed to deliver to a farm outside Cali. When he got there, Los Machos grabbed him and began a lengthy interrogation, which included several beatings with baseball bats.

Then they waterboarded him.

This is the same technique used on Al-Qaeda prisoners to force confessions through simulated drowning. First they covered Dos Mil's head with a plastic bag, then they held it under water for long periods of time, bringing him close to the point of asphyxiation, before yanking him out of the water.

After each near drowning, they gave him a little time to recover, so that he didn't go into shock and die before telling them what they wanted to hear. But the only thing that Dos Mil had to say was that he'd been detained very briefly when he landed in Miami, while border patrol officers checked his travel documents. At every turn, Dos Mil denied being a cooperator.

The beatings continued until they killed him. Los Machos then cut him up and threw his remains into a river.

Word of Dos Mil's murder eventually got to the DEA, which added it to the list of charges which would, eventually, face Don Diego and Eugenio.

In the meantime, the FBI in Florida uncovered Eugenio's British Virgin Islands connection, seized two luxury waterfront condominiums worth $2.5 million, and an eighty-foot yacht, valued at $3.5 million. The bureau had gotten too close and that really shook up Don Diego, who'd already been indicted in Florida. It also unsettled his family, to the point that most of them fled back to Colombia.

In December 2003, Juan Carlos Montoya Sánchez, Don Diego's kid brother, was arrested. He oversaw the family's processing labs. Along with him, the Colombian police grabbed Carlos Felipe Toro Sánchez. He handled shipments to the States. Both were deported to Miami and both were sentenced to long jail times.

A rumor then circulated throughout the Norte Valle that the man who'd tipped off the police, at least about Juan Carlos if not both men, was the retired Colombian National Police (DAS) colonel, Danilo Gonzalez Gil.

He was a celebrated cop in Colombia, a twenty-three-year veteran of the force who'd earned acclaim by being one of the men to track down Pablo Escobar and kill him. But like so many other former cops, Danilo had also been working with the traffickers—as a sort of go-between for the good guys and the bad guys—and getting paid lots of money by both. The DEA knew he was bent because Bustamante had named him when he met with the DEA in Panama. So it made sense that, at some point, the DEA would try to flip him.

For years, Danilo had maintained a special relationship with Don Diego. But as tensions grew, he realigned himself on the side of an ex-cop who'd once served with him—Wilber Varela.

That seriously displeased Don Diego, who had reason to believe that, somehow, Bustamante was also mixed up in this.

That's because the DEA had been careless.

They'd run that investigation against Danilo—Operation Rainmaker—and were meeting secretly with him in Panama. His lawyer always accompanied him. That man's name was Gerardo Candamil. The same Gerardo Candamil who'd tried to negotiate Bustamante's surrender with Bonnie.

Rooney knew him, too, having met him in Colombia, in the DEA offices at the U.S. Embassy. What struck Rooney at that meeting was how two of the DEA agents treated him in an odd way. It was, he thought, almost as if Candamil himself was an informant. No one ever said that to Rooney, but that's the impression he got.

Everyone in Bogotá knew that Candamil was Bustamante's lawyer, and his association with Danilo gave way to suspicions that Danilo and Bustamante were linked.

That was reinforced the day that Candamil, Danilo, and a group of DEA agents returned to Bogotá after their meeting in Panama, on the same commercial flight together.

If not a serious breach of security it was, at best, a pretty stupid thing to do. Especially because some bad guys at the Bogotá airport saw Candamil and Danilo come off the plane with guys they perceived to be DEA agents and, possibly, other informants.

The rumor was that Danilo was going to turn himself in. But neither Danilo nor Candamil—who didn't seem to know that they'd been spotted—were warned by the DEA that their lives might be in danger. The two were seen often together in Bogotá.

On Thursday afternoon, March 25, 2004, they'd been out to lunch together.

Arriving at Candamil's north Bogotá office in the lawyer's chauffeured car, Danilo received a phone call on his cell. He elected to stay in the backseat of the car to continue the call, while Candamil got out and went upstairs.

Two minutes later, as Danilo stepped out of the car, several of

Montoya's men ran up to him—reportedly including a former FARC guerrilla named Gildardo Rodriguez Herrera, who was sometimes called "the lord of the red shirt" for his typical choice of clothing—and put fourteen bullets into Danilo's head and torso.

Candamil heard the shots, crawled under his desk to hide, and after a few minutes phoned the DEA to tell them. Right away, the agents said, you have to get out of the country. They fetched him, brought him to the embassy, and put him on a commercial flight, unaccompanied, that night for the States.

Back in Central Islip, the news of Danilo's death was not news at all. The first Rooney heard of it was when he received a call from Miami Airport that Gerardo Candamil had arrived.

A few years before, Rooney had decided that as long as Candamil was Bustamante's lawyer, he might be an interesting asset. In the normal course of business, there was no way Candamil could discuss anything he'd ever discussed with his client. That was protected by privilege. But there was no "normal course of business" when it came to dealing with Bustamante, so Rooney had put Candamil's name into the system, just in case he ever showed up and might be in a position to talk.

This was that time.

The note Rooney had put into the database said, "If you encounter him, please detain him." The agent who stopped him notified a very senior agent who was working Miami Airport, the legendary Ed Kacerosky. He was the U.S. Customs agent widely credited with getting the Orejuela brothers.

Kacerosky called Rooney to say that they had Candamil in custody. He repeated what Candamil had told the other agent, that there'd been a murder that afternoon in Bogotá and for his own safety, the DEA had shipped him off to the States. But nobody was with him and nobody was there to meet him. Kacerosky asked Rooney, "What do you want me to do?"

Rooney said, "Interview him. Take him into the back room and pump him for every bit of information you can about Bustamante, the Norte Valle Cartel, corruption, people in Cali, everything."

Candamil was a nervous type to begin with, but for the three hours that Kacerosky interviewed him, he was really nervous.

As luck would have it, one of the AUSA's in Bonnie's office, Wayne Baker, was on his way to Miami to interview some people on another investigation, and was traveling with a few El Dorado agents. Rooney got in touch with Baker and told him about Candamil. He said, "They're going to admit him into the country, so can you please hook up with Eddie Kacerosky and see what you can get from Candamil."

Rooney arranged to have Candamil put up in a hotel for the night, and early the next day, Baker—along with an El Dorado ICE agent—when to meet him.

Somehow, and Rooney isn't sure how, word leaked back to the DEA in Bogotá that ICE was interviewing Candamil. Furious, a pair of agents jumped onto a plane and flew to Miami, found the hotel, barged into the room, and announced, "The interview is over."

They physically tried to yank Candamil out of there.

Baker tried to stop them, and he and one of the DEA guys almost came to blows.

Rooney never understood what the DEA's problem was. Candamil would make a fabulous witness in a variety of NVC cases—and he seemed more than willing to cooperate—but the DEA wasn't going to stand for it. They grabbed Candamil and hid him, and refused to let Baker or Rooney know where he was. They refused to let anyone else near him.

The DEA agents got so stupid about it that they proceeded to file formal complaints against Baker, Kacerosky, and Rooney for interviewing their "informant."

The fact that the DEA and Rooney were on the same side apparently eluded them.

But Candamil was a registered DEA informant—Rooney doesn't know if Bustamante ever knew—and they weren't going to share him, no matter what. Rooney then had to write up a long report saying that he asked Kacerosky to interview Candamil, which meant none of this was Kacerosky's fault. He got Baker off the hook, too. He wrote, "Blame me."

Those two DEA agents did. But no one else bothered.

Rooney never found out what Candamil was telling the DEA, if anything, while he was working for Bustamante and Bustamante was still slamming drugs. The relationship was, he still believes, suspect to say the least.

Once the Miami incident blew over, the DEA moved Candamil to New York. He decided to stay in the country because he feared for his life back home. The DEA lodged him in a hotel in Hempstead, Long Island, a working-class town in the middle of Nassau County, surrounded by much wealthier communities. Candamil lasted only two days before he rang Rooney to complain, "I'm scared. There are too many Negroes in the neighborhood."

Knowing that the guy wasn't too tightly wrapped, Rooney figured he might still be able to turn Candamil into a useful cooperator. So he rang one of the El Dorado agents whose wife, he knew, was in the real estate business. Through her, Rooney helped Candamil find an apartment in Whitestone, at the northern tip of Queens.

Of course, Candamil had no credit, and no income in the States, which meant Rooney and El Dorado had to go out on a limb for him not just to get the apartment, but also to furnish it. Rooney also arranged for Candamil's wife and children to join him there.

That lasted a week.

This time the excuse wasn't as idiotic as "too many Negroes," it was, "My wife doesn't like it here."

He said they were going back to Colombia.

Rooney bellowed, "Are you fucking nuts? We just got you an apartment, you've got furniture, Danilo was shot outside your office. We had to jump through all these hoops to keep you safe, and now you're leaving? What the hell are you going back to Colombia for?"

It turned out he missed his girlfriend.

To this day, every now and then, Rooney phones him in Bogotá, and there are long periods of time when there is no answer, and even when he leaves messages, Candamil doesn't always phone back. There are long periods of time when Rooney wonders, Have they killed him yet?

16

The Colombian police were closing in on Bustamante and might have had him within days except, as the media reported, he got killed in a roadside assassination plot hatched by the FARC, not far from Cartago.

A lot of people breathed a big sigh of relief. Good riddance, they decided, to bad rubbish. Many other people were annoyed. Bustamante had been offering to come in and, in a way, they regretted that he was dead. All the information he might have divulged had been blown to pieces, along with him.

But some people knew better.

Bustamante was feeling the heat and needed to buy some time to make his escape. The roadside explosion ruse distracted the police hunting him long enough that he could run to the Cordoba region, where he holed up at a jungle camp, protected by his friend Carlos Castaño, while he made more suitable arrangements.

Buried inside the Justice Department in Washington, D.C., there is an office called the Narcotics and Dangerous Drugs Section (NDDS).

It was originally created to help federal prosecutors around the country complete highly complicated cases. The NDDS was there to take up the slack when prosecutors in the field were overwhelmed, or a case was too sophisticated, or the office in the field didn't have sufficient expertise.

That was then, this is now. The DEA came along one day and joined forces with the NDDS to create the "959 Group." Their cases are born out of Title 21 of the United States Code, Section 959, which confers international jurisdiction on drug cases. As long as they can establish that a trafficker is moving, or intends to move, drugs into the United States—whether or not they know where the drugs actually are—they can claim jurisdiction.

Prosecutors across the country note that the NDDS doesn't develop anything, that they're just glory seekers who help themselves to everybody else's evidence and witnesses. In response, the NDDS argues that it takes a big-picture view. On paper, the NDDS claims, 959 allows the government to up the ante against organized criminals. In practice, 959 creates yet another level of interagency warfare.

In the beginning of the Bustamante matter, Bonnie felt she had a slam-dunk case. But the NDDS decided it could make a better case. Because she wanted to do the right thing, she offered to supply them with her evidence. Months went by and nothing happened. The NDDS did not indict. They claimed to be waiting on some additional undercover evidence which, in the end, never panned out.

Bonnie didn't complain because she really wanted to make her own case against Bustamante. After waiting long enough for nothing to happen in Washington, she indicted him.

Then, at the end of 2003/beginning of 2004, the 959 Group decided that they would indict him, too, along with several other big hitters. They added to their list, Don Diego, Bento Renteria,

Arcangel, and Chupeta. Except Miami had already indicted Don Diego and Bonnie had already indicted the others.

This was going to be different, the NDDS pointed out. This was going to be a RICO case against the NVC leadership.

The Racketeer Influenced and Corrupt Organizations Act, or RICO, provides extended criminal penalties for organized offenders, plus the right to pursue them in civil court where the government can claim back the criminals' assets and, also, impose additional monetary damages. It has been effectively used against the Mafia since 1970, and continues to work well in the fight against the drug cartels.

But Bonnie saw the NDDS indictment—which did little more than piggyback her's—as a duplication of effort and a prime example of just how inefficient the government can be. She suggested, as long as we're working the same targets, wouldn't it be better if everyone worked together?

Hoping to make that happen, she phoned a really good guy named Boyd Johnson, who prosecuted big drug cases out of the U.S. Attorney's office in Manhattan (SDNY) and offered to pool evidence.

The one place they could do that was Washington, hand in hand with the NDDS. She and Johnson agreed that it was a great idea, although Bonnie's bosses were not enthusiastic, fearing that SDNY and/or the NDDS would try to cut them out.

It's a fact of life that there is a natural rivalry between Bonnie's EDNY and Johnson's SDNY. Some people in the EDNY claim that the Manhattan office is arrogant. Some people in the SDNY claim that the EDNY is the jealous cousin from the boondocks. The truth is that both offices are territorial. There is money at the end of a RICO rainbow and both offices want the biggest slice of any forfeited assets. They also want the biggest slice of the glory. They also want the defendants, especially if they can get them to cooperate. Each one becomes a source of new intelligence and that, in turn, brings in new cases. Ultimately, it comes down to who controls the defendant, who controls the witnesses, and who makes the cooperation decisions.

Bonnie and Johnson got along fine, and started putting everything together, until the DEA—under the banner of the 959 Group—demanded certain things, like control of the witnesses. At Rooney's headquarters, ICE said no because the case was originally theirs out of EDNY. The DEA said, tough.

In the end, someone at EDNY decided they didn't want to be part of it, so Johnson's SDNY and the NDDS proceeded on their own.

That left Bonnie and the EDNY out in the cold, at least as far as the 959 case was concerned.

Aeropostal flight VH830 took off from Simón Bolívar Airport in Caracas, Venezuela, at noon on Tuesday, June 29, 2004. Three hours later, the McDonnell Douglas MD80 jet touched down at Havana's José Martí International Airport.

Passengers disembarked and made their way into Terminal 3 where Señor Arturo Sanchez Cobarrubia stepped up to the Cuban Immigration booth and handed over his Mexican passport complete with a Cuban tourist visa stamped inside.

The Immigration officer opened the passport, checked the photo and visa, looked at the gentleman in front of him, and asked some basic questions. Typically, those would have been along the lines of, where are you coming from, how long are you planning to stay in Cuba, where are you staying, and why have you come in from Caracas?

Judging from the gentleman's answers, the Immigration officer grew slightly suspicious. He held up the passport and asked, "You are a citizen of Mexico?"

The man answered yes.

"Then who," the Immigration officer wanted to know, "is your president? What is the name of the president of Mexico?"

When it became obvious that Sr. Sanchez Cobarrubia didn't know the answer, other Immigration officers were summoned. By early evening, the Cuban authorities determined that the Mexican passport and tourist visa were both fake, and placed Sr. Sanchez Cobarrubia under arrest.

He was not allowed to see a lawyer. He was not charged in any court of law. He was simply carted off to Villa Marista and thrown unceremoniously into a small, filthy, stench-and bug-ridden holding cell.

Once an elegantly ornate Catholic school for boys run by Marist monks, Villa Marista was expropriated after the Castro Revolution by the Ministry of Interior's Directorate-General for External Security (DGSE). Today, part of it houses the Operations Department of the Ministry's Directorate of Counterintelligence, the other part is a grimly fortified, dilapidated jail for political prisoners.

Modeled on the old Soviet system, Villa Marista is the Cuban equivalent of the KGB's infamous Lubyanka prison.

Also like the Russians, Cuban justice is modeled on cruelty. Anyone branded an enemy of the state—for whatever reason, or without any reason—risks being put to death. Anyone who steals a cow risks being sent away for twenty years.

According to a Cuban dissident Web site, the cells in Villa Marista are nine-by-six feet, with an iron bunk chained to the wall. Windows are blinded so that prisoners cannot see out, although some light does come in. The toilet is a hole in the corner of the floor with a weak stream of water running into it. That also serves as drinking water.

In the ceiling, there is a single lightbulb fixed behind a metal mesh that is always on. As there is no ventilation, the cells are swelteringly hot in the summer and can get very cold in the winter.

The guards are known to be particularly sadistic. Interrogations are conducted by surprise, often in the middle of the night when barely awake prisoners are disoriented.

There are regular beatings.

And the food is foul and inedible.

After three days of this, Señor Sanchez Cobarrubia decided he had a card to play which might get him out of there. Hoping to impress them, he admitted that he'd paid five hundred dollars for the passport and visa from someone in Juarez, and that he was, in fact, the famous Colombian drug trafficker, Luis Hernandez Gomez Bustamante.

The Cubans were impressed enough to toss him back in his cell and add a few more beatings to his daily routine.

One version of the story has it that Bustamante planned to go from Havana to Mexico, where he would be protected by his trading partners in the Juarez Cartel. Another version of the story is that he planned to stay in Cuba, protected there by the exiled chief of the Juarez Cartel, Vicente Carrillo.

That is probably the most likely. According to what Alejandro Bernal Madrigal once told a Colombian journalist, "If you reach the island and live there quietly, and pay $5 million to Fidel, no one bothers you. Cuba is a paradise. As long as you do not kill anyone or talk politics."

It is likely that by the time he gave the Cubans his real name, they already knew who he was because, when they arrested him, he was carrying his computer. Later, he said that much of what he had on his laptop documented his trafficking activities for 2003 and part of 2004, and also bribes to Colombian politicians. Even if his files were coded, which presumably they were, Cuban counterintelligence wouldn't have had too much trouble cracking the codes.

Bustamante was never formally charged with any crime. His only offense in Cuba was attempting to come into the country with a false passport. In most countries, they might detain you overnight, or just confiscate your false passport and put you on the next plane out. Under Cuban law, it's punishable by up to one year in jail.

Instead, Bustamante was locked up in that holding cell for thirty-two months.

As soon as they knew who he was, on July 2, the Cuban Foreign Office notified the government of Colombia that they had captured Bustamante. Negotiations opened between the two countries to repatriate him. The Colombians told the Cubans they had an arrest warrant for him, and that the Americans had also filed for arrest and extradition. The Cubans said that they would send Bustamante back to Colombia, but only on the condition that the Colombians did not then give him to the Americans. The Colombians said keep him, and that was the end of the Cuban-Colombian negotiations.

Four or five months later, the inimitable Oscar Rodriguez was notified by some people in Colombia about Bustamante's predicament, and asked to represent him.

Knowing that Bonnie was deeply involved with the Bustamante case, Oscar reminded Bustamante's benefactors that he had a very good professional relationship with her, that she was very straight, and that he could deal with her.

He told them, "Bonnie is a special person. Very talented. Very smart. And she always keeps her word. Unlike some of the others. You can take Bonnie's word to the bank."

But getting Bustamante to Bonnie so that he could work out a deal was much easier said than done. The two major hurdles standing in Oscar's way were the four-decade-old "Cuban embargo," and the Bush administration's unalterable hatred for the Castro regime.

Still, Oscar made arrangements to go to the island of his birth. "I went there and spoke to the government people, and met with some people I know, and petitioned everyone on Bustamante's behalf. I sent messages to him and got messages back from him, but they wouldn't let me see him."

Home in Miami, refusing to give up, Oscar started phoning Bonnie, almost weekly, saying, "Bustamante wants to come to America, can't you extradite him?"

She had to remind him, "We can't talk to the Cubans."

Oscar begged her, "Please, Bonnie, his back is killing him. He needs surgery. It's too damned hot in his cell."

"What can I do?" she asked.

He answered, "Anything you can."

Under normal circumstances, she could start the extradition process. But as long as the United States and Cuba did not have diplomatic relations, that door was firmly shut.

Except, she found out, there was a "United States Interests Section" in Havana.

The handful of Americans who manned it operated out of the old U.S. Embassy, which had been renovated in 1997, by the Clinton administration, to create a more efficient presence on the island. There was a consular services officer, a political and economic section, a public diplomacy program, and a refugee processing unit. Another part of their mission, she read on their Web site, was "to help reduce global threats from crime and narcotics."

She wondered if the Cubans would agree that sending Bustamante to Central Islip was a big step in that direction.

The people in Havana need to speak to "their people" in Washington, Bonnie reasoned, and went looking for "their people." That's when she discovered a "Cuba desk" in the State Department. And a few days later, she was in Washington meeting with the men who manned the Cuba desk.

It was, Rooney recalls, a surreal experience.

With the Bush administration holding a hard line on Cuba, the five men who sat around the table with Bonnie and Rooney did not hide their total contempt for Castro's Cuba. They were especially contemptuous and somewhat paranoid about having a communist regime threatening American democracy only ninety miles off our southern coast.

Bonnie found them straight out of some bad 1960's Cold War movie.

These men were so determined to show their loathing for all things Cuban that they refused to utter the name Fidel Castro. Instead, they only ever referred to him—and through clenched teeth—as "the bearded one."

She told them that she was looking into the possibility of asking the Cubans to extradite Bustamante to the United States.

They reminded her, it's impossible.

She wondered if, short of formal extradition, there was some way to ask the Cubans simply to hand him over.

They reminded her, that, too, is impossible.

She suggested, "We could just ask and then if they say no, we can make a big deal out of it in the press. You know, with headlines like, Cuba shelters drug trafficker."

They pronounced her notion, "Ill informed and impossible."

She didn't want to explain to them that Bustamante was begging Oscar to get him out of there. Instead she argued, "The longer he stays in Cuba, the more stale his information becomes. If we can get him, we can get his whole gang. But we need to do it sooner rather than later. Guys, this is about the war on drugs. This is about stopping cocaine coming into the United States." She really played up to their view of the world. "We need to try because this is about protecting America."

At least one of them seemed to understand, because he agreed, "All right, we'll try." But then he cautioned her, "We will send a diplomatic note. But a diplomatic note is not a formal request. And, be warned, if they ask for a quid pro quo, there is no deal. Impossible."

She thanked them and went back to New York, expecting to hear from them in a few days. Or, a few weeks. Or, a few months. She phoned them several times, and e-mailed them several more times, always asking, what's going on?

She never heard anything from the Cuba desk.

In January 2007, a Cuban prosecutor announced that he was going to ask the courts to sentence Bustamante to life in prison. His case was based entirely on legal proceedings against Bustamante that he claimed were taking place in the United States, Colombia, and Panama.

Oscar was outraged. "Cuba's intentions are very sinister. They're condemning him with Internet clippings."

Which is pretty much what the Cuban prosecutor was doing. There were no trafficking allegations against Bustamante in Cuba. He wasn't even charged with his only crime there, trying to enter the country with a false passport. The prosecutor was proposing to put Bustamante away forever based entirely on hearsay allegations from three countries, one of which had no diplomatic relations with his.

It was so bizarre, even by Cuban justice standards, that no one was willing to approve it. One month later, word came from Cuba that they were fed up with Bustamante. He had become a nuisance, always complaining to them about his prison conditions—he was still in that disgusting pretrial detention cell—and about his back, and about his regular beatings, and about the heat, and about how the whole place reeked because the toilet didn't really flush and was only cleaned once a week.

The Cubans decided to get rid of him. They announced, he's served his time, and gave the Colombians seventy-two hours' notice to come pick him up.

On February 8, 2007, guards removed Bustamante from his cell, drove him in chains to the airport, and handed him over to the Colombian police. He was flown immediately to Bogotá.

But the Colombians didn't want him, either.

They worried that he could use his resources to escape. Or that he could create all kinds of havoc by giving newspaper interviews. They wanted to ship him off to America as soon as possible. And Bustamante said he wanted that, too.

He was held at the heavily fortified compound of Bogotá's chief prosecutor. The idea was that the Americans could pick him up there. But then, a Colombian magistrate ruled that Bonnie's original extradition request wasn't sufficient and wanted her to file another one.

As she hustled to put that together, the Colombians decided that, for Bustamante's own safety, he needed to be in solitary confinement in a high-security part of Combita Prison.

Oscar flew to Colombia to see Bustamante. But the man he found this time was very different from the man he'd met at El Vergel all those years before.

"Jail changes these men," he says. "When they're out in the world, free, and trafficking, they think that their life is going great. When they get locked inside a cell, they have to come to terms with the fact that their life is going another way, someone else's way, the government's way, and that they have to play by certain rules. They may or may not be ready to do that. Jail changes these men. It can break them."

He says that because most of these men come from very poor backgrounds, they are easily blinded by their sudden and extraordinary wealth. "They started working for other big people when they were young and, particularly this group, they lasted long enough to become very rich and very powerful themselves. But they lose both their wealth and power very quickly. It gets taken away, and they find themselves, like Bustamante did, spending three years in that Cuban prison, then facing the rest of his life in an American prison. The end for them comes fast and they all find it terribly difficult to deal with."

Bustamante told Oscar he was resigned to go to the States, that he'd asked to go straight from Cuba, and that he wanted to get on with the next step of his life. He said he wanted to put all this behind him. He also said he would feel safer in the States.

"When they're trafficking," Oscar goes on, "their life is lived in a giant golden jail because they need to protect themselves. They're looking over their shoulders all the time. They go to a meeting with someone, and bring with them a lot of men with guns, and the other fellow has a lot of men with guns, and no one knows what's going to happen. They have to hope they will go home alive. Bustamante's life has always been tough. All these traffickers, they're always afraid of everybody. They know that most of them wind up in jail or dead. It's a life of distrust."

Oscar did what he could to help Bustamante move the process forward so that he could get to the States quickly. He knew that the best thing for his client was being in America where he would be dealing with Bonnie.

During those months in Colombia waiting to go to the States, Bustamante did give interviews to the press. Which wasn't necessarily the smartest thing he could do because it ignited resentment toward him.

The most telling interview, which appeared only a month after his return, appeared in the newspaper *El Tiempo*.

Bustamante said that once he got to the United States he intended to tell everything he knew about how he and other traffickers had funded political campaigns.

In many ways, the interview sounded less like a prisoner's remembrances and more like a naked attempt at blackmailing the government into keeping him in Colombia.

He admitted that he'd "owned" a few members of congress and at least eight mayors in the Norte Valle. He said he never paid any money directly to President Samper, but he knew the men who did; that they'd paid him somewhere between $1 to $2 million in cash, and that Samper knew where the money was coming from. Bustamante also said, at one point, he was spending up to $250,000 a month in bribes to policemen and prosecutors.

What's more, he said, he intended to talk about the paramilitaries and to explain how they continue to run trafficking operations from jail.

It was exactly the kind of bravado that could get him killed while he was in Colombia. But then he said he recognized how his life had been one of distrust and betrayal, and told the newspaper that he intended to retire. "There are only two certainties in this world, the cemetery or a jail cell."

Of course, the certainty of Bustamante's retirement was already assured by the U.S. government.

He said he was aware of the growing threats against his life as long as he stayed in Colombia. In fact, the authorities had uncovered no fewer than five assassination plots against him in Combita.

As soon as he'd returned to Colombia, he said, he'd written to Don Diego, Varela, and Chupeta, encouraging them to come to the U.S. with him. He did not say whether or not they ever responded. But he did talk about his laptop, confirming that it contained many business records. He said he knew for a fact that the Cubans had turned the laptop over to the Colombians.

The files on his laptop would show, he admitted, many of his dealings with the Mexicans, which anyway, had grown too complicated and too expensive. "You send them one thousand kilos and four hundred go to them. They also charge twenty percent for landing it in Guadalajara or Mexico City. And you have to put up your own capital."

The interview was broad and rambling. At one point, the journalist asked him about Pablo Escobar. Bustamante said he'd only known Escobar slightly, but insisted, "The guy was nuts."

There was an incident, he said, when he stole two trucks with dynamite from Escobar, and two helicopters carrying weapons. He admitted that he used to call the cops whenever he could to report cars filled with Escobar's guys.

Then, he said, Escobar had once tried to kill him. "They almost did me in Cartago on his orders."

When Escobar died, Bustamante said, he thought about getting out of the business. "But there are so many expenses, that you have to go back. Maintaining your bodyguards and that deluxe lifestyle, which is not a good life at all, is very expensive.

He talked about the Orejuelas—he said he didn't work with them but had a landing strip that he occasionally let them use—and about the FARC. He said he bought finished product from Bolivia, Peru, or from the FARC in the south of Colombia.

He also talked about his friend, the AUC leader Carlos Castaño, who'd been reported missing since 2004 and was assumed to have been murdered. His body had never been found. Referring to Castaño as "the professor, Bustamante claimed he was probably hiding somewhere, reorganizing the paramilitaries. "The professor is a great friend of mine. He must be on his home turf in La Costa."

Finally Bustamante spoke about Colombia's neighbor, Venezuela, which was firmly under the control of the socialist dictator, Hugo Chávez. "Venezuela is the temple of drug trafficking. There is a collaborative relationship among Venezuelans, Colombians, Brazilians. It is very easy to traffic through there because they can't catch anybody."

On Thursday, July 19, the Colombian courts gave final approval to Bonnie's new request that Bustamante be extradited to the United States, as everyone expected they would.

Immediately, he was returned to Bogotá where, dressed in light pants, a lime green sweater, and a bulletproof vest—and in handcuffs and in chains—a heavily armed police SWAT team handed him over to a group of heavily armed DEA agents.

The Americans quickly bundled him into a Learjet and rushed to get out of Colombian airspace.

Knowing that the transfer was about to happen, Rooney had been waiting in Miami. As soon as he got word that Bustamante was being handed over, he and a group of armed ICE agents left in a small prop plane for Guantánamo Bay.

The reason Rooney had to pick him up there was because the DEA plane couldn't make it all the way to New York without refueling, and refueling presented a legal problem.

The law says that a foreign trafficker being brought to the United States on a 959 charge must be tried either in Washington, D.C., or in the first district where he lands. That he was coming to the States on Bonnie's charges didn't matter. The NDDS's separate indictment meant that, regardless of why he was being brought into the country, wherever he landed first, that's where the jurisdiction had to be.

If the DEA had flown Bustamante from Bogotá to, say, Miami to refuel there, she could still have prosecuted him, but she'd have to do it in Miami. Or the NDDS could prosecute him in Washington, D.C. But refueling in Miami would mean that Bustamante could not be prosecuted in New York.

When someone suggested that the plane refuel in Puerto Rico, Bonnie had to remind them that the jurisdictional rule applies wherever there is a federal district court.

Then, she realized, there is no federal district court at Guantánamo Bay. So the DEA jet landed at the naval airstrip there, which is across the way from where terrorists were being housed.

Rooney was waiting on the tarmac to take control of the prisoner.

The DEA jet taxied up close to the ICE prop plane, and came to a stop. The door opened, some agents came down the stairs, and then other agents escorted Bustamante out of the plane. Now the ICE pilots started their engines.

Rooney took control of the prisoner. And as they walked from one plane to the next, he said to Bustamante, "Welcome back to Cuba."

17

The 1,450-mile flight from Guantánamo Bay to John F. Kennedy Airport in Queens, took over six hours in the tiny, single-engine turboprop Pilatus.

Although there was no real danger that Bustamante could, or would, do anything, he was handcuffed, chained, and buckled into a last-row seat—there were only twelve seats on the plane, two rows of six—so it was easy for Rooney, another ICE agent, and a DEA agent to keep a constant eye on him. For most of the flight, Bustamante was pensive, looking out the window, not talking.

The DEA agent on board had a brown bag filled with sandwiches. Rooney offered one to Bustamante, along with a bottle of water. He took it, said, *gracias,* and ate quietly.

Rooney got the impression that Cuba had really softened him up.

Landing at Kennedy, the little plane taxied to a secure hangar in a remote corner of the airfield where a ten-car convoy was waiting.

There were heavily armed ICE agents, New York State Troopers, the NYPD, and Port Authority Police.

It was far more muscle and firepower than they needed to escort Bustamante, in handcuffs, chains, and a bulletproof vest, from the plane to a car and then to the MDC in Brooklyn. But no one was taking any chances. They were there to keep him in custody, and also to keep him alive, should someone try to silence him. Toby rode with Bustamante.

Arriving at the MDC, Bustamante was processed, then booked into the top-floor SHU and solitary confinement. Early the next morning, he was brought downstairs, where even more cars, and more heavily armed men, were waiting to take him to court.

There were agents in full body armor with shotguns, state troopers in marked cars, and armed agents in unmarked follow-up cars. Bustamante was kept in handcuffs and chains, and loaded into a black SUV with dark windows. Now Rooney joined Toby to ride with Bustamante.

A state trooper, with red lights flashing on his car, led the way, clearing traffic as the convoy sped along Southern State Parkway. Overhead, an ICE helicopter shadowed them at low altitude for the entire forty-seven-mile ride.

The prisoner was just as quiet now as he had been in the plane.

Arriving at Central Islip, the motorcade pulled into the secure garage at the courthouse. Bustamante was transferred from the SUV to a holding cell. At exactly noon, he was brought upstairs to courtroom 1010 where Judge Seybert and Bonnie saw him for the first time.

His head was shaven. He looked drawn and sullen. He certainly didn't look like one of the most dangerous and vicious criminals in the world.

The charges Bonnie had lodged were read to him, and the judge remanded him to the MDC, without bail, to await trial. Eventually, he would be shipped down to Washington, D.C., to face the RICO indictment that the NDDS and Boyd Johnson at SDNY had filed against him.

Now, he was led out of the courtroom, taken down to the basement, and put into the SUV. Then the motorcade, complete with helicopter, delivered him safely back to the SHU in Brooklyn.

Bonnie watched as Bustamante left the courtroom and thought to herself, we've come a long way since the Tele-Austin raids.

Flashback to January 2004.

It had been seven years since Bonnie and Rooney got their first peek inside the Norte Valle Cartel, and even if they didn't know at the time that's what it was called, the first of the big name NVC traffickers was on his way to America.

When Arcangel Henao was still in the Cartago region, there is evidence to suggest that the Colombians knew exactly where he was but couldn't, or wouldn't, go after him because he was being protected by the AUC.

After war broke out between Don Diego and Varela, Arcangel fled to Panama so that he didn't have to take sides. The DEA located him living on a farm along the Colombian-Panamanian border. They waited, watching him all the time, until the various indictments against him were in place—not just Bonnie's, but also the RICO case in Washington—then asked the Panamanians to get him.

The farm was raided on Saturday morning, January 10, and Arcangel was arrested without incident. His girlfriend, Diana Monsalve, was with him at the time. She was Arnoldo's daughter—Juan Albeiro Monsalve's niece—and she would later tell Bonnie and Rooney that she was convinced it was Bustamante who had ordered her father killed.

Instead of sending Arcangel to Colombia, where he would sit in Combita until someone approved an extradition request, the Panamanians had agreed to short-circuit the system and, based on Bonnie's indictment, officially expel him.

You can have him, they said, but you have to come get him.

Rooney was more than happy to fly down to Panama to bring Arcangel back, but ICE couldn't get its act together in time. In fact,

Rooney had asked for country clearance on Thursday, two days prior to the raid because he wanted to take part in Arcangel's capture.

Normally, country clearance for an agent on official business is handled between Washington and the embassy and takes fifteen minutes. But ICE headquarters sat on it.

On Monday, two days after the capture, headquarters informed Rooney that he'd have country clearance within twenty-four hours. He told them, don't bother, it's too late. So the DEA flew Arcangel out of Panama, and took all the credit—along with the ensuing publicity—for bringing him back to the States.

The forty-nine-year-old Arcangel arrived on Wednesday, January 14, at MacArthur Airport on Long Island—in the country where he would, almost surely, spend the rest of his life—with nothing but a small backpack.

Rooney and other ICE agents took custody of him. They couldn't handcuff him because he had no left arm. So they cuffed Arcangel's right hand to a chain belt, then motorcaded him to the MDC in Brooklyn.

The temperature in Panama when Arcangel flew out was eighty-eight degrees. The temperature on Long Island when he arrived was nine degrees. Arcangel said that he'd never been in cold weather. He said that he was freezing.

Rooney gave him his coat.

Bonnie didn't call him by his nickname, "Mocho," because it means, "amputee." She called him Arcangel, and told him it was a beautiful name.

Rooney decided Arcangel's mother had given it to him because he was born deformed and wanted him to have the blessings of the higher angels.

But Bonnie didn't dwell on that. She found him to be a pathetic soul. He was an uneducated farmer who'd became titular head of the Henao family when his older brother Orlando was murdered in jail on the orders of Pacho Herrera. Whenever the NVC hierarchy met, Arcangel had a seat at the table, but no one seemed to pay much attention to him. No one seemed anxious to deal with him.

Whatever money he made, he invested in cattle and his farms. Although, he once invested in a submarine.

The Colombians have always used every means they can think of to move drugs, from speedboats, container ships, planes, vehicles, and people to balloons, animals, and microlites. In 1995, they flirted with the idea of landing a big submarine somewhere along the East Coast of the United States, filled with four hundred tons of cocaine.

It was a Russian strip club owner in Miami named Leonid Fainberg who suggested to some of his Cuban friends that what the Colombians really needed was a sub. His Cuban friends told their Colombian friends, and the Colombians said they were interested.

The owner of Porky's, a club in Hialeah that was sleazy even by Hialeah strip club standards, Fainberg liked to call himself "Tarzan" and tried to look the part. He was pumped up through steroids and weight lifting, sported a goatee, and wore a blond ponytail. His business card had a caricature of himself as Atlas holding the world in the air with one hand.

In the past he'd helped the Colombians buy six surplus Russian helicopters and some bulletproof Zil limousines. Now, he promised, he had all the right contacts to get them a submarine. Even if he didn't.

Someone in Colombia, and it's not clear who—but most likely one of the last vestiges of the Cali Cartel—funded Fainberg to go to Russia, and budgeted up to $35 million for the purchase, delivery, crewing, and maintenance of the boat, plus Fainberg's commission.

Traipsing around the old Soviet naval base at Murmansk, he actually managed to find a Tango Class diesel sub for sale and negotiated a price of $5.5 million. Fainberg also located a retired admiral who, along with his crew of twenty-five, was willing to sail it.

The problem was, how to get the submarine to Colombia.

Fainberg arranged for the Colombians to meet the admiral, who explained to them that he didn't want to sail across the Atlantic because the boat would need a complete overhaul as soon as they got into port. His idea was to tow it. But a submarine in tow would be visible and the Colombians worried that someone—for instance, the U.S. Navy—might wonder what was going on. Fainberg reassured everyone that all they had to do was say that the submarine was being used for oceanographic research. But the Colombians got cold feet and the deal fell through.

Five years later, the Colombian National Police raided a warehouse outside Bogotá where they discovered Russian engineers building a 98-foot submarine. It was double-hulled, designed to have a range of 2,000 miles, could dive to 330 feet, and carry up to 200 tons of cocaine.

Since then, traffickers have settled on forty to fifty foot "semi-submersibles" which they can build easily in the jungles by the dozens.

Little more than a fiberglass hull powered by a small diesel engine, the boats sit very low in the water with just a tiny conning tower visible above the waterline, making them difficult to spot, even by electronic means.

They're painted ocean-green, which also helps camouflage them, and are manned by a crew of up to four. They stand in the cramped conning tower for the entire trip. The boats have a range of around six hundred miles and sail at an average speed of ten to fifteen knots. Most trips last two days.

The cocaine is off-loaded onto go-fast boats at a rendezvous point. Earlier models carried four to five tons of cocaine. Newer models are said to carry twelve to fifteen tons. The cocaine serves as ballast to keep the semisubmersibles upright. Without its ballast, the minisubs are unstable which is why, once they're emptied, they're sunk.

Making semisubmersibles all the more attractive, at least in the beginning, was a law of the high seas that said, in order to charge a ship's crew with drug offenses, you have to arrest them with the drugs. So whenever a minisub was interdicted, they scuttled the boat. According to maritime law, anyone found at sea without a boat is designated a castaway and other ships are required to rescue them.

To get around that, the United States pushed through a law that made the crewing of an unregistered semisubmersible illegal. So, now, with or without the drugs, crew members can be arrested and prosecuted. It's made the business of working these boats that much more dangerous. But there doesn't appear to be any short supply of willing sailors. One estimate has it that, these days, semisubmersibles are carrying nearly one-third of Colombia's cocaine exports.

Arcangel was almost a semisubmersible pioneer.

He had been one of several investors, along with Don Diego, in the construction of a small submarine. Everyone liked the idea and had high hopes for the project. When it was built, he went to see the test run. They put the boat into the water and two sailors started steering it back and forth along the coast, going farther out to sea with each pass. Everyone was impressed until they got about twelve hundred feet offshore and capsized.

His investment of $750,000 went down with the boat.

An utter failure, that ended his submarine days. He never recovered his money and decided to go back to the old ways of moving drugs. He also went back to investing in cattle. That's what he loved.

Over time, he talked to Rooney about Bustamante, Don Diego, Cano, Chupeta, Dagoberto and many of the others. He went into detail about Abelardo Rojas, brother of Jaime and El Loco, who ran a stash house in New York and moved both drugs and money for him. He went into detail about Aldemar Rendon Montoya, his cousin and chief money launderer.

He also talked about money laundering. Rooney thought that he would tell some great stories and reveal brilliant new methods. But Arcangel surprised him with how spectacularly unsophisticated the Norte Valle bunch was when it came to that.

"They brought me boxes and suitcases with cash in them," he said "We bulk-shipped cash. We'd sell drugs to the Mexicans, get paid right there in dollars, then put the money in suitcases and our couriers flew with the money as passengers on planes with the suitcases. Or we stuffed air conditioners with hundred-dollar bills, really big air conditioners, and drove them from Mexico City back to Colombia."

And he talked about his friend, Javier Montanez, who was at the time third in command of the AUC. His real name was Carlos Mario Jiménez, but most people referred to him by his nickname, "Macaco," which he got for looking like a "macaco," which is a type of small monkey.

Born not far from Cartago in 1966, Macaco had been captured by the Colombian police in 2002, trying to escape by plane to Venezuela, but got out of jail very quickly. As soon as he was released, he went back to the jungles to oversee several clandestine airstrips and cocaine-processing labs. He was an extremely tough and violent man.

Yet, Arcangel's lawyer told Bonnie and Rooney, "Macaco shivers when he hears your names."

She couldn't believe it. "What?

Apparently, ever since *La Semana* had published their names, every trafficker in Colombia knew that "Doctora" Bonnie Klapper and "Agente" Romedio Viola were after them.

Arcangel confirmed it. "You two are the most feared people in Colombia."

Bonnie and Rooney both liked the thought of that, even if they didn't necessarily believe it.

It's understandable why Arcangel might believe it, however. Some reports would later credit him with being the smartest trafficker of all, the man who understood high-tech and embraced the digital age to triumph over the other groups, and law enforcement. It is, flatly, untrue. Nothing in his story bears that out, and the people who know him, and have gotten to know him in recent years, are united in saying that he is hardly intelligent enough to go to the bathroom alone.

When Rooney returned his backpack to him, the one he'd flown with to the States, a delighted Arcangel opened it and started pulling out the few things that were inside. One was his pajama bottoms.

Bonnie couldn't believe it. It was a Daffy Duck and Goofy pajama. Like something a seven-year-old would wear. She told him, "Those are for kids."

Arcangel smiled broadly. "My seventeen-year-old girlfriend loves them."

18

Toward the end of 2004, the Colombians arrested the NVC's elder statesman Gabriel Puerta-Parra.

Indicted in Miami and by the NDDS in Washington, the "Sensitive Investigative Unit" of the CNP arrested him, acting on a hotline "La Recompensa" tip that he was hiding in the mountain village of La Vega, south of Cali. He was extradited to the States in 2006 and has since pleaded guilty to trafficking and money-laundering charges.

Making Puerta-Parra a particularly good catch, he'd worked as legal counsel at the DAS, and had once been Pablo Escobar's attorney. He was also the bag man for funds going back and forth between the NVC and the AUC. He knew how the Colombian intelligence services worked, had a close working relation with Don Diego and Carlos Castaño, and set up an array of legitimate businesses through which money could be laundered. There were investment companies, finance houses, real estate developers, construction companies, and even an airline.

He owned Intercontinental de Avacion, along with Arcangel Henao's family and other active investors in Norte Valle cocaine shipments.

Based in Bogotá and Cali, Inter flew short-haul flights to neighboring countries. The airline eventually went out of business after a series of crashes due to failing safety standards.

For drug-trafficking organizations, owning their own airline is almost as good as owning their own bank.

Then, over Christmas 2004, they nabbed Dagoberto Rios Flores.

He'd gone to spend the holidays with his family on a farm outside Medellin, "for the last time," he said, because he was intending to surrender right after the new year. Maybe he was, maybe he wasn't. But his timing was off, because a poor dirt farmer somewhere nearby—a man raising a child alone because his wife had abandoned him—spotted Dagoberto, recognized him from Bonnie's billboards, and phoned the reward hotline.

That ten-cent call earned the dirt farmer $1.75 million.

Because it was much too dangerous to let the now very rich dirt farmer stay in the country, Bonnie and Rooney arranged to get him out immediately. They moved him and his child to Florida. Today he owns four condos there and complains regularly to Rooney that the real estate market has fallen through the floor since he became a millionaire.

Nicely enough, the sixty-five year-old former dirt farmer turned real estate mogul, spent the first fifty-grand of his fortune with a high-end plastic surgeon. Rooney notes that, after his face-lift and liposuction, he now looks like a sixty-two-year-old former dirt farmer. But the man himself must believe that he got his money's worth and, accordingly, he has a certain appeal to the ladies. No sooner did he have his new nose and waistline than he asked Rooney to ask Bonnie if she would like to go to Hawaii with him.

A month after putting Dagoberto in jail, they grabbed José Aldemar Rendón Ramírez.

A short and stocky middle-aged man with black hair and brown eyes, Rendón was a trafficker on his own account and a fixer for hire. As a trafficker, he dealt mainly in small parcels, fifty to two hundred kilos. As a fixer, he seemed especially adept at paying bribes to prosecutors and judges to get criminal charges dismissed.

But most of all, Rendón was Bustamante's principal money launderer. And as a money launderer, he was big-time.

Although his laundering method was really very basic—wiring cash from one place to another—it was Rendón who, on a trip to New York in 1992, actually came up with the idea of opening storefront remitters.

He'd known Monsalve for nearly thirty years, and convinced him to set up the Tele-Austin operations for Bustamante. The way it worked was, Monsalve had to come up with his own lists of senders' names, but Rendon would provide the lists of recipient names. He came up with those through contacts he established at *cambios* in various places around Cartago, notably Armenia, Pereira, and Manizales—the three cities which received nearly $70 million from Monsalve's operations and which, eventually, led Bonnie and Rooney to the Norte Valle Cartel.

In addition to those crimes, Rendón was carrying some additional baggage. According to authorities, at one point he had a falling-out with the manager of a *cambio* in Pereira. The manager said he no longer wanted to be involved. Rendón said that wasn't an option. The manager went to the police and the next thing that happened was that he turned up dead. Somewhere along the way, Rendón also allegedly ordered the murder of a drug courier.

About eighteen months after his arrest, he was escorted north to Central Islip, where Bonnie confronted him with the evidence she'd compiled. Among the people now willing to testify against him was none other than Monsalve.

Understanding that he was done for, Rendón acknowledged that he'd worked for Bustamante, that he'd brokered drug deals for him, and that he'd laundered money for him. He also said that he'd often recommended and recruited transporters and other money launderers for Bustamante, receiving a commission on their revenue for the service.

But Rendón insisted that he was not "the big guy." He needed Bonnie to know that, while he was definitely guilty of some things, that didn't mean he was guilty of everything.

The crime he didn't get charged with was being stupid.

He'd been included in the $5 million reward program, and with that kind of money hanging over his head, he probably should have been more careful in his choice of girlfriends. At least, he should never have chosen one whose other boyfriend was a cop.

At the age of fifty-five, he was getting it on with a girl in Pereira who was only seventeen. She found out that he was one of the men named in "La Recompensa" and decided that reward money easily trumps sex with old men. So the next time he invited her to Medellin for a dirty weekend, she told her cop boyfriend. He followed her to the rendezvous, and long before the lights went off, her cop friend called for his cop friends and Rendón was busted.

The seventeen-year-old walked away with $1.5 million.

Later, when someone asked Rendón what he was doing with women so much younger than himself, he said he liked them young.

Hardly atypical among these men, the following question was, what about your marriage? He admitted, it failed. Why? He explained, "Because I told my wife I wanted to go out with many different younger women and she didn't approve."

The next big name to fall was one of the biggest, Jhonny Cano.

He is said to have started life as a teenaged assassin for hire, and by the early 1990s was working directly for Bustamante, whom he'd known all his life. They came from the same village. His alleged specialty was killing people from a motorcycle.

According to legend, one of Cano's earliest assignments was to murder a minor-league trafficker who'd had the mishap of nearly crashing his plane. The fellow encountered an engine problem and was forced to make an emergency landing. He brought the plane down on a jungle airstrip at a farm owned by Bustamante.

When Bustamante heard about it, he sent word back to the hapless pilot that he couldn't leave the plane on the airstrip indefinitely, that he had to get it out of there.

For whatever reason, the fellow decided he didn't want the plane anymore, and walked away from it, forever. Bustamante had to remove it, and sent the fellow a bill. When the man foolishly refused to give Bustamamnte his money, Bustamante ordered Cano to kill him. And that's what he did.

As Cano got older and Bustamante's business grew bigger, he assigned Cano greater responsibilities. One of them was to supervise workers in various jungle processing labs. After that, Bustamante put him in charge of his personal security.

Witnesses told Rooney that Cano went on to kill scores of other people, including at least one Colombian police officer, many rival traffickers—in one of those hits, a two-year-old child was killed in the crossfire—and several other assassins.

It is reasonably believed that Jhonny Cano has murdered, or at least been involved with the killings of, at least, three hundred people.

As a reward for his loyalty, Bustamante allowed him to traffick on his own account. Cano moved drugs through Miami on their way to New York, then funded Jaime Rojas Franco and a few others to set up stash houses where his drugs—and Bustamante's, too—could be stored safely, waiting to be sold.

The first notable shipment that Bonnie and Rooney were able to track back to Cano, was a 1998 wholesale deal of 720 kilos that Cano did with various individuals at $17,000 per kilo. That comes to $12.24 million.

A year later, Cano moved 390 kilos to Jaime Rojas and another 320 to a trafficker named Gonzalo Arango. But the shipment to Arango was intercepted by the NYPD. Cano wasn't amused, although he allowed the people to whom he'd given the cocaine to pay him back through future sales. Like two separate shipments of one-half ton each. And a third, where he hit the ton mark in a single shipment.

Cano suddenly had so much money coming in for himself, in addition to what he was paid by Bustamante, that he set up a rudimentary laundering system along the lines of the so-called "black market peso exchange" (BMPE).

A parallel currency market, it is, basically, a barter system where goods move and money stays put. A broker in Colombia arranges to buy drug cash in the United States, Canada, or Europe at a discount. At the same time, the broker takes pesos from a legitimate businessman in Colombia to pay the trafficker. The businessman, who now owns the overseas cash, can stash it in a foreign bank account or spend it whenever he is outside the country, free from Colombian income taxes. Or, he can use the money to purchase goods—whisky, household appliances, consumer electronics, cigarettes, used auto parts, precious metals, footwear, vehicles, boats, computers, cell phones—which he smuggles back into Colombia. One official government estimate suggests that 45 percent of the consumer goods on sale in Colombia come through the BMPE. A huge percentage of those goods are sold in the *sanandrecitos*.

BMPE brokers make money on the spread between buying and selling dollars and pesos, and sometimes also take a commission on the overall deal. Some of them can command fees as high as 25 percent. Otherwise legitimate companies outside Colombia, the ones selling their goods through the BMPE, have made a sale they might not have otherwise made. The banks handling the money transfers also earn fees. On paper, it's a good deal for everyone involved. In reality, those companies, and those banks, are facilitating drug-money laundering.

The first of the major BMPE cases—the one that really defined the problem for both big business and law enforcement—was back in 1998 and involved the Bell Helicopter company. It sold a $1.5 million, seven-seat Bell 407 to a Colombian who paid for it in 30 different installments, using 16 third-party sources. None of the 16 people paying for the helicopter had any relationship with Bell. Nor did they have any relationship with the man buying the helicopter. They were simply being used by the BMPE broker to launder street cash. And, at the time, Bell couldn't have cared less.

Since then, dozens of corporations have been caught out by the BMPE.

Testifying in front of a congressional committee, one BMPE broker catalogued deals she put through Sony, Procter & Gamble, John Deere, Whirlpool, Ford, Kenworth, Johnnie Walker, Swatch, Merrill Lynch, and Reebok. As she explained, "These companies were paid with U.S. currency generated by narcotics trafficking. They may not have been aware of the source of this money, but they accepted payments from me without questioning who I was or the source of the money."

In each of these cases, the companies insisted they did not know that they were being paid in dirty money. But then, the better the laundryman disguises the payments to the legitimate company, the easier it is for him to wash drug cash through the BMPE.

Cano's version of this was nowhere near as sophisticated. He simply sold the dollars he earned in New York to traffickers in Miami and let them do their own deals with the BMPE brokers, as long as someone paid him pesos in Cartago.

Of course, Cano had to discount his dollars off the regular exchange rates, and there were people taking commissions at both ends, but he didn't care what the Miami-based traffickers did with the dollars, or who cut themselves in on the deal. He didn't want to depend on bulk shipping. He didn't want to risk losing his money, or having to exchange huge amounts of dollars in Colombia which could draw attention to himself. All he wanted was pesos at home.

Again, making life as simple as possible, he managed his money laundering with cell phones and pagers, keeping transactions relatively small, between $200,000 to $300,000 at a time.

Helping him were two women. His wife, Marta Agudelo Cano, and her sister, Julia Agudelo. He also brought their brothers, José Ignacio and Leonardo, into his money-laundering scheme. Later all four would be arrested and extradited to the States, and all four would plead guilty to money-laundering charges. Bonnie felt their participation was very minor and asked for no more than time served and probation. The judge agreed.

Cano himself, however, was never going to get that lucky.

A group of three people came into the U.S. Embassy one day and said they knew where Jhonny Cano-Correa was. They asked if "La Recompensa" really meant they would get a reward. The embassy officials assured them they would. So they gave up Jhonny.

The Colombian National Police (CNP), together with ICE and DEA agents, located Cano right where the informants said he was, hiding in a jungle farmhouse south of Caucasia, in the Antioquia region, some 190 miles to the north of Medellin.

Protected there by a heavily armed security force, the police realized there was no way they could take him in a simple raid. Instead, they mounted an air assault with helicopters.

At noon, on Saturday October 29, 2005, the CNP's special "jungle assault unit" hit the farm. Guards on the ground fought back. One Colombian policeman was wounded in an intense firefight. But the attack had come too fast and too ferociously, and Cano—who was there with most of his family, including several young children—feared for their lives and gave up.

At the hideout, the cops confiscated grenade launchers, grenades, automatic assault weapons, and a substantial cache of ammunition.

Cano was helicoptered to Bogotá, held there briefly for processing and questioning, then delivered to Combita where he was kept in isolation.

Eleven months later, acting on Bonnie's request for extradition, Cano was flown directly to New York. It was a Friday night. He was met at the airport by a whole cavalcade of heavily armed police and cars with flashing red lights. He spent the weekend at the MDC and, first thing Monday morning, in another cavalcade of heavily armed police and state troopers with flashing red lights to clear the way, he was rushed off to Central Islip where he found himself standing in front of Judge Seybert. Cano was charged with various versions of conspiracy to traffic narcotics and various money-laundering offenses.

Like the others who'd been appearing before her—now, with increasing regularity—she remanded him to the MDC, to be held there awaiting trial, without bail.

Initially, Bonnie decided they would not talk to Cano. Given his record as a professional assassin, she told his lawyer, "There's only so low we'll sink."

Anyway, the evidence she had against him was so substantial that there didn't seem any reason to do anything more than leave him alone, in his cell, and wait for him to understand he had no choice but to plead guilty.

Then his AUC buddy Macaco got extradited.

Carlos Mario Jiménez was first arrested in 2002. At the time he was wanted for several murders, among other crimes. The DAS, Colombia's intelligence service, considered him to be the AUC's number three man, and believed that he was in a position to become, one day, Carlos Castaño's successor.

Somehow, he managed to got out of prison very quickly, and reestablish himself by taking over a number of cocaine-processing labs and hidden airstrips. He controlled an army of six thousand men. Before long, the DAS was talking about Macaco in terms of also being Bustamante's successor.

Then the Colombians jailed him again. This time, in 2005, it was under the terms of the "Law of Peace and Justice."

If you were a member of the AUC and you surrendered, made a public statement, and confessed your sins, you would receive a vastly reduced sentence, be allowed to serve it at a much nicer jail than Combita, and not get extradited to the United States. You also had to agree to pay reparation to the family of your victim.

However, these were not men who were ever going to play it straight. Like the others, Macaco continued trafficking from jail.

Eventually, President Uribe decided he'd had it with this crew, pulled the plug on their jailhouse businesses, scooped up a bunch of the leaders who were under indictment in the States, and announced they were on their way north, en masse.

There was a last-minute effort to keep many of them, including

Macaco, in Colombia. The victims' families fought to prevent extradition, fearing that if they were gone they would never get their reparations. The country's supreme court ruled they should stay. But Uribe was so anxious to get rid of them that he found a judicial panel willing to overturn the supreme court's decision. Uribe handed them over to the DEA, and they were rushed out of the country.

No one in Washington or New York or Miami expected them to be there quite so soon. Suddenly there were fourteen of these characters to deal with. And it drove the prosecutors crazy.

A few of the prisoners were willing to cooperate. But the crimes they'd committed were so horrendous that there wasn't something that could automatically be done.

Macaco was going to be dealt with in Florida, but Bonnie heard that the prosecutors there were in desperate need of additional witnesses to testify against him. She knew that Cano had information which could be useful, which is why she and Rooney finally started talking to him.

Rooney says that of all the people they've interviewed in connection with the Norte Valle Cartel, Cano turned out to be the most honest. "He never lies. He looks you in the face, thinks the question through, and if he doesn't know he doesn't embellish."

These days, Bonnie speaks with him on a regular basis. He is a beneficiary of her "cookie campaign for honesty." He is not in the SHU but mixed in with the general population at the MDC, and has been known to encourage others to talk to Bonnie, reminding them about the cookies she bakes. At the same time, he continues to be a good source of information about the Norte Valle's business dealings both inside and outside Colombia.

Prison has, definitely, made him a more pragmatic man. He tells Bonnie and Rooney often, "I was stupid, uneducated, and good with a gun, so they picked me. I look back at what I did and I pray to my savior that I don't burn in hell."

Mellowing or not, the problem is that his reputation as a stone-cold professional killer has preceded him, and that's not made life easy for him.

He's a target.

Generally speaking, the Colombians try to keep to themselves. But word gets around about who's who, and there are always plenty of street thugs looking to make a jailhouse reputation for themselves by taking on some major guy.

In 2009, a Dominican kid targeted Cano and a fight broke out. Cano got beat up pretty badly and suffered the humiliation of a broken nose.

Rooney was concerned and rang Cano's lawyer. He wanted to know, "How did that happen? After all, he's a professional killer."

The lawyer spoke to Cano, asked him the same question, and Cano gave him a straight answer. "I've never had to use my fists."

When Rooney spoke to him about it, Cano repeated the same thing. But by now, there was something else on his mind.

"When you took me to court," he said, "and you had all those men with body armor and their assault weapons and the cars with the flashing lights, that was just like Rasguño, yes?"

Rooney assured him, "Yes, you got the same treatment as Bustamante."

"So how come," Cano asked seriously, "there was no helicopter?"

19

As more and more of the Norte Valle mob arrived in the United States, what had been a trickle of people willing to surrender was becoming a flood. It was as if everyone with something to hide suddenly feared that everyone else with something to hide would denounce them as part of a plea bargain, and that they'd be arrested and sent to Combita for several years before being extradited, anyway.

A lawyer Bonnie knew in Miami rang one afternoon to say that he had a client who'd been very involved in trafficking for the NVC, and insisted, "He wants to cooperate."

She asked what his name was. The lawyer told her.

Priding herself on always being forthcoming, Bonnie had to confess, "I never heard of this guy."

"He's Colombian," the lawyer said. "He happens to be in Mexico at the moment. He's had enough. He wants to come in."

"That's fine," she said. "But I still don't know who he is and I can't tell you that he's on my list of people to charge."

The lawyer was doing the best for his client. "He's a straight-up guy. Eventually, you will get to him. But he doesn't want to wait. His wife is giving him a hard time to get out of the business and he really wants to come clean."

Obviously, turning this down would be foolish. "Okay," she agreed, "we'll meet him."

The lawyer said his client would come to Florida as long as Bonnie would write him a letter of safe passage, stipulating that he would not be arrested while he was in the States to negotiate a surrender.

Bonnie provided the letter and a date was set. Rooney flew to Florida and met with the man in his lawyer's office. He admitted that he'd been trafficking since the days of Pablo Escobar and had made a fortune working for Bustamante. He didn't go into numbers, didn't stipulate quantities, but Rooney found him very credible.

Rooney followed up a couple of more times, believed the man when he said that he'd never been involved in violence and agreed to sign him up. He put together a plan—he wanted to leave him where he was so that he could help bring in other people—and phoned his lawyer to explain what he was willing to put on the table. Rooney said that the man had to come to New York and that he had to plead guilty to trafficking offenses. He said he would not be held in jail awaiting sentencing, and could return to Mexico, but only as long as he was willing to help him find people that he needed to find. He said he'd be supervised by ICE agents in Mexico and that he'd have to wear a wire to tape conversations.

The lawyer put the deal to his client and quickly phoned back to say that his client was willing to do what he wanted.

That's when Rooney apologized, "I hope he doesn't mind flying to New York for the plea. He'll have to pay for his own ticket, and I don't know how much money this guy's got, but I'm just too busy to come to Florida again."

"No problem," the lawyer said, "he can afford the ticket and he can afford to stay in a good hotel." There was a pause, and then the lawyer asked, "Speaking of his money, have you thought about what kind of number you want for forfeiture?"

Actually, no one had. But he didn't want the lawyer to think forfeiture was his idea because he'd probably feel foolish for having mentioned it. "What kind of numbers are we talking about?"

The lawyer offered, "How about half a million dollars?"

Nice sum, he thought to himself, especially for a guy he'd never heard of. But instead of agreeing right away, he said, "No. Come on. You can do better than that."

"All right," the lawyer said, "let me get back to you."

An hour later he phoned to say, "What about two and a half?"

"That sounds a bit more like it," he decided. "How is he going to get us the money?"

The lawyer said, "Cash."

"And," he needed to know, "where is the cash?"

He told Rooney, "Mexico."

"In a bank?" he asked.

"No," he said. "He's got it all at home."

He wondered, "How's he going to get it to us?"

The lawyer volunteered, "Why doesn't he just drop it off at the embassy?"

"All right," Rooney said, and made the proper arrangements.

On the given day, at the given time, the man in Mexico climbed into a taxicab with four cardboard boxes, all wrapped tightly in masking tape. He arrived at the U.S. Embassy, was met by the proper people outside, and helped inside with the boxes. They were opened and the money was counted.

It was supposed to be $2.5 million exactly, but the first count came up with another number, so they counted it again. The second time they had the same number as the first, which was $2,499,999.

Someone at the embassy then noticed that one of the $100 bills was counterfeit. The man who brought the money clearly didn't know that, but the government couldn't give him credit for it.

Still, even with the bogus $100, he was $1 short.

After the embassy people phoned Rooney to tell him about the money, he got on the line with the man and said, "You did that on purpose, didn't you?"

210

"Of course," he answered right away. "I was checking to see if you would really count it all."

Another cooperator who just showed up at Bonnie's and Rooney's door one day to surrender mentioned to Rooney that Ariel Rodriguez—the fellow known as El Diablo—was the man who actually pulled the trigger on Monsalve's brother Arnoldo.

El Diablo had been working as a transporter for Bustamante, moving drugs from the Norte Valle to the coast. He was someone with a lot of violence in his past, having killed a number of people. Rooney wanted Bonnie to indict him, but Bonnie had heard a rumor that he was dead.

Except, El Diablo kept popping up in various investigations.

Rooney reminded Bonnie that they had a tremendous amount of evidence on El Diablo, so in July 2006, she added his name to Superceding Indictment #5. She charged him with conspiracy to possess with the intent to distribute cocaine, conspiracy to import cocaine, international distribution conspiracy, conspiracy to launder money, and money laundering.

That put El Diablo right up there on their wanted list with Bustamante, Jaime Duran, Jhonny Cano, and all the others.

Many months later, a lawyer brought in another man who wanted to surrender.

Because Rooney needed to know what crimes he'd committed, he asked, "Did you ever murder anyone?"

He said, "No."

Rooney asked, "Did you ever kidnap anybody?"

He said, "Never."

He asked, "Did you ever beat anyone up to collect a drug debt?"

"No," he said, "I am a peaceful man. I never killed anyone. I never kidnapped anyone. But . . ." He stopped and looked at Rooney for a long time. . . . "Does Tasering count?"

"Tasering?" He shrugged. "It depends. Tell me what you did, then we can figure it out."

He said, "Okay . . . see . . . Jhonny Cano found out that El Diablo had put a contract out on him."

"El Diablo?" He said, "You mean Ariel Rodriguez."

"That's right," the man went on. "Jhonny told me I had to bring El Diablo to him. So I invited him to come with me to one of Bustamante's farms. He said okay, because he didn't know what was going to happen. We got to the farm and as soon as he got out of the car, I Tasered El Diablo."

Rooney thought for a moment. "That doesn't sound like such a big deal. What happened next?"

"Well . . ." the man said. ". . . next, you see, the other guys who were waiting there dragged him into a barn, beat him to death, cut off his arms and his legs, then cut off his head, and put his body in one barrel of lye and the rest of him in another barrel of lye, then threw both barrels into the jungle."

Rooney was stunned.

The man continued, "The one who cut up his body . . . he did it with a machete. His name is . . . we call him Goofy."

Rooney looked at him incredulously. "Goofy cut up El Diablo with a machete."

"Yes." The man nodded several times. "But I only Tasered El Diablo."

Later Rooney told Bonnie, "Look at the dates. He says they killed El Diablo more than a year before we indicted him."

Bonnie reminded him, "I asked you if you were sure he was dead, you made me indict a dead man."

Rooney shrugged. "Who's going to complain?"

Later, Rooney decided, "I'm thinking about starting a Norte Valle clothing line."

Bonnie assumed Rooney was kidding. That is, until he showed up with T-shirts. They had a drawing of a devil with his hands up, and a guy with a gun shooting a lightning bolt into him.

Under the drawing in bold writing it said, "I Tasered El Diablo."

Then there was the arrest of Orlando Sabogal Zuluaga, yet another "Oscar Rodriguez Production."

Considered to be one of the world's most wanted and violent traffickers, Sabogal was on the run and rumor had it he'd gone to Spain.

Rooney had witnesses and cooperators who were willing to testify that Sabogal was, indeed, Bustamante's chief assistant, and that he not only brought multi-ton loads into the United States, he laundered hundreds of millions of dollars.

One witness provided an account of meetings with Sabogal in Los Angeles where he was recruiting transporters and distributors for loads of up to one ton. It was Sabogal, the witness said, who set the prices, quantities, and arrival times. After a while, it was Sabogal who increased the quantities to more than a ton and a half.

Another witness told Rooney that Sabogal had sold him the transport rights for Bustamante's cocaine from Medellin through Uruba to Cancún and Cozumel. But to do that, the witness had to cut a separate deal with the AUC which provided protection for the loads. Later, Sabogal would bring him to meet Bustamante at El Vergel, where they discussed moving drugs by go-fast boats and tankers to Mexico. At one of those meetings a deal was cut where Bustamante and Sabogal agreed to pay the witness $250,000 to $300,000 for each 600 to 1,200 kilo load. It was Sabogal who handled the details of these shipments.

Rooney then found a cooperator who told him how Sabogal helped Bustamante set up a crude money shipment scheme, using a crooked car dealer in Bogotá named Miguel Fajardo.

At Sabogal's instructions, cash in New York was stuffed inside stereo speakers, then sent to Miami via UPS or Airborne Express. The money was taken to a garage in Homestead, where it was hidden inside cars specially outfitted with traps, usually in the gas tanks. Fajardo then legally imported the car.

A variation on the old "French Connection" scam, everything worked fine until people started getting busted.

At that point, Sabogal recruited a team of couriers in the States who regularly flew to Colombia with cash-stuffed suitcases containing around $150,000 each. For a while, Sabogal's couriers were bringing $10 to $15 million per month to Colombia.

Rooney also had a witness who recounted the details of a strange incident that took place in 1998.

Sabogal had instructed one of his people in New York to meet a Canadian man who handed him $1.5 million. The money was then delivered to some Arab gentlemen at a rendezvous point on Forty-sixth Street. Three days later, a $2.7 million cash pickup was also delivered, on Sabogal's instructions, to these same Arab males.

This was around the same time when John Forbes and the El Dorado team spotted money going through the storefronts, being remitted directly to Pakistan.

Forbes questioned it then but no one in Washington did anything about it.

And no one in Washington seems to have bothered going back to look into it since.

Sabogal moved money around Florida, and on a few occasions, according to Rooney's witnesses, he transshipped drugs through Jamaica.

Yet another witness spoke about a meeting at El Vergel where Bustamante, Sabogal, and Sabogal's pilot outlined how the pilot made regular runs to Peru to pick up cocaine base. At that same meeting, Bustamante and Sabogal learned about a client in San Diego who was looking for 2.3 tons. The cocaine was flown out of Pereira on two small planes to Mexico and from there, trucked to Los Angeles. The value of such a deal is staggering, made all the more obvious by Bustamante paying $2,000 per kilogram just for the transportation.

It was Sabogal who also opened new transport routes, moving drugs by go-fasts from the small port of Necocli, on the west coast of Colombia, to Mexico and from there, to the States. But that wasn't always a very lucky route.

The suburban mom, Bonnie Klapper. *(Private photo)*

The coal miner's son, Romedio "Rooney" Viola.
(Private photo)

The El Dorado offices in Building 6 of the World Trade Center were destroyed on 9/11. *(U.S. Customs)*

The site of the TeleAustin remitter, 70-13 Austin Street, Queens, New York, where the case began. *(Private photo)*

The arrest of Juan Albeiro Monsalve, the Norte Valle Cartel's man in New York, led Bonnie and Rooney to Cartago, home of the cartel. *(ICE)*

Monsalve was moving 600 to 800 kilos of cocaine into New York every month. *(ICE)*

Fifty kilos of cocaine translates into fifty kilos of street cash. *(ICE)*

Bonnie Klapper with El Dorado supervisor John Forbes. *(Private photo)*

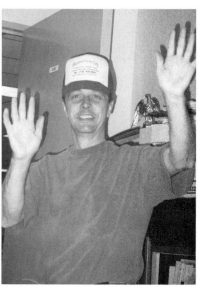

A young "Rooney." *(Private photo)*

Luis Hernando Gomez Bustamante, aka Rasguño, is less than pleased about being photographed during the finger-printing process. The bulletproof vest is to protect him from being assassinated by his former colleagues. *(DIJN)*

A subdued "Don Diego" on his way to the United States, seemingly resigned to his fate of life in prison. *(DIJN)*

Viola (r) and a team of ICE agents land in New York with Arcangel Henao Montoya, the ampu-tee trafficker known as "El Mocho." *(ICE)*

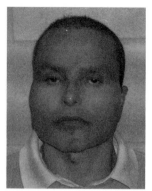

Bustamante lieutenant and chief enforcer Jhonny Cano-Carrero. *(ICE)*

The extremely violent Wilber Varela set off a war that saw thousands murdered. *(ICE)*

Years of plastic surgery while in hiding in Brazil didn't help Juan Carlos Ramírez Abadía, aka "Chupeta," avoid arrest and deportation to the United States. *(ICE)*

Orlando Sabogal, nicknamed "Caraqueso" (Cheese Face) had been Bustamante's right-hand man almost from the beginning. *(ICE)*

Jaime Maya Duran surrendered in Mexico and might still be in jail there had Rooney not managed to get him on a plane to New York without any ID. *(ICE)*

When the hapless "El Diablo," Ariel Rodriguez, put a contract out on a rival, revenge came quickly. He was Tasered, then cut up with a machete, by his own friends. *(ICE)*

Varela had worked his way to the top of Bonnie's and Rooney's list, when his own men wreaked revenge while he was in hiding in Venezuela. *(Venezuela Federal Police)*

Rather than be caught with the evidence, Norte Valle Cartel fast-boat runners set the boats, and the cocaine, alight, then jump in the water and try to swim for their lives. Often, the ones who don't get captured, drown. *(ICE)*

Carlos Arturo Patino, alias "Pate-muro," worked for Wilber Varela and allegedly told fellow prisoners in Combita prison that he could avoid extradition by murdering the American prosecutor Bonnie Klapper, and the federal agent Romedio Viola. He became the last of the Norte Valle Cartel to be prosecuted in the States, and was found guilty on multiple charges. *(ICE)*

Although Rooney retired, he returned as a civilian employee to help Bonnie and join in the hunt for Norte Valle Cartel associates in Mexico. *(Private photo)*

First stop in New York was the Metropolitan Detention Center in Brooklyn, where the top floor Special Housing Unit meant no contact with other prisoners, 23-hour-a-day lockdown, and one hour of daily exercise in a cage with only a tiny window for natural light. *(Jim Henderson)*

Colombia's dreaded Combita prison, where the "extraditables" were held, with no hot water and in appalling conditions, while awaiting their deportation to the United States. *(DIJN)*

Conditions in the Special Housing Unit are among the harshest in any U.S. prison. *(DoJ)*

Map of Colombia, showing Armenia, Pereira, and Manizales, the three cities near Cartago, where the Norte Valle money was wired from Queens.

On one of the first trips out of Necocli, the go-fast boat carrying 950 kilos of cocaine tons sank in bad weather. The bales of coke floated, were reloaded onto another fast boat and that boat also sank. This time the shipment was lost. They tried again. Another 950 kilos were loaded onto a go-fast boat in Necocli, but again, along the way to Cancún, bad weather struck and the boat was lost at sea.

Eventually the transporters figured out how to get around the hazardous weather conditions and loads started arriving regularly at their final destination, which was Houston, Texas.

Once that was in place, the witness—who had helped establish the Houston route with Sabogal—was kidnapped by Bustamante and held for nearly one month, until the previously lost loads were paid for. The witness didn't have the cash so, under threat of death, he handed over deeds to several properties, as well as a number of valuable paintings.

Sabogal clearly knew that his days on the run were numbered, because he contacted a lawyer to try to work out a surrender. Oscar was called in to help.

"He was a very poor guy who came up the ranks the hard way," Oscar says. "That doesn't excuse anything he ever did, but it tells you something about him. I met him a couple of times in Spain while he was hiding out there. I found him very reserved. I had to be careful because I was representing Bustamante, but I tried to get him to surrender. And he wanted to surrender. The last time I saw him in Spain I said, you've only got a few days. Either you come in on your own or they'll find you."

Obviously, Oscar says, Sabogal didn't understand that the clock was about to run out, because a few days after Oscar spoke to him the Spanish police grabbed him.

A tip had come into the reward hotline, not just that Sabogal was in Spain, but it was so specific, that the Spanish police were able to locate him in Majadahonda, a town some six miles northwest of Madrid. They arrested him on a warrant request from Bonnie, in a shopping center, carrying false identity papers. That same day, the

U.S. Treasury Department moved to ask the Colombians to freeze his and his family's assets.

"All I could do for him at that point," Oscar says, "was tell Bonnie that Sabogal wanted to come in and was about to come in. And you know what? Bonnie being Bonnie, because he was planning to come in, she was willing to work things out for him."

Bonnie being Bonnie, whenever Oscar phoned, she took the call.

And it wasn't long before he was calling her again, this time about somebody just as big.

20

Annamaria Lopez, a thirty-three-year-old, dark-haired, slightly heavy Colombian woman stepped off her American Airlines flight from Mexico City to Miami, and proceeded along with the other passengers to Immigration. She'd come to see friends in South Florida and do some shopping. She planned to stay a week and had a valid return ticket. She had more than enough money to buy a first-class ticket, but she flew economy so she wouldn't stand out from any of the other passengers.

This was her first trip to the States since she and her boyfriend, Jaime Maya Duran, had fled to Mexico.

And even if he told her she shouldn't go—she was so sick and tired of being cooped up with him, always looking over her shoulder, always worrying that there would be a knock on the door—there was no way he could stop her.

She needed to get away for a while. She told him that she loved him and promised him that they would always be together, but she said she was near breaking point, that she was going crazy with the constant stress of being on the run.

Now in the Immigration Hall, she presented her Colombian passport to the officer and waited for him to stamp it. He saw her visa and checked her name on his computer screen. A couple of minutes later, the officer signaled for a second officer, and then a third officer arrived and that's when Annamaria was instructed to follow them into some offices at the other end of the hall.

They sat her down in a small, windowless interview room and began asking her questions about her identity, what she planned to do in the United States, and who she was meeting.

Five hours later, she was still sitting in that room.

Right from the beginning, she told them the truth, that she was there to see old friends and to go shopping. They asked for the names and addresses of her old friends, and sorted through her credit cards. Her suitcase was brought in and, in the presence of two Customs officers, she was told to open it. She did and they rifled through everything.

On several occasions throughout that very long day, she asked for something to drink but all they would give her was a glass of water. When Annamaria demanded to know why she was being held, no one gave her any answers. She argued with them about being treated like this, then got angry, then demanded to see a lawyer, then cried, then got angry again.

Finally, one of the officers announced that she could repack her suitcase but that she was being denied entry into the United States. Her visa was cancelled. She was put into the Immigration system database as an undesirable. And then she was escorted onto the next flight back to Mexico City.

By the time she arrived at her apartment, more than eighteen hours after she'd left, she was so furious at Jaime that, he later said, it took him over an hour to calm her down so that he could find out what had happened.

Bonnie was looking forward to Labor Day weekend.

Her older son was home for a while and having the family unit together again was good. He needed attention. No one ever knew when he would fly off the handle and suddenly become violent, but the new medication seemed to be working and she couldn't wait for some sorely missed quality time with him.

It was Friday morning, September 1, 2006.

Most people had already taken off. But she enjoyed it when the office was quiet like this, and had time to finish some paperwork and go through the last few e-mails she needed to deal with. Anyway, she planned to leave by noon. The long weekend was for her husband, her sons, the beach, and barbecues.

She almost made it.

At 11:40, the phone on her desk rang. She told herself, don't answer it. She'd already said "Have a great weekend" to everyone she wanted to say that to, and she couldn't think of anybody that she really needed to talk to.

It rang a second time.

She told herself, it can wait until Tuesday.

Then it rang a third time.

If it was her husband or her boys, she knew, they would call her cell.

But when it rang for the fourth time, her conscience got the best of her and she picked it up. "Hello?"

A booming voice said, "Bonnie? This is Oscar. And this time it's going to happen."

She was always happy to hear from him, but she didn't know what he was talking about. "This time? What's going to happen?"

He answered, "Jaime Maya Duran."

Born in April 1963 in Cartago, Jaime was a prime catch. According to his DEA file, before he fled, he'd taken over the day-to-day running of Bustamante's operation. And in one of Bonnie's interviews with Bustamante, he'd actually spoken in glowing terms about Jaime, although Bustamante always referred to him by his alias, "Alejandro."

"How come all of a sudden, now?" She wanted to know

"He's been on the run for more than two years and his girl-friend got fed up." Oscar told her the story of how Annamaria had been turned away by U.S. Immigration in Miami. "She talked him into it."

Bonnie asked, "Where is he?"

"Mexico," he said. "But before I give you his address and phone number, shouldn't we be talking terms?"

So for the next hour and a half, Bonnie and Oscar talked terms.

Oscar explained that Jaime wanted to surrender because he knew that, if the authorities down there got him, he'd have to sit in a Mexican jail for a year or two until they sent him back to Colombia. Then, he'd wind up in Combita for another year or two before the Colombians sent him to the United States.

Time spent in a Mexican prison and in Combita waiting to be de-ported didn't count as time served for the Americans, and Jaime didn't want to start all over again in the States from the bottom. He under-stood that if he gave himself up, he'd be earning some credit with the U.S. courts.

Normally, bringing a fugitive in from Mexico can be a long, com-plicated procedure. If he's already in custody there, it can involve the Department of Justice, Department of Homeland Security, the State Department, the Mexican Embassy in Washington, D.C., the U.S. Embassy in Mexico City, the Mexican Foreign Ministry, the Mexican Justice Department, and a whole lot of bureaucracy, especially Mexi-can bureaucracy.

But Jaime wasn't yet locked up and, as far as Oscar could ascertain, there was no Mexican warrant out for him. He told Bonnie, "They probably don't even know he's there."

"That makes it much easier," she agreed, and suggested that Jaime might just want to walk into the U.S. Embassy and surrender. If he did that on, say, Wednesday morning, she figured she could bring him back on a direct flight to New York that same afternoon.

"This wouldn't be an extradition or a deportation," she ex-plained, "he would simply be another guy flying out of Mexico."

That sounded like a plan to Oscar, but if it was going to happen, Bonnie needed to put a lot of things in place right away.

Phone calls took up the rest of Friday. Paperwork took up most of Saturday and Sunday.

Bonnie then spent Labor Day Monday in the office making sure that the embassy would be waiting for Jaime when he walked in the door. She also needed to be sure that the Mexicans would be properly informed and allow it to happen, that Jaime would be escorted back to the States by U.S. Marshals, and that Rooney would be there, too.

Working over Labor Day weekend turned out to be the easy part.

Rooney arrived in Mexico on Tuesday afternoon and had dinner that night with Jaime, Oscar, and another lawyer. He found Jaime to be a pleasant man, who stood five foot seven, weighed 170, and had a thick crop of brown hair. He was soft-spoken and otherwise polite. Jaime kept repeating, "I am tired of running."

As planned, the next morning, September 6, at exactly 9:30, Jaime, Oscar, and the other lawyer arrived at the embassy where Jaime formally surrendered to Rooney and the U.S. Marshals. While the necessary paperwork was being processed, three economy seats were booked for the three o'clock Delta flight to New York. The two lawyers had already made their own arrangements to fly first class on Aeromexico at five o'clock.

Typical Rooney, he made certain that Jaime paid for his own ticket. He knew how much money these traffickers were making and how they threw it around, and never understood why, if they were coming to America to surrender, the U.S. government should pay for their plane ride.

At this point, Jaime's second lawyer said to him, "How much cash have you got on you?"

Jaime opened his wallet and counted out just under one thousand dollars.

Rooney said, "Leave it with your lawyer because when we get to

New York you're going to go to jail and you won't be able to keep it. We'll have to confiscate it from you. Give it to him."

But the lawyer said to Jaime, "No. Hold onto it until we get to New York and I'll worry about it then."

So Jaime kept the cash on him, which turned out to be very lucky.

Thinking everything was just about ready, Rooney phoned Bonnie to confirm that they'd be on the three o'clock Delta flight. She promised to arrange a proper welcoming committee. He then phoned Toby to tell him, "We're coming in on the three o'clock but I don't have my car, so can you please meet me?"

Toby promised to be there.

That's when the U.S. Marshal who would accompany him on the flight, asked Jaime for his passport. But Jaime didn't have one.

Rooney wanted to know, "How can you not have a passport?"

Jaime explained that just before he and Annamaria sneaked into Mexico, he destroyed all his paperwork and had been living there without anything.

"You've got to have something," Rooney insisted.

Jaime shook his head. "Nothing."

"Driver's license? Anything at all?" Rooney wondered, "How are we going to get you on the plane without any ID?"

One of the embassy officials suggested, "We'll write a letter."

"What kind of letter?" Rooney didn't understand. "I mean, how's he going to get on a plane without a single document saying, I'm Jaime Maya Duran?"

"Don't worry." The embassy official was very reassuring. "It will be an official letter from us to Delta Airlines stating that it's okay to let Mr. Duran on board, that we know him, and that we're vouching for his identity."

Deep down, Rooney knew that wasn't going to work. "You sure?"

"We're sure," the embassy fellow said. "Don't worry."

Rooney made the mistake of taking his word for it.

"What's this?" The Delta check-in agent said when Rooney handed him the letter from the embassy.

"The gentleman lost his passport," Rooney said, "and we need to get on the plane. If you want, you can call the embassy and they'll verify it . . ."

"No good." The Delta agent shook his head and handed the letter back to Rooney. "He's not even an American. He needs a passport."

"Normally, yes, he needs a passport . . ." Rooney showed him all the paperwork on Jaime's arrest. "But he's got this instead. He's my prisoner."

"Sorry," the Delta representative said, looking at Jaime in a strange way, perhaps wondering why, if Jaime was a prisoner, he wasn't in handcuffs.

Neither of the lawyers were there to help. Oscar had a lunch date with an old friend who was an ambassador in Mexico City, and Rooney didn't have a clue as to where the other lawyer was. Anyway, they were scheduled on the later flight and probably wouldn't even check in until after the Delta flight was gone. So it was down to Rooney and the U.S. Marshal to reason with the airline. But this man wasn't having any of it.

Rooney asked to speak to his supervisor. Within a few minutes there were five Delta staff huddled not far from check-in, discussing the situation. Rooney insisted that it was all right to let Jaime onto the plane, but that they had to do it fast because the flight was almost ready to board.

Except, the Delta people said, it's not all right.

"Unless," one of them offered, "Mexican Immigration says it is." He pointed to an elevator. "They're just upstairs. If you get them to say okay, we'll let you onboard."

Rooney reckoned, cop to cop he could make this work, and told the Delta people, "We'll be right back."

But the Mexican Immigration office wasn't just upstairs and it took time to find them. Then, it took more time to make the officers on duty understand what they wanted, because until Rooney,

Jaime, and the marshal came to bother them, they were sitting around the office having a pleasant time doing nothing.

"Please," Rooney begged, "just stamp the letter so we can leave."

One of the Mexican officers ruled, "Can't be done."

"It can be done," Rooney insisted. "It's not like we're bringing him in to stay. We're taking him out forever. We're taking him off your hands. All you have to do is stamp this letter and he'll be gone."

"It isn't possible," one of them said, and all the others were in agreement. "If he came here illegally, then he cannot leave legally."

Rooney asked, "Can we speak to your supervisor?"

Three officers arrived from the back office and Rooney started all over again. "We just need you to stamp the letter."

These three merely repeated what the other three already said. "Can't be done."

"How about this?" Rooney tried, "Let's get the U.S. Embassy on the phone and they'll tell you it's okay."

One of the officers said they couldn't do that because it wasn't possible to make an outside call from that office. The U.S. Marshal said he had a Mexican cell phone, only to discover that his battery was dying.

Rooney kept pointing to the embassy letter, promising these officers, "All you have to do is stamp this. It's all right. Delta said that would be enough."

One of the Mexican officers motioned to Rooney, "Wait," as if he had an idea. He mumbled something in fast Spanish to the others, took the letter into the back office, and came out five minutes later. "Okay. If he will pay the fine for staying here illegally, perhaps my chief will let him leave."

Rooney knew a shakedown when he saw one but, at this point, that hardly mattered because the flight was ready to leave. "How much is the fine?"

The six Mexicans huddled, decided that Jaime had been in the country for so many days and came up with, "Eight hundred and forty-two dollars . . . U.S."

Shaking his head at the blatant way they'd simply pulled a number out of thin air, Rooney told Jaime. "Pay it."

Jaime took the money of his pocket—the money he hadn't given to his lawyer—and handed over $842. One of the officers counted it, nodded, took it to the back room and stayed there for quite a while, before coming out with a receipt.

"Good," Rooney said. "Now can we leave?"

But another officer stopped them. "You'll have to wait for the rest of the paperwork."

"What rest of the paperwork?" Rooney asked.

"The rest of the paperwork that needs to be done," the officer said. "It won't take long."

And there they waited for the rest of the paperwork until 3:45, by which time the Delta flight was gone.

Eventually an officer came back into the room with some paperwork.

Rooney thought to himself, *There's still time to get on the Aeromexico flight at five.* "Okay." He handed the man the letter from the embassy. "If you would just stamp this please . . ."

But the officer said, "I'm afraid . . . no."

"What?" Rooney was dangerously close to losing his temper, which he knew wouldn't help the situation. "You said if he paid the fine . . ."

"But it is not that simple," the officer tried to tell him.

Desperate, Rooney grabbed the U.S. Marshal's dying cell phone and called the embassy. He had just enough time to tell someone there, "We're fucked. They're not letting us get on the plane. We've already missed the Delta flight and at this rate we'll miss the five o'clock Aeromexico. Then what? You'd better start making calls to Mexican Immigration at levels you deal with to get us the fuck out of here."

If they missed the Aeromexico flight, Rooney feared that the Mexicans would lock up Jaime. If that happened, they'd then have to start all over again, this time going through normal extradition channels to get him back. Which was exactly what everyone hoped to avoid by doing it this way.

"Come on . . . just stamp the letter . . ." Rooney tried reasoning with the Mexican officer again, but it was like talking to a brick wall.

They were still there at 4:00. And at 4:15. And at 4:30.

By this time, Rooney noticed a marked increase in phone calls coming into the office. From the way the officers spoke on the phone—constantly looking at Jaime and him—he assumed the embassy was beginning to make this happen.

Finally, some senior guy they'd never seen before appeared from the back office carrying even more paperwork. He told Jaime that if he signed these forms, he could leave. Jaime signed them, an officer stamped each page, then handed the copies to Rooney.

A third officer pointed to the door. "You can go."

Rooney, the marshal, and Jaime raced for the Aeromexico counter, only to be told, "The flight is sold out."

"We need three seats," Rooney wasn't having it. "This is very important . . ."

"Sorry," the agent said, "we're overbooked."

Rooney knew Oscar had to be in the airport, somewhere, by now. The marshal's phone was dead, so he had to beg someone at Aeromexico to dial Oscar's cell.

Oscar answered and Rooney explained the problem.

Unfortunately, the plane was boarding and Oscar was already in his seat.

Rooney begged him for help, so Oscar got off the plane and came back out through security.

When he arrived at the check-in counter—dressed in a tracksuit because he was tired and wanted to sleep on the flight—Rooney said, "We're fucked. You've got to get us on the flight." He handed Oscar the paperwork from Mexican Immigration that said Jaime could leave.

Oscar pulled one of the Aeromexico supervisors aside and spoke quietly to him. "I need three seats."

The man answered, "The flight is overbooked."

Oscar kept trying—"Three seats anywhere on the plane"—until he saw it wasn't going to work and asked for the man's supervisor.

Now a fellow appeared who seemed to have some authority.

Oscar pulled him aside. "I am a high U.S. government official."

"What?" The man looked at Oscar in his tracksuit. "You are?"

Oscar said. "I am here on official business of the United States of America. This is of the utmost importance. I need to get these men on the flight with me back to New York."

"But," the fellow repeated, "we are overbooked."

Oscar said again, "Of the utmost importance."

Rooney never knew how Oscar managed it, but suddenly the fellow nodded, went to check the availability, and came back to tell Oscar, "Perhaps there are two seats."

This time Oscar took a wad of bills out of his pocket, went to the counter with the supervisor, handed over money to pay for the tickets, and came back to Rooney with two boarding passes.

"There are no other seats on the flight," Oscar said. He turned to the marshal. "I'm afraid you can't come."

The marshal gave him an odd look, as if to say, who the hell put you in charge?

Oscar handed 37H to Jaime and 9C to Rooney. "Come on, let's go."

Except now there were new problems.

Each airline has its own policy about transporting prisoners but all of them need to be told that there's a prisoner on board; prisoners need to be identified to the pilot and the aircrew before being boarded; prisoners need to be seated in the last row, handcuffed, next to the officers escorting them; and U.S. rules require the U.S. Marshal to be there, too.

Except, Rooney hadn't informed anybody at Aeromexico; Jaime wasn't handcuffed; even if the prisoner was seated in the last row, Rooney wasn't next to him or, for that matter, anywhere near him; and the U.S. Marshal was staying in Mexico.

But there just wasn't enough time to get into that discussion with Aeromexico. Anyway, Rooney suspected, if Aeromexico knew the truth, they'd probably deny Jaime the right to board.

Instead, the three of them raced for security.

Oscar stepped through the magnetron, and Jaime stepped through the machine, and that's when Rooney remembered he had a pair of handcuffs hanging off the belt loop at the back of his jeans. If he went through with them, he'd set off alarm bells, someone would ask why was he carrying handcuffs, and Aeromexico would figure out that he was escorting a prisoner.

Thinking fast, Rooney said to the guy at security, "I have a pacemaker."

The man motioned for Rooney to step around the side of the magnetron so that he could pat him down. As he did, Rooney slipped the handcuffs off his belt loop and into his back pocket. And prayed.

The pat down was so sloppy that the man doing it never felt around under Rooney's jacket and along his back.

By the time Rooney, Jaime, and Oscar reached the gate, the plane door was actually starting to close. Rooney had just enough time to borrow Oscar's cell phone and call Bonnie to tell her that they were on the five o'clock and ask her to please call Toby to pick him up.

Oscar went into first class, Jaime went to 37H, and Rooney sat down in 9C. The seat belt sign came on and the pre–takeoff announcement began. Rooney took a deep breath and settled in. He kept telling himself, the flight crew and the pilot will be seriously pissed if they find out what's going on. And as the plane took off, he reassured himself, they'll never find out.

And they didn't. At least, not until the plane pulled up to the gate at Kennedy Airport.

Bonnie had put all the proper procedures in place to arrest Jaime as he stepped off the plane. But because jurisdiction at JFK falls under the New York City Port Authority, the moment the Aeromexico crew opened the door, ten armed Port Authority detectives were standing there demanding, "Where's our prisoner?"

Passengers were out of their seats and in the aisles, taking belongings out of the overheads and lining up to get off. But the Port Authority detectives weren't letting anyone off.

The pilot came out of the cockpit to see what was going on.

Passengers grew more and more restless. The crew started to get angry because no one was being allowed off. The detectives became more and more aggressive because they wanted their prisoner.

Rooney somehow worked his way through the crowd to the cabin door and identified himself to the detective in charge. "It's okay, let everybody off first."

The detective in charge barked, "Where's our prisoner?"

The pilot wanted to know, "What prisoner?"

Rooney told the detective in charge, "He's in the back."

"What the fuck!" The detective in charge started lambasting Rooney, "You're on a plane, alone with a prisoner, and he's in the back and you're in the front? Where's the marshal?"

Rooney let him have it. "Listen, prick, you don't know what I went through to get on this fucking plane and bring this fucking guy back here."

The pilot kept saying, "What prisoner?"

Rooney told the detective in charge, "Just let everyone off. Don't worry. Jaime will come off. He's back there. He has no place else to go."

More than 150 people were clamoring to leave, so the detective in charge had no choice but to permit them to exit, while the pilot and the chief flight attendant were now both demanding to know, "What prisoner?"

Jaime, who had no idea what had been going on or what was awaiting him, came up the aisle casually and was the last one off the plane.

Because the Port Authority detectives were now so furious at Rooney—"How can you be so fucking stupid as to fly him up here without fucking handcuffing him and fucking sitting next to him and fucking watching him every fucking second of the way"—they took it out on Jaime. They grabbed him, dragged him off to a holding cell, and strip-searched him.

The pilot was now also so irate that he turned on Rooney. "How dare you bring a prisoner on board. I'm going to report this incident. This is a direct violation of Aeromexico policy. . . ."

Rooney spotted Toby, said aloud to no one in particular, "I refuse to face any more abuse," dodged around the side of the pilot, sidestepped the aircrew, motioned to Toby to follow him, and ran for it.

Two days later, blurbs like this appeared in newspapers around the world with a Mexico dateline: "Mexico Hands Over Colombian Drug Lord to U.S.—The Mexican government has handed over Colombian drug lord Jaime Maya Duran to the United States. Maya Duran was captured on Wednesday, 6 September, by Mexican police and agents of the Mexican attorney general's office and flown immediately, and without incident, to New York."

21

And they continued to come.

Abelardo Rojas, who ran Bustamante's stash houses in New York, got caught, was extradited, and pleaded guilty. Davinson Gomez, one of Bustmante's henchmen, got caught, was extradited, and pleaded guilty. Gabriel Villanueva, another Bustamante henchman, got caught, was extradited, and pleaded guilty. Victor Lopez, a Bustamante money launderer, gave himself up and pleaded guilty. Gilberto Monsalve, Juan Albeiro Monsalves's nephew, got caught, was extradited, and pleaded guilty. Edgar Castaño, a money launderer, gave himself up and pleaded guilty. Gabriel Montoya, one of Don Diego's relatives, gave himself up and pleaded guilty to drug charges. Luis Escobar Uribe, who managed air transport for Bustamante, got caught, was extradited, and pleaded guilty. Jair Rendón, Aldemar Rendón's cousin who did quality control for Bustamante, got caught, was extradited, and pleaded guilty. Juan Carlos Giraldo Franco, a load broker for Bustamante, got caught, was extradited, and pleaded guilty. And Hector Salazar, a cocaine transporter and load broker, surrendered and pleaded guilty.

As members of the gang got arrested or walked in to surrender, other people worried that that person was going to talk, so they came in, too. In a few cases, they came forward not realizing that neither Bonnie nor Rooney had a clue as to who they were. They simply figured that she'd get to them eventually and didn't want to hide or spend a year or two in an extradition jail.

With many of the cartel's top echelon already accounted for, and their lieutenants accounted for, Bonnie was now reaching down to the foot soldiers, several of whom fell into the nonviolent category. They heard that she was fair, that she could be trusted, and so they hired lawyers to work out a deal.

Under normal circumstances, when she prosecuted someone, that person would be remanded to jail, awaiting trial. But after proffering some of these smaller fish, who were surrendering before there were even charges, and knowing that they wouldn't be testifying for months or years, she was willing to offer them a different deal.

Bonnie didn't want a situation in which people were sitting in jail for longer than they otherwise would have served, and recognized that some of these people could serve as eyes and ears for her in Colombia. So she allowed them to remain out on bail on the condition that they would continue to cooperate and report back information that she wanted to know.

In many cases that worked well. In a couple, it failed miserably.

She warned the people whom she allowed to stay out, that it was dangerous. She made a point of telling each of them, "If you're going back to Colombia, do not go to Cartago. You can go to Bogotá. But you must not go to Cartago."

Not everyone believed her.

One of those was a family man in his mid-forties who'd been on radar screens in Miami and N.Y.C. as a money launderer, mob bookkeeper, and part-time cocaine load investor. His lawyer had phoned Bonnie to say that he wanted to come in, and after she proffered him, he agreed to cooperate. She allowed him to stay out. She knew where to find him if she needed to—he was living on a farm in Panama—but, admittedly, there was no way she could supervise him or protect him. That said, whenever she needed him he would show up. And Rooney regularly went to see him in Panama.

Then came the day when he announced that he was planning to visit relatives in Colombia. She warned him again about Cartago. But that's where he intended to go. He told friends that he felt a tremendous longing to see his farm again.

He arrived in Cartago on a Tuesday night. Fifteen hours later he was dead with a dozen bullets in his chest.

It was the first time Bonnie had ever lost a witness, and she was sick.

No one could say for sure that he was murdered because they knew he was a cooperator, but in Colombia, where alliances change daily, even the appearance of being an informant is enough to get you killed.

Then she lost a second witness.

This man had come in on his own and brought with him a lot of general information that corroborated many things she already knew. But mostly he had tremendously important information about Macaco.

It was, in fact, so substantial, that Bonnie wanted to share it with Macaco's prosecutors in Florida.

In that regard, some people in her own office have found Bonnie "unusual." Not everyone, especially her supervisors, always appreciated her willingness to share. They want big cases to stay in their district. They want the publicity. They want the credit. And on those occasions when they're thinking about sharing, they want quid pro quo.

Bonnie says she could have indicted Macaco in New York, but, "I've always operated under the delusion that we're all one country, in the same fight against the same criminals. So when we've got a cooperator and we don't need him right away, rather than indict someone who is already indicted somewhere else, I call the other district to say, we've got a witness for you."

She offered the fellow with the information on Macaco to Florida, and he helped them put together their case.

He was known as "the air-conditioner man."

A transporter and money launderer, he made his living in Mexico bulk-shipping cash back to Colombia. He worked a scam where he stuffed hundred-dollar bills into big, industrial-sized air conditioners, then sent them as legitimate cargo from Mexico City to Cali or Bogotá.

When the Mexican police got wise to him, they seized $20 million from his stash house.

In Mexico, a police raid can mean the end of your business. Or it can simply be an introduction to your new partners. It didn't take long for the air-conditioner man and his friends to make the cops understand that seizing money like that wasn't a good idea, and once those particular Mexican policemen understood that Señor Bustamante would be a very grateful fellow if they left him alone, the same cops started escorting the trucks carrying the cash-laden air conditioners to the airport.

The air-conditioner man managed to launder $150 million that way, in just two years.

Because Bustamante was grateful to the air-conditioner man for his efforts, he had enough readies to buy himself an expensive farm and think about getting out of the business.

That's typical, Bonnie found, of many people involved with drug trafficking. "They're farmers and farming, and cattle, and coffee growing is what they really love. They invest in shipments, or handle some money laundering, make a ton of money, buy some land, and quit the business."

In the air-conditioner man's case, he and his partner eventually had a falling-out and he left Mexico for Medellin. His problem was that the farm he'd bought to retire on was an important farm that Macaco had once owned. And the two of them got into a title dispute.

Whenever a major trafficker puts money into a business or property, he always uses nominees and shell companies. That's why asset forfeiture investigations can take years. These guys make it as complicated as possible, on purpose, to prevent anyone from finding out that they own the place. They understand that the only way to keep the assets in the family is to mine the money trail so heavily with financial duck blinds that it will be nearly impossible for anyone to identify and eventually seize those assets.

Macaco had put the farm in the names of several nominee owners, who may or may not have legally sold it. But Macaco, or someone acting on his behalf, or someone claiming to act on his behalf, now wanted it back.

Air-conditioner man wasn't interested. And the more they tried to pressure him into giving it up, the more he told Bonnie and Rooney about them.

To resolve the problem, Macaco's guys called a meeting in Cartago. Air-conditioner man was dumb enough to go. That's the last anyone saw or heard of him. His body was never found.

So after never having lost a witness in twenty-three years, she'd suddenly lost two.

And she nearly lost a third.

This poor soul who was cooperating on a different matter, wound up shot in the stomach. He was university educated and well traveled, but chose drug trafficking as a profession. He was involved with a group moving tons of cocaine bound for the States via Venezuela and Mexico. He came to see Bonnie before she'd indicted him. She let him stay out because she believed he had very good information about Luis Enrique Calle Serna, the man who called himself "Comba."

Serna was Wilber Varela's right-hand man.

But he must have known something was up, because a hit man found Bonnie's cooperator coming out of a night club at 3 A.M., and started shooting into a crowd.

Life for Bustamante in the SHU at the MDC was always going to be hard. The only time he was taken out of there was when he was shipped off to Washington to answer the charges levied by the NDDS. Then, he was kept in some horrible D.C. holding facility.

He was alone twenty-four hours a day. The steel bed in his cell in Brooklyn had a thin mattress and was in the middle of the floor. There was no wall to sleep against.

Oscar Rodriguez thinks that Bustamante imagined things would go differently for him once he got to the States. "But they didn't. And it affected him tremendously. He deteriorated."

Later Oscar would remark, "Combita was a piece of cake compared to the MDC."

Bustamante complained to Oscar, for example, that his cell was freezing cold. He said he wanted out of there. Oscar had to explain that, as his lawyer, he could do some things but not everything, and getting him out of *el hueco* would be very difficult.

The truth is, the SHU was very cold. Even the interview room where Oscar would meet Bustamante, was freezing. At one point Oscar phoned Rooney to see what could be done, saying right away, "I'm freezing my butt off. It's so damned cold, just to get Bustamante out of here, I'll plead guilty."

The best the two of them could arrange was to get Bustamante some long underwear.

At various times, Bustamante seemed forthcoming. He admitted that he'd ordered the killing of Monsalve's brother Arnoldo. He admitted to being responsible for shipping, or investing in or in some conspiratorial manner having something to do with around 2,000 tons of cocaine. When the Colombians seized some of his assets in 2004, they were valued at $270 million.

At times he spoke about his wife, his nine children, and his girl-friend. He said he once owned eight planes, but moaned that they all since disappeared and he didn't know who took them.

But most of the time he lied.

Bonnie and Rooney both speak some level of Spanish, which she says helps them because interpreters tend to make people sound better than they do. "Bustamante had his own way of speaking; not sophisticated as the translator made out. So when you sit there and understand what he's saying, you get a better understanding of the man. That was really important with Bustamante because he doesn't look like a killer. Monsalve did. You could tell by looking at Monsalve that he had no sense of right or wrong. But with Bustamante, it wasn't the same. He wasn't scary. But he reeked of being amoral. There is no light behind his eyes. You listen to him speak and you realize that he's playing games. To this day, Bustamante is still looking for an angle."

Oscar tried to get Bustamante to see that, with time, things might get better. He kept saying, "You've got to get over a few humps."

But Bustamante didn't see those humps.

"My job," Oscar notes, "was to try to get him to earn the government's confidence. It's a process where the government has total control. Prisoners are told what the consequences are if they cooperate or what can happen if they don't. The government can write a "substantial assistance" letter. The government has the right to explain to the court, under a presentence investigation, all the relevant facts that got this guy to this position. They can help him or the prisoner can hurt himself. It's a tightrope. And it starts with the prisoner telling the truth."

Unfortunately for Bustamante, that wasn't the way he played it.

"I tried to make him understand," Oscar says, "that things would get better if he cooperated. While he was here he had some visits from some people that changed his attitude. But you can only do so much in certain situations. I tried to make him understand that he had to tell Bonnie the truth. She always treats prisoners very well, except Bustamante, because he lied. You can't lie to Bonnie. Anyway, I was substituted. He brought in a new lawyer. And for me, that was the end of it."

It was also, pretty much, the end for Rooney, too. "Bustamante lies. So we stopped talking to him."

With no one else to talk to, Bustamante sent word to *El Tiempo* newspaper from jail—through a Colombian lawyer—that he had fresh information about the bombing of Avianca Flight 203 in November 1989.

That was the flight that Pablo Escobar blew out of the air, murdering 107 people, because he thought that a few important Colombian politicians, all of whom were in favor of extradition, were going to be on the flight. None were. César Gaviria Trujillo had booked a seat—a year later he'd be elected president of Colombia—but he changed his plans at the last minute. Two Americans were killed on the plane.

A man named Dandeny Munoz Mosquera was arrested in the States for the crime, put on trial, and was found guilty. He was given multiple life sentences and is spending the rest of his life at ADX Florence, a "supermax" federal penitentiary in Colorado.

Other people were tried in Colombia and convicted there. Because the bombing was preextradition, they could not be sent to the U.S.

Now Bustamante was claiming that Dandeny didn't do it, and said he knew who did. Except, he wasn't going to reveal what he knew unless someone came and talked to him.

Rooney wasn't having it. "No one believes him. He's sitting in jail for the rest of his life and nobody is talking to him. He wants some attention."

Anyway, Bonnie and Rooney were now much too busy. The Norte Valle Cartel was splitting open at the seams.

Just as Bustamante was being sent from Cuba back to Colombia, and would soon be on his way to the States, Eugenio Montoya Sánchez, Don Diego's kid brother, got busted in Colombia. He'd been running the family business while Don Diego was too busy trying to hide.

A few weeks later, the CNP raided four addresses in Cali where they seized more than $50 million in cash and gold. The money belonged to Chupeta.

Then the Colombians nabbed Laureano Renteria, who'd been Chupeta's right-hand man. They caught him at a stash house where they were also able to seize $19 million.

When the police first stormed into the place, Renteria tried to convince them that he was only a construction worker, there to do some remodeling. He eventually pleaded guilty and worked out a deal to trade cooperation for a reduced sentence. When a DEA informant in the States told them that Renteria was actually the man responsible for managing Chupeta's finances, they applied for his extradition and the Colombians moved him to Combita. The same day that the extradition order was to be served, Renteria was found dead in his cell. He'd been poisoned so that he couldn't talk.

Next, Eduardo Restrepo Victoria was arrested. He was supposedly Varela's right-hand man.

And then the DEA found Chupeta.

Juan Carlos Ramirez Abadia had been hiding for nearly five years in the lap of luxury, with his wife, in a secluded, gated, and very well-guarded condominium complex on a hill, about twenty miles from São Paulo, Brazil.

Back in 1996, when Chupeta originally surrendered to the government as part of the amnesty program, effectively ending his working partnership with Don Diego, he'd been sentenced to thirteen years. But he got out in six. With civil war brewing between Don Diego and Wilber Varela, and fearing for his own safety—in addition to worrying that he could be rearrested and extradited because while he was in jail he continued trafficking—Chupeta decided it was time to get out of the country.

The favorite hideout of many criminals wanted in the U.S. has always been Brazil, which was once famous for being one of the few places on Earth that didn't have an extradition treaty with America.

In fact, there are nearly sixty countries that don't, except that Brazil does. The treaty was signed in 1961 and entered into force in 1964, although it prohibits the extradition of Brazilian citizens. The U.S. also signed a 1997 treaty with Brazil for mutual legal assistance in criminal matters.

Chupeta didn't know that, so he opted for Brazil.

He smuggled a huge amount of money into the country with him, and arranged for more cash shipments on a regular basis. He bought property all over the country and, for good measure, went through at least three major operations with plastic surgeons to change his appearance.

Looking very different now than he had in Colombia, he settled into a daily routine, changing locations every few months, but apparently feeling safest at the condo outside São Paulo.

He hardly ever left the compound, was rarely seen during the day, lived on food delivered from local restaurants, and never answered his own phone. Neighbors told reporters that they thought he was Italian. The press later reported that 150 unused cell phones were found in his house. They said he used one a day, after which he threw it away, so calls could never be traced.

In 2005, Brazilian police were called to a minor accident with a small plane in Curitiba, in the south of the country, and discovered a multimillion-dollar load of cash on board. It was obviously being smuggled in, and they wanted to know who was behind it. A two-year investigation led them to Chupeta.

Except that the man they believed to be Chupeta in Brazil didn't look anything like Chupeta once had looked in Colombia, and they couldn't find any witnesses to swear it was him.

The DEA tried to help, but they couldn't come up with anybody who'd known him in both countries and with both faces.

Although they had an informant in Brazil who'd dealt drugs with Chupeta there, they'd never met face-to-face. Then, someone in the DEA reckoned that just because his face had changed, it didn't mean his voice had changed, and maybe the informant who knew his voice in Brazil could identify him by hearing his voice in Colombia.

Later, the story got out that, thanks to advanced voice-recognition technology, the DEA was able to identify him. Even Chupeta's lawyers seemed to confirm, in statements to the press, that the Americans put wiretapped voice recordings through various forensic techniques to establish a match. The same techniques are said to be used to identify Osama bin Laden's voice on radio broadcasts.

The Brazilians had tagged twenty-two different locations for Chupeta all over the country, and swooped down on all of them. He was arrested at the condo in São Paulo. He put up no resistance.

It was later reported that, when they arrested him, Chupeta asked to be extradited immediately to the United States. There had been several charges lodged against him in Brazil, for money laundering, corruption, and gangsterism, and he was plainly worried that he might have to sit in a Brazilian jail for thirty years before they extradited him.

The Brazilians imprisoned him for money-laundering offenses, and held him at a remote high-security location in central Brazil. His money, however, still made him an influential man. The American extradition request was just about to be approved when armed gunmen tried to break into the prison and free him, along with a major Brazilian trafficker. The attempt failed. A second attack on the prison was foiled before gunmen had a chance to do anything.

Within an hour of the extradition request being approved, Chupeta was helicoptered from the prison to Manaus, in the Amazon jungle, where he was handed over to DEA agents who immediately put him on a plane to New York.

He was arraigned in Brooklyn on multiple charges, including murder, trafficking, money laundering, and racketeering, then moved to Washington to be prosecuted there.

That's when the real story came out about the DEA's voice-recognition system.

Looking for a sample of Chupeta's voice from his days in Colombia, a DEA agent in Brazil rang one of his guys in Brooklyn to ask if anyone had phone taps recorded in Colombia. And there were some. So a DEA agent in Brooklyn fetched them, and got a tape recorder.

He then phoned back the DEA agent in Brazil, who put the informant on the line while the fellow in Brooklyn ran the tape, holding the phone close to the tape recorder.

The informant in Brazil confirmed that the voice he was hearing was the same voice he knew from his phone discussions with Chupeta in Brazil, and that was good enough for the Brazilians.

So much for high-tech.

22

Chupeta's old partner, Don Diego, was still on the run.

But only just.

In an elaborate attempt to disappear, he faked his own death. But, knowing that a similar ruse hadn't worked for Bustamante, Don Diego went one better and also faked his own funeral. It was a suitably impressive affair, complete with priests, a coffin, and a lot of mourners. Unfortunately for him, the old adage is right—you can only fool some of the people some of the time—and this time he couldn't fool the cops. They checked the corpse.

The men closest to him were in prison. Not just his brothers Juan Carlos and Eugenio, but his cousin, Carlos Felipe Toro Sánchez, was in jail, too. So were most of his old partners in the NVC. So were most of his rivals, although Varela was still out there somewhere. So Don Diego still had to worry about Varela.

The police were looking for him, the army was looking for him, and his face was plastered all over billboards promising anyone who turned him in "La Recompensa." He didn't know if he could even trust the men he was trusting, and paying huge sums to protect him. He was forced to spend more and more time moving from one hiding place to another, always looking over his shoulder, never knowing when or where someone would arrest him, or trap him, or turn him in, or simply sneak up behind him and kill him.

Life on the run is never easy. People who have done it say it is filled with stress. But most of all, they say, it is filled with fear.

Don Diego was so wary of everyone, that he started demanding very peculiar receipts from the people who were buying his cocaine and the officials who were taking his bribes. After writing out how much they received, each had to place a fingerprint on the receipt, meaning that, should they ever be tempted to betray him, Don Diego could prove they were corrupt.

Being named by the FBI as one of their "Ten Most Wanted" criminals didn't make things any easier for him. Since May 2004, he'd been number seven on the list.

For an uneducated, former altar boy from the Cauca Valley village of Trujillo, Diego León Montoya Sánchez had come a long way. He was only six places behind public enemy number one, Osama bin Laden.

His father ran a coffee and cattle business. The family also owned a bus line. As a child, he later told prosecutors in Miami, he was an altar boy who wanted to go to a seminary. But in 1975, when Don Diego was just fourteen, his father died. As the oldest son, he had to go to work in the family businesses.

It happened at a time when there was a big increase in guerilla activity throughout Colombia. The AUC, FARC, and ELN were all extorting small businessmen and landowners saying, pay us or we will steal your land and kill your entire family. In response, many landowners, especially in the Cauca Valley, turned to cocaine to raise money quickly so that they could fight the guerillas.

Big and menacing, Don Diego earned a reputation for himself in town as a hothead who couldn't control his temper. He was a tough kid who'd get into bar fights without any provocation. That got him hired by the man who owned the local cocaine laboratory and wanted a truck driver who could protect his loads. That's how Don Diego got to know all the small traffickers in the valley, and through them all the bigger traffickers in the region.

In 1984, he hooked up with the Urdinola family, already highly successful traffickers through their associations with the Orejuela brothers in Cali. It was Ivan Urdinola who loaned Don Diego the funds to set up his own operation.

Before the decade was out, Don Diego was flying in cocaine base from Peru on his own planes, landing them at his own jungle airstrips, and processing the base into cocaine hydrochloride at his own laboratories. Producing multiton quantities, he became a major source of supply for the Urdinolas. As his business grew and his production increased, he added Orlando Henao and Juan Carlos Ramirez Abadia, aka "Chupeta," to his list of clients.

By then, authorities had implicated him in two horrific massacres of several hundred innocent people in his own hometown of Trujillo. Referred to as Trujillo I in 1988 and Trujillo II in 1994, elements of the Cali Cartel, local traffickers like Don Diego, and rogue factions of the Colombian police are said to have spent months torturing, decapitating, castrating, and dismembering 342 guerrilla supporters with chain saws. They even murdered the local priest.

Many of the Colombian policemen who took part in these killings would later wind up working for Don Diego and his NVC cohorts.

His ugly predisposition toward gratuitous violence, which Don Diego never hid, helped him to expand his cocaine business. He became a notorious player who always made certain that other players did not stand in his way. The more important he became, the more he surrounded himself with men who shared his propensity for violence.

At the same time, he acquired more and larger planes, leased them out to other traffickers, and did joint ventures with Chupeta. Together they transported other people's cocaine into Mexico, bound for the States. Depending upon the size of the plane, they could move 1 to 1.5 tons per flight. Don Diego also established working partnerships with rising-star traffickers in the region, like Eduardo Restrepo and, of course, Bustamante.

In time, the Mexican authorities got wise to the airlifts. If bribes weren't paid on time, planes and cocaine were confiscated. So Don Diego and Chupeta, and the others, too, turned to the sea and established maritime routes to Mexico. In the beginning, they used fishing ships and go-fast boats. They soon escalated to cargo ships and sometimes even tankers.

As a team, Don Diego and Chupeta quickly established a huge network of transporters between Colombia and Mexico, and maintained this extremely lucrative partnership well into the mid-1990s. They shipped from ports along the Caribbean coast into Cancún, and from ports along the Pacific coast to any of a hundred small ports along Mexico's Pacific coast. That's where they hooked up with Victor Patino Fomeque and his half brother, Luis Alfonso Ocampo Fomeque, who'd established a maritime smuggling business that pretty much dominated trafficking between Buenaventura and Mexico.

Their seagoing ships could carry four to six tons of cocaine, their go-fast boats could carry up to two and a half tons. The go-fasts would usually rendezvous on the high seas with those bigger ships to offload. Then the go-fasts would be sunk to avoid capture back at the home port.

Had it continued, there's little doubt that they would have easily surpassed anything the Orejuela brothers accomplished, and put themselves on par with Pablo Escobar at his highest point. But the partnership came to an abrupt end in 1996 when Chupeta accepted the government's surrender program.

With him out of the picture, at least for a while, Don Diego shut down his processing labs. He'd been producing four tons a month but decided that he didn't need to manufacture when he could obtain cocaine cheaply enough from third parties. Instead, he concentrated on his maritime smuggling operations.

And the quantities he was now dealing in were astonishing. You can tell how much by what he could afford to lose.

All traffickers accept the reality that a certain percentage of their cocaine en route to the North American markets will get seized. They write off their losses to the cost of doing business. They then factor in those costs to the price of the goods that get through.

In spring 2001, Don Diego took two big hits when authorities confiscated one shipment of six tons, then another of twelve tons. Eight months later, they seized a Don Diego shipment of 9.3 tons. Two and a half years later, he suffered another loss of 2.2 tons.

It goes without saying that whenever there was a loss, he'd turn to the people responsible and try to collect from them. Sometimes they paid. Sometimes, when they didn't or couldn't, he'd presumably murder them. They'd go on the run, hide and hope he never found them, or hide and wind up dead, anyway. But in order to sustain a business that could afford to lose 29.5 tons of cocaine in only a few years, and maybe never collect on the losses, Don Diego had to make sure that eight to ten times as much got through.

At around $17 million per ton wholesale, the money quickly adds up.

While his trafficking grew to be colossal, his money-laundering problems became just as big. That side of the business was handled by his brother Eugenio.

Because drugs are bought and sold for cash, and a ton of cocaine roughly translates into a ton of cash, Don Diego and Eugenio needed to get out of paper money as quickly as possible. It was too dangerous to keep, too expensive to store, and too difficult to get rid of in such gigantic quantities. Once, when the Colombian police stumbled across a Don Diego hiding place, they found more than $50 million in cash and 150 kilos worth of gold bars. Don Diego and Eugenio found out the hard way, like all of them do, that it's one thing to move a few hundred thousand in one hundred dollar bills, it's a whole other operation to wash $50 million in tens, twenties, fifties, and hundreds.

Obviously, one of the things they did was pay for everything in cash—salaries, bribes, properties, their lifestyle, and their toys.

Wherever they could, they poured cash into land and businesses, including one of the most important computer equipment wholesalers in Colombia. But the cash was coming in faster than they could get rid of it. They also worked out ways to settle debts through bartered goods—computers, vehicles, planes, property, boats, cars—whatever they could in order to lessen their reliance on cash.

On the other hand, they never lessened their reliance on violence. For foot soldiers in Don Diego's private army, Los Machos, life wasn't just cheap, it was worthless. One U.S. government estimate has it that Don Diego and his mob were involved in the killing of one thousand and five hundred people. That figure is most likely wrong. Given the size of his empire, the need to enforce rules, the need to maintain discipline, and the civil war with Varela, it is almost certainly much higher.

Just after Eugenio was arrested, a tip came in to the police telling them where Don Diego was hiding. Hoping that they were finally going to grab him, a U.S.-trained Colombian commando team was sent to a psychiatric hospital two hundred miles south of Bogotá. They'd been assured that Don Diego was there, disguised as a patient.

They broke down the doors looking for him and got ambushed. A horrible gun battle ensued and eleven commandos were killed. It turned out that the guys who killed them were members of another Colombian military squad—in other words, they were all supposed to be on the same side—except that these military killers were also on Don Diego's payroll.

The government had been trying to close in on him for seven years, and thought they'd cornered him several times. He'd long since had to abandon his main hideout, a twenty-seven-room fortress protected by one hundred heavily armed soldiers in his "Machos" army, and was now hardly ever sleeping more than a night or two in the same place.

In another major gun battle, when army commandos were convinced they had him, they killed eight "Machos," only to discover Don Diego wasn't anywhere in the vicinity, and hadn't been.

His bribes and payoffs to high-ranking members of the Colombian armed forces and various police organizations were legendary. More than once, Colombian soldiers stationed in Cartago and Zarzal hid him from the authorities, dressing him and his men as soldiers and moving them around the countryside in military vehicles. Eventually, ten Colombian army officers, including two colonels, plus three NCOs, would be arrested and tried for complicity.

Needless to say, Don Diego's ability to reach that far inside the army made any intelligence from them and about him, totally unreliable.

Which is how the British got involved.

According to a very credible source in London, an officer working for the British Intelligence Service (MI-6) and stationed in Bogotá, received some precise information on Don Diego. The source was so good and the information so explicit, that the MI-6 agent was reluctant to tell anyone, for fear that a leak could get back to Don Diego. If it did, he would easily figure out who'd betrayed him, there would be killings, and he'd flee.

So the British decided to keep this secret on a strict need-to-know basis and, in fact, right up to fifty minutes before the raid, only four other people in the country knew the details of what came to be called, "Operation Simeon." There was a government minister, two highly trusted army generals, and the colonel commanding the soldiers of the search teams.

The FBI and the DEA were specifically left out of the loop.

An elite surveillance team had been in the general area of Don Diego's location for two months and they'd reported spotting him ten times, up to and including Thursday, September 7, 2008. But no one on the surveillance team knew about the raid.

On Friday, allegations emerged from sources inside the Colombian government that Don Diego had been paying a Colombian admiral to pass along positions of U.S., British, Dutch, and Canadian warships in the Caribbean working drug-cargo intercept missions. The story came out when one of Don Diego's transporters was captured at sea off Cartagena and was found to have in its possession up-to-date navigation charts giving exact locations for the ships.

It was also revealed that Don Diego was increasingly dependent on semisubmersibles to move his shipments.

None of the five people privy to the details of Operation Simeon—the Brit and the four Colombians—knew if the story would spook him and set him off on the run again. But that was a real concern.

Saturday morning, the surveillance team reported Don Diego moving between farms in Zarzal and La Tebaida.

His security was set up to establish an outer perimeter in a forty-mile radius. Anyone coming within that distance of him set off alarm bells, which gave Don Diego sufficient time to flee.

On Sunday, at around 2 P.M., the informant—whose identity has never been revealed—pinpointed Don Diego's location. He was at his uncle's farm, El Pital, which was just outside Zarzal, some twenty miles northeast of his own hometown, Trujillo.

Six hours later, the same informant said that Don Diego only had around thirty men with him.

That evening, an elite Colombian commando unit that had been trained by the British SAS, assembled in seclusion at a base near Cali. None of those fifteen soldiers knew what or when the mission was. They were not even told the name of it. They were sequestered and put on immediate standby. They spent the night on couches, in chairs, and sleeping on the floor, in full battle dress with their assault weapons next to them.

At the same time, troops were summoned to bases and put on alert in El Cairo, El Dovio, and El Aguila, simply to distract attention away from the men waiting near Cali.

At 4:30 on Monday morning, the Operation Simeon attack force, which had grown in number to forty-five and now included air-assault helicopter crews, was given the green light from Bogotá. The commandos took off, still not knowing where they were going or why.

Fifty minutes later, all hell broke loose at the farm.

Helicopters came screaming out of the sky. Commandos dropped down ropes to storm the various buildings. Firefights broke out all over the large property.

On the way in, one of the helicopter pilots spotted a man running away.

The commandos quickly secured the area. Some of the resistance force had scattered. The ones who were captured were handcuffed and left guarded on the ground.

Inside the main house, they arrested Don Diego's uncle, his bodyguard, his girlfriend, and his seventy-year-old mother. On Don Diego's still-warm bed, they found his wallet and two sets of IDs, one of them in his own name.

A search team was dispatched to follow the man the pilot had seen running away. Tracking him proved to be easier than anyone thought because he was dragging a leg and left a very clear trail.

They knew that had to be Don Diego. He'd suffered injuries in a car accident many years before, leaving one of his legs seriously injured.

The commandos followed the trail for half a mile, until it led them to a creek bed, where they found him hiding beneath leaves, still in his underwear.

According to one report from an officer on the scene, the first thing Don Diego did when they yanked him out of the ditch was to offer his captors $5 million if they would release him.

He was told no, and secured in chains.

At that point he was said to mumble, "I lost."

A helicopter managed to land close enough that they could fly him back to the farm.

Only later did anyone realize that he'd positioned a jeep, a motorbike, and horses close to the house as escape routes, just in case. He never explained why he ran, rather than use any of those other options.

Before he was flown away, his mother was allowed to hug him good-bye. She then shouted angrily at his captors, "My son is not a bad man."

That morning, when news of Don Diego's apprehension got back to the DEA, instead of celebrating, they lodged a complaint against ICE and attempted to have the ICE attaché thrown out of the country for not telling them that they were trying to capture one of their fugitives.

Don Diego was shipped off to Miami where he admitted to conspiracy to import cocaine; conspiring to participate in conducting the affairs of an enterprise through a pattern of racketeering activity; and with knowingly and willfully, and with malice aforethought, aiding, abetting, inducing, and procuring the torture and killing of Jhon Jairo Garcia Giraldo, aka "Dos Mil."

He was sentenced, effectively, to life imprisonment, which he is serving at Coleman, a high-security federal penitentiary in central Florida, fifty miles northwest of Orlando.

Except they couldn't call it life.

Under the terms of the extradition treaty with Colombia, a specific number of years must be attached to a sentence. Legally, of course, American judges can impose whatever sentence they want. But the Justice Department has promised the Colombian government to make every effort possible to convince the courts not to impose "a life sentence." Complying with that, the judge in Don Diego's case effectively gave him life but put an official release date on it of November 22, 2046.

Prosecutors have decided to worry about what happens to the ninety-year-old Don Diego after that, sometime in 2045.

Only a small handful of the Norte Valle Cartel was still on the run. For all intents and purposes, as a functioning organization, they were out of business. But that didn't mean the hunt was over.

High on everyone's list was Wilber Varela.

In March 2004, the Colombians launched "Operación Resplandor," raided locations all over the Cauca Valley, and came home with seven high-ranking members of Varela's gang. They seized $2.96

million in genuine dollars, $4.7 million in counterfeit dollars, and 71 million Colombian pesos, which sounds like a lot but was under $40,000. They also got three cars, five motorcycles, and a whole lot of automatic weapons and explosives.

Two months later they came back for more. "Operación Resplandor II" went looking specifically for financial documents so that they could take apart the organization's money-laundering businesses. They got some cash, but more important, they found a computer hard drive. That led them into front companies and businesses, which they could eventually seize.

With Bustamante and Don Diego out of the picture, Varela's market share was bound to increase. Demand hadn't changed, and the new players looking to fill the void in Colombia were, just that, new players. None of them were on a scale with Varela, which worried both the Americans and the Colombians. Varela had the wherewithal and experience simply to step into the void left by the others and build an even more powerful empire.

But the $5 million that was still hanging over his head, plus arrest warrants issued by the Colombians based on Bonnie's indictment in Brooklyn and the NDDS indictment in Washington, D.C., made life absolutely impossible for him in Colombia.

He fled to Venezuela. And that changed the dynamics of the game. Everybody knew Varela was there. The DEA was tracking him and so, presumably, was the CIA. That's one of the things the agency customarily does, hand in hand with the DEA. But everybody also knew that, as long as Hugo Chávez was in power in Caracas—with all his anti-American, anti-Colombian rhetoric—Varela was safe.

Varela thought so, too.

Chávez was a career military officer who'd led an unsuccessful coup d'etat in 1992. He came to power through the ballot box six years later on a left-wing socialist ticket, promising to take care of the poor. In the meantime, the right-wing AUC, looking for fresh territory to extort and exploit, drifted across the Colombia-Venezuela border and began taking hostages. Chávez, who had a relationship with the left-wing FARC, threatened to shut the border. Tensions rose between the two countries, and both governments began posturing.

For Varela to operate big-time inside Venezuela, he needed Chávez to look the other way. But Varela's connections to the AUC were never going to please Chávez, which made Varela more dependent on the AUC for his own safety than he would otherwise want to be.

And those AUC men who remained close to him, knew that.

It didn't matter that the AUC had been officially disbanded a few years before in an agreement with the Colombian government. Or that Castaño was probably dead, even though they never found his body. Or that Macaco was in jail. It's like when a college officially closes an errant fraternity. The brothers still think of themselves as brothers.

The four brothers who surrounded Varela were Comba, Daniel Rendón, Daniel Becerra, and Pedro Guerrero. Rendón was the loudest. He was offering one thousand dollars to anyone for each policeman they killed, and was named by the Colombians as the most dangerous man in the country. But the leader of the band was Comba, who commanded Varela's mercenaries, Los Rastrojos.

And sometime between Tuesday afternoon, January 29, 2008, and Wednesday morning, January 30, he left no doubt about his own ambitions.

It happened in Loma de Los Angeles, in the Venezuelan state of Mérida, just across the border with Colombia in the western part of the country. A small vacation spot in the shadows of the Pico Bolívar, it's one of the few places in the northern half of the continent where you can ski.

On that Tuesday, four men arrived at a small hotel in two cars.

The oldest of the four, a man in his mid-fifties with a thick black moustache, rented a cabin under the name José Antonio Perez Chacon. He had a driver's license with him showing that name.

The man who shared the cabin with him was Weimar Perez Aramburu, Perez Chacon's bodyguard.

The names of the other two are not known for sure, but one of them is reasonably believed to have been Comba. The other is suspected to have been his brother, Javier Antonio, or possibly Diego Rastrojo—the man who "invented" Los Rastrojos—whose real name was Diego Perez Henao.

The next morning, when a maid came to make the beds and clean the cabin, she knocked, got no response, stepped inside, and found two bullet-riddled bodies.

It was Chacon and Perez Aramburu.

The men they'd been with the day before were nowhere to be seen.

At first, the police believed the name on Chacon's driver's license. His body showed seven gunshot wounds. Both men had been dead less than forty-eight hours.

Not recognizing the second man, they fingerprinted him, then lifted prints off Chacon's left hand.

The results came back that Chacon was Wilber Varela.

But the face on the corpse didn't look enough like the face on Varela's mugshots to be absolutely certain. Given the proclivity of these men to undergo plastic surgery, and also to fake their own deaths, further tests were conducted. It was determined that the general shape of the dead man's face matched Varela's, and that the shape of his moustache was the same, although the moustache on the corpse was much thicker. Before long, the Venezuelan police announced that extensive tests had confirmed the identification, matching no fewer than thirty-two verified characteristics.

Varela was history.

23

The suspicion was that Comba himself pulled the trigger, but that he was acting on the orders of Macaco.

Bonnie could only shake her head at how alliances in Colombia were like shifting sands, as she crossed Wilber Varela off the list of possible visitors to Central Islip.

With Varela out of the way, Comba and Los Rastrojos soon moved to concentrate their authority over the shipping ports along Colombia's Caribbean coast, careful not to wind up in a war with a small group operating there called the North Coast Cartel.

In Cartago, a young sleazebag named Jorge Blandon decided to become the new kid in town, and let it be known that he would not tolerate anyone cooperating with the Americans. He proclaimed death to "*los sapos*" and is said to have sent his men on a killing spree to reinforce the point.

For Bonnie and Rooney, Blandon was little more than a vicious small-time hood. Even Comba was only a few steps further up the ladder. Those two would have to wait in line before she could deal with them, because there were still a few old-timers left.

One of them was Juan Carlos Arturo Patino Restrepo. Known to his associates by the nickname, Patemuro, no one is quite sure what it means.

A trafficker and murderer, he was born in 1964 in La Virginia, a small village high in the mountains, about ten miles north of Cartago along National Route 25 where, according to Colombian legend, the best killers come from.

He's heavyset, of medium height, has an elongated oval face, dark hair, a large nose that looks as if it has been broken, and a small mouth. DEA intelligence files show that, as a trafficker, he purchased coca from the FARC and processed it in labs that he operated in Los Llanos, a region of northern Colombia deep inside AUC territory, where that group could protected him. He arranged for multithousand-kilo shipments to the United States and often invested in the shipments of his NVC friends. He ran a private army of several hundred men out of Los Llanos, north of Medellin, and allegedly kept a large squad of professional hit men on his payroll in La Virginia. He was known to be extraordinarily violent.

Like the others, he was uneducated. Like the others, he had amassed a great fortune very quickly. But unlike the others, he didn't seek a place in the hierarchy. He never became part of the inner circle. He maintained his independence and mostly operated apart from the others.

Bonnie had already indicted his friend, associate, and transporter, José Luis Vallejo Tangarife. That was in July 2006. Vallejo made her list at the same time as El Diablo and the Aguedelo sisters. But Patemuro wasn't yet there.

He was definitely a player, though, and that same year the Treasury Department's Office of Foreign Asset Control set the wheels in motion to seize nearly $60 million of his assets—businesses, farms, shops, houses, apartments, and vehicles—throughout Colombia.

It wasn't until mid-April 2007 that Patemuro jumped onto Bonnie's radar screen. The last crime they had documented for him was for trafficking, dated early May 2002. Although he had a working association with Bustamante, he'd spent so much of his criminal life aloof and apart from the others that he almost wasn't in the system, at all. Five years later, the statute of limitations was about to run out on that earlier crime.

Bonnie realized she had to do something fast. If the statute lapsed, someone would have to go out and find a whole bunch of new crimes, and a whole bunch of new witnesses, essentially starting all over again. That would be a major pain because witnesses and cooperators never seemed anxious to roll over on him. The word was, Patemuro is too dangerous.

The obvious thing was to indict him on the 2002 matter. But she had only one witness and she knew that Miami had three. It wasn't cricket to indict out from under another district, and even though he wasn't at the top of their list either, she was hoping she could convince them to take the lead on this. So she phoned Florida and offered to provide her witness to them. That would give them four and a fairly easy case.

The answer was, we'll get back to you.

When they didn't, she tried again.

And again, the answer was, we'll get back to you.

Before she could make a third call down there, she got one from a DEA agent in Miami who was beside himself. "They're not going to charge Patemuro."

"Why not?" She wanted to know.

"It's not going to happen. They say they don't have enough evidence. They say the evidence is old." He pleaded with her, "You've got to do it."

Bonnie immediately told Rooney, "Miami says no."

He said that didn't leave them any choice. "We have to charge him. We can't let the statute expire."

"But if we charge him," she asked, "then what?"

"Then nothing," Rooney said. "It's business as usual. We've got him in the system."

Indicting Patemuro wasn't really the problem. A skillful prosecutor can convene a grand jury and indict their lunch. But looking back at the evidence she had against him, and at the quality of the witness she had, it's clear that she didn't have enough to convince the Colombians to extradite him.

If she indicted him on that evidence, and one day the Colombians caught him and she filed a PAW and then sought extradition, the Colombians could easily decline to send Patemuro to the States, claiming that her case was too thin. Deferring to Miami made good sense. But because that wasn't going to happen, it left her with no other option.

The best Bonnie could do was indict him before the statute ran out, then wait on the PAW and extradition request until she got more witnesses.

"Somebody will show up and roll on him," she assured Rooney, as if she was also trying to convince herself.

"Absolutely," he reassured her as best he could. "It always happens. Somebody will show up . . . eventually."

The two of them spent the next several days running around, putting a case together against Patemuro—naming him along with sixteen other Norte Valle Cartel members—for his part in a "continuing criminal enterprise."

On Thursday April 5, Bonnie convened a grand jury and charged Patemuro as part of an international distribution conspiracy, with conspiracy to possess with the intent to distribute cocaine, and with conspiracy to import cocaine.

Officially, the next step would be to ask the Colombians for a PAW, giving them the authority to go out and look for Patemuro, but there was no urgent reason to do that. If he showed up in the States the feds could arrest him. Back home, he was protected by the FARC and his hit men, and almost certainly with plenty of well-placed bribes paid to politicians in the business of protecting drug traffickers.

But on Friday the thirteenth, Patemuro's luck ran out.

A high-ranking officer in the DIJIN happened to spot him on the street in north Bogotá. Patemuro was just there. The officer realized who he was and pounced.

Because this was so unexpected, DIJIN headquarters wasn't totally sure what to do with him. They could hold him in prison while his case worked its way through the system, but because he was such a dangerous prisoner, they didn't want to hold onto him any longer than necessary. Drug cartels and the terrorist groups were known to respond to captures with unimaginable violence, not only putting policemen and their families at risk, but the civilian population as well.

The Colombians "usual best idea" for situations like this was to ship these guys to the States as soon as possible and let the Americans deal with them. If nothing else, getting them out of the country eliminated the risk of a paramilitary assault on the jail to free them.

But in Patemuro's case, there was no pending extradition request.

Bonnie received a panicked phone call from a DEA agent she knew in Colombia, to say, "They've arrested Patemuro."

She asked, "What have they arrested him on?"

"Nothing," he told her. "They don't have any charges."

"Huh?" She didn't understand. "How can they arrest him? I didn't seek a provisional, and if they don't have any charges . . ."

He explained, "He was somewhere they didn't expect him to be. They spotted him, figured they'd never have another chance, and grabbed him."

In order to keep him in custody long enough for Bonnie to put together an extradition case, the DEA agent reminded her, she had to file a PAW. And that had to be done within forty-eight hours.

In the meantime, the Colombians themselves started running around looking for a reason to hold Patemuro. They needed somebody who could testify against him. That meant finding somebody willing to risk his life. And it wasn't as if people were lining up to volunteer. Everyone who knew him, or had anything to do with him, understood the possible consequences.

Somehow they came up with a poor day laborer who said his job was digging graves on Patemuro's farm so they could bury the people that Patemuro killed.

As weak as that was, it gave the DIJIN enough to hold Patemuro on "a disappearance" which, in Colombia, is a murder charge where there is no body. Not surprisingly, Patemuro's lawyers argued that it was a trumped-up charge. Unfortunately for Patemuro, the magistrate disagreed.

The problem now became the PAW. There was no way Bonnie was going to let him walk so she worked nonstop with the Department of Justice, and the State Department, to put it together and rush it through the proper channels to the DIJIN.

She only just beat the deadline.

Coincidentally, while this was going on, Rooney happened to be in Colombia dealing with another matter unrelated to Patemuro. At one point, he found himself at DIJIN headquarters just as Patemuro was being processed. The two men met for the first time. It lasted all of thirty seconds.

Patemuro looked Rooney in the eye and said, "Mr. Viola, I know of you. But I have never sent a single kilo of cocaine to anywhere ever in my life."

That Patemuro knew who he was unnerved him. "If that's your story, then I'll see you in New York when you get there. If you have nothing else to tell us now, I'm not here to talk about your family life."

Rooney went his way and Patemuro was escorted his way.

Now, having bought enough time for Bonnie to put together an extradition request, the Colombians moved Patemuro to Combita.

Of course, Patemuro chose to fight extradition. He knew if they sent him to the States, he was never coming back. And there is a certain irony in the fact that he did fight it. Based on publicly available documents, it's obvious that Bonnie's indictment against him was weak. Everything she was able to add to it came after he was extradited. Had he not fought extradition, Bonnie would have been in a more difficult position to make her case.

Five days after he was arrested, Patemuro tried to bring charges against the Colombian authorities for wrongful arrest. He also launched corruption accusations against everyone involved in the process. He hired a human rights attorney in Colombia to claim, among other things, that sometime around March or April 2004, he'd paid Rooney $500,000 to get his name off the list of people whom the United States intended to extradite. According to Patemuro, the money had been delivered to Rooney by Nancy Cadavid's sister, Libya.

Of course it was a lie. Patemuro hadn't been indicted yet and therefore wasn't on any list anywhere for extradition. But, Patemuro didn't know that, so as soon as he made up the 2004 date, the charge was dead in the water.

But that wasn't going to stop him from doing whatever he had to do.

Two months into Patemuro's time at Combita, his old friend Vallejo showed up. The extradition request that Bonnie had lodged against him was based on much harder evidence than Patemuro's, even though they both contained all the usual charges, such as distribution, possession, and conspiracy to possess violations.

Over the next sixteen months that Patemuro spent at Combita waiting to be sent to the States, he and Vallejo were always together. And Patemuro was always showing off. On more than one occasion he told some of his fellow inmates that he was collecting millions of dollars from associates to fight extradition and the legal battles—plural—that faced him if and when he got to the States.

"But I won't be extradited," he liked to brag, "because I've paid off enough people."

That was just jailhouse bravado. Deep down, he had to know that the odds were stacked against him. Very few of *"los extraditablos"* ever manage to walk out of Combita and go home. He was never going to be the exception.

He kept up appearances, anyway. "All of this aggravation," he told anyone who would listen, "is because of Special Agent Romedio Viola and Assistant U.S. Attorney Bonnie Klapper."

In his mind his hardship was somehow their fault. And in his mind, there was a very simple way to put an end to it. He said to some fellow inmates, "I know where they live, and I know about

Bonnie's older son and his health problems, and I know where her boys go to school."

On several occasions, Patemuro explained to fellow inmates, "As long as Viola and Klapper are the ones trying to extradite me and put me in jail, then they are my main problem."

And when it came to that, he boasted, "I know how to solve it. The Colombian way."

Before long, Patemuro dispatched Libya Vallejo to the authorities in Bogotá where she made a formal corruption claim against Rooney. She repeated Patemuro's original lie, that Rooney had been paid half a million dollars to prevent Patemuro's extradition to the United States.

It was one thing hearing that from a prisoner, it was another hearing it from someone who may or may not be a credible witness. So a prosecutor was assigned to investigate.

Right off the bat, she requested Rooney's full cooperation and, of course, he agreed to do whatever she wanted. To begin with, she said, she wanted a full sworn statement. He gave her that during a long day with her at the Colombian Consulate in Miami. In it, he totally refuted all of the claims being made.

Unbeknownst to Rooney, and under the prosecutor's supervision, Libya had secretly recorded two phone conversations with him, patently trying to lead him into some sort of self-incrimination. But, at no point during either conversation, did Rooney say anything incriminating.

Although the prosecutor would not allow Rooney or anyone in the States to have a copy of the tape, she did permit a Justice Department official at the U.S. Embassy to hear it.

On the tape, every time Libya tried to lead Rooney into a certain answer, he plainly didn't know what she was talking about. The DoJ official who listened to the tape wrote, in a confidential report back to Washington, that the two conversations exonerated Rooney.

The Colombian prosecutor also spoke with some of the witnesses Bonnie and Rooney had in the Patemuro case. They helped to substantiate Rooney's version of the events.

To counter that, Patemuro tried to bring Bonnie into this by alleging that Rooney kicked back half the money to her.

Not long afterward, an attorney representing Patemuro brought Libya's allegations to the Office of the Inspector General at ICE—which later became IG's office at Homeland Security—and, acting according to regulations, a formal investigation was opened into both Rooney and Bonnie.

Later, an attorney representing Vallejo would repeat these same allegations in open court.

As a result of those allegations, Bonnie and Rooney were both taken off the Patemuro case.

Specifically, Libya was lying that Rooney had asked for $1 million to keep Patemuro from being extradited and after some bargaining, agreed to settle for half. According to her, the most important meeting took place, ironically, on April Fools' Day, 2004, at the Bogotá Plaza Hotel. Rooney had agreed to meet them there for lunch because Libya had phoned him to say that Patemuro wanted to come in and was hoping Rooney could help.

After lunch, Vallejo claimed, he handed Rooney a bag with $250,000 in it, promising that the rest would come later.

Rooney said that Libya had given him a bag that contained a gift she wanted him to take back to Nancy. Rooney promised to deliver the gift, and did. His mistake, of course, was taking it from her in the first place.

The DHS proceeded with their investigation, despite the fact that the Colombians closed theirs, having concluded quickly that Libya's allegations were unfounded and false. In fact, the Colombians even opened an inquiry against Libya for lying to them.

Yet, in the face of evidence which clearly disproved the allegations being made, the DHS kept their investigation open for more than five years. During that time, they never once bothered to ask Bonnie or Rooney about the allegations.

Agents working for the Inspector General questioned dozens of informants, all of whom denied that Bonnie or Rooney ever did anything improper. Those agents allegedly read Bonnie's and Rooney's e-mails and allegedly warned witnesses they might be deported if they didn't admit that Rooney had stolen money.

Eventually, Libya herself recanted.

It was six months later when the DHS formally closed the case against Bonnie and Rooney. And then, it was only under pressure because the Patemuro trial was about to start.

And then, no one from the DHS bothered to notify either of them. The case was shut down. Under DHS rules, they still won't admit publicly that it was ever opened.

In the meantime, several prosecutors working out of the Brooklyn U.S. Attorney's Office petitioned to bring charges against Libya. They believed she should be held accountable for wasting hundreds of hours of investigative time, attempting to harm Bonnie's and Rooney's reputations and lying to federal officers. But those requests were turned down by other federal prosecutors in Puerto Rico, which had jurisdiction because that's where she told the lies.

They deemed the case "not important enough."

In January 2007, the DIJIN had captured a trafficker named Octavio Cardona Echeverry, also known as "the Doctor."

A former associate of Pablo Escobar, he'd been handling some shipments for the NVC when the police found him in Medellin and arrested him. They got his brother, Guillermo, too.

Warrants for both were outstanding, having been issued way back in the 1990s on numerous drug-related charges, by the U.S. Attorney's office in Miami. Octavio had also been considered a "person of interest" for at least a decade, by U.S. Customs, the DEA, and even the CIA.

The DIJIN informed Miami that the Cardona brothers were in

custody and extradition proceedings were begun. Eleven months later, in early December, the two men were delivered to Florida.

A week or so after they arrived, Bonnie received a call from an FBI agent—and friend—in Miami who wanted her and Rooney to come to Florida to interview Octavio, who had something really important to say about Patemuro.

He warned her, "This guy is telling me that Patemuro wants you dead."

The two of them flew down there and found Octavio to be a very credible fifty-three-year-old who'd been picked up for a three hundred-kilo deal. He wasn't a major guy by any stretch of the imagination. But when he was in Combita, he said he got to know Vallejo and Patemuro very well.

Octavio told Rooney that he regularly heard Patemuro brag, "I'm never going to get extradited because we trumped up corruption charges against the agent. And, if that doesn't work, I'm just going to have him killed."

Among other things, Octavio, Patemuro, and Vallejo had taken English classes together, and after one class, an agitated Patemuro started running off at the mouth about the Colombian police officer who'd been instrumental in his capture and extradition. He claimed that the officer had fabricated the disappearance case against him by providing false witnesses to give evidence. He said that, together with "an American agent," they'd set him up.

Patemuro told Octavio, "I have two options. I will accuse them of corruption. And if that doesn't work, I will have them both killed."

Of course, the American agent was Rooney.

On another occasion, Octavio said that Vallejo confided in him how he and Patemuro had been rehearsing a story that Patemuro had come up with, which they were both going to tell once they were extradited. Vallejo explained that Patemuro's intention was to blame the charges against him on the Tasered, now-dead trafficker El Diablo—Ariel Rodriguez. He said that Patemuro had ordered him to lie about El Diablo, and that if he didn't, Patemuro would murder members of his family.

By creating enough confusion about El Diablo's role and who did what to whom, Vallejo went on, Patemuro was hoping to produce sufficient doubt about the Colombian police officer's honesty.

But just in case, Vallejo told Octavio, Patemuro was also setting into motion a story to trump up charges against Rooney. He was going to say that Rooney was selling secrets to the cartel people.

According to Octavio, Patemuro had paid Vallejo's wife Libya to tell the Colombian tax authorities that Special Agent Romedio Viola had placed Libya's sister, Nancy Cadavid, under protection and was selling the information she gave him back to the traffickers.

Octavio then mentioned that Patemuro and Vallejo both bragged that they knew a lot about the prosecutor. They said they knew her name, knew she had a son who was not well, and knew where her children went to school.

It was at that point, Octavio said, Patemuro stated that he "intended to take care of Bonnie Klapper."

Bonnie and Rooney came back to New York and did what they were supposed to do. She went to the DoJ people who investigate death threats against prosecutors, and Rooney went to the ICE people who investigate death threats against agents. They filed all the proper paperwork.

And, nothing happened.

24

Undeterred, Bonnie and Rooney kept doing their thing.

On the assumption that Patemuro would someday wind up in the United States, Bonnie began lining up witnesses to testify against him. But, knowing what she already knew about him, she wasn't surprised to find many potential witnesses saying that they would not take the stand, for fear of retribution.

Patemuro still blamed Bonnie and Rooney for his predicament, but now he was blaming Arcangel Henao for his arrest. Witnesses said they heard Patemuro on several occasions threaten to kill members of Arcangel's family. In response, Arcangel was fast to say that Patemuro is "a violent man with a known reputation for seeking retribution."

Everybody knew that, and Patemuro was counting on everybody believing that he was a violent son of a bitch. Lawyers in Colombia are still trying to find witnesses to take the stand against him in a corruption case down there.

Patemuro had a good idea of who might testify against him and wanted the word out—if you speak against me, you are putting your family in harm's way. He wanted people to know, your family will not be safe anywhere, not in Colombia, not in the U.S., because someone will kill them wherever they are.

Arcangel took those threats seriously and said that he would fear for the safety of his family if he testified.

Another potential witness claimed that Patemuro told him about five separate individuals he'd killed. The witness shook his head. He knew if Patemuro even suspected he was cooperating, his entire family would be in danger.

A trafficker whose identify is being kept secret, and was incarcerated in Miami, claimed that Patemuro told him how he'd shot a man in Mexico. But he didn't want to have to say that on the stand.

Another potential witness, at that point working as a confidential informant, has described how Patemuro had ordered the killing of a woman and her family after the woman had allegedly stolen some heroin from him. He said, because of that, ten people were murdered. He repeated that Patemuro often warned him, if you ever testify, I will kill your entire family.

Yet another witness said Patemuro told him he was going to murder Arcangel. But the witness wouldn't say that in court because, "He is a violent, crazy man who knows where my family lives in Colombia."

Apparently there were loads of potential witnesses, but many of them categorically refused to testify against Patemuro because they feared their families in Colombia would be instantly murdered and they, too, would eventually be killed.

Potential witnesses seemingly all agreed: "Patemuro is a ruthless, nasty individual."

One even insisted, "I would rather spend the rest of my life in jail than testify against him."

On September 22, 2008, Rooney was in Miami to interview a cooperating witness who cannot be named. He, too, had been in Combita with Patemuro. He told Romedio he'd had three or four private discussions with Patemuro, during which Patemuro warned him not to talk to anyone in the U.S. about him.

He said, Patemuro was convinced that Arcangel was giving the Americans information that would be used against him, especially about one particular cocaine shipment they were both involved with. Patemuro insisted that load was going to Europe, and not the U.S. But that didn't matter, he said, because Arcangel was talking and he was going to get killed.

This man said Patemuro told him that he was collecting millions of dollars from associates to fight his legal battles. He then ordered this man to tell another trafficker who was also awaiting extradition at Combita, that he'd better not speak to the Americans about any AUC meetings Patemuro attended because he did not want to be linked to terrorism.

At the same time, Patemuro warned this man never to speak to Bonnie Klapper, and actually used her name.

When this man asked Patemuro about her, he flatly replied, "I am going to solve that problem in the Colombian way."

Rooney asked this man, "How do you interpret that statement?"

This man answered, "When a man of Patemuro's reputation and power says he is going to solve a problem in the Colombian way, it means that he will have the person killed."

Exactly one month later, Rooney interviewed another trafficker, a former member of the AUC, who said that while he and Patemuro were together in Combita, Patemuro told him he'd met with a DEA agent and an assistant U.S. attorney in Panama—this was supposed to be sometime in 2002—and paid them both to ensure that he would not be indicted.

Patemuro also told this man, "When I refused to pay any more money, the DEA agent and the AUSA joined forces with the Colombian tax authorities to ensure that I was charged."

Of course, it was another lie. The meeting never took place. There never was a bribe. But, according to witnesses, Patemuro was naming names. Patemuro was saying that the DEA agent was

Romedio Viola—except he wasn't a DEA agent—and that the AUSA was Bonnie Klapper.

Six days later, on Tuesday, October 28, 2008, Patemuro lost his extradition appeal.

The Colombians hustled him out of Combita in the middle of the night. The DEA flew him to New York, escorted by heavily armed U.S. Marshals. Rooney and several heavily armed ICE agents then took custody of him at Long Island's MacArthur Airport.

Patemuro was given the usual escort honors—heavily armed ICE agents in full battle gear, plenty of state troopers with red lights flashing on their cars, and several SUVs with darkened windows with more men inside carrying big guns.

But he didn't get a helicopter. Given that Patemuro was talking about killing an agent and a prosecutor, Rooney found something even more appropriate. A bearcat.

The moment Patemoro stepped off the plane, in handcuffs and chains and a bulletproof vest, Rooney rushed him to the huge armored personnel vehicle and secured him inside.

Even though intelligence had not picked up on any threat against Patemuro, the bearcat was an extra guarantee that nobody could get to Patemuro inside, and that there was no way at all he could get out.

The escort party seemed pretty pleased with themselves for having arranged that, except Rooney. He was upset that they wouldn't let him ride up front in the bearcat.

The arraignment was set for the usual place, the Federal Courthouse in Central Islip, Courtroom 1010.

Patemuro showed up but Bonnie didn't.

Because of Patemuro's threats, her boss refused to allow her to be in court that morning. To her dismay, and to her anger as well, another AUSA was brought in to pinch-hit.

But that didn't change anything as far as Patemuro was concerned. Given the charges lodged by the U.S. government against him and the fact that he was a definite flight risk, Judge Seybert ordered him held without bail at the MDC.

Patemuro was put back in the bearcat and taken to Brooklyn where they locked him up in the SHU.

Unbeknownst to Bonnie or Rooney, or anyone else, by that time, Patemuro had stopped talking about settling things the Colombian way and had already made the necessary arrangements.

Paid informants come with a caveat: Their information is only as good as their subsources.

In other words, whether or not anyone can trust information from a paid informant depends entirely on whether or not the people feeding information to the paid informant are trustworthy.

Rooney was now interviewing a paid informant named Miguel, and in the past, there were times when Miguel proved to be reliable. But there were other times when the information he provided was absolutely unreliable. Some of his information led to arrests of high-level fugitives. Some of his information led to wild-goose chases and dead ends.

Miguel told Rooney that, according to one of his subsources, Patemuro had dispatched an assassin to the States to kill Bonnie.

Although the credibility of this particular subsource was questionable—the person had once worked for the Colombian government but had been fired for corruption and mental instability—when Miguel said that a second subsource confirmed the first, and that the information from the second subsource was precise, Rooney quickly admitted that this was worrisome.

That second subsource even named the man who'd taken the contract. Call him "Jaime." He was known to be involved with trafficking, but not otherwise associated with violence. Miguel said that Jaime owed money to Patemuro and that killing Bonnie was how Patemuro wanted the debt repaid.

The plan was for Jaime to travel from Colombia to Spain, then fly from Spain to New York.

Just because Patemuro was now secure in a cell in Brooklyn didn't mean the investigation into him stopped.

Bonnie and Rooney continued interviewing everyone they could find.

A gun had already been made available in Brownsville, Brooklyn.

Then a bizarre e-mail arrived from an informant who, after going through the lot of interesting intelligence about some traffickers, added this PS: "By the way, Patemuro has hired an assassin to kill you."

He, too, named Jaime.

He, too, said that Jaime was traveling from Colombia to Spain and from there into the U.S.

He finished the e-mail with, "Be careful."

It turned out that Jaime was someone they already knew, and he was associated with Patemuro.

The Colombians confirmed that he held a Spanish identity card.

The marshals came storming into Bonnie's life.

As she puts it, "They went from zero to one hundred in ten seconds."

They arrived at her office, just like that, a group of very large guys carrying very serious weapons, and ordered her to come with them. She protested that she was busy. The marshal in charge explained, in no uncertain terms, that this wasn't an invitation, it was an order.

And they whisked her away.

By the time they got her home, local police were crawling all over her house installing surveillance cameras to watch every door and every window, to create a perimeter around her garden, and to put panic alarms in various rooms in case someone heard something or spotted something and needed the cavalry.

For the next three months, there were armed marshals with her wherever she went.

They transported her back and forth to work in an armored SUV with darkened windows. Anytime she had to leave the office, it was back in the SUV. Three agents spent every night in her den at home, all night, with M-6 machine guns at the ready.

At first, she told the marshals that she always took her younger son to school every morning, and that nothing was going to change just because they were protecting her.

They said they'd take him to school.

She protested. But they refused to let her drive her own car. So, every morning, two armed marshals—with two more in a follow-up car—piled Bonnie's son into their SUV, and Bonnie got in, too, usually in her bathrobe, and so did her dogs. One of them, Checkers, especially thought this was fun because he liked to ride on the armrest in the front seat. The marshals told Bonnie that this was not permitted.

Bonnie said, "You tell him to move."

A marshal tried, Checkers growled, and that was the end of the discussion.

They'd get her son to school, then take Bonnie home, wait for her to get ready for work, then drive her into the office. They'd stay with her all day, change shifts, and take her home. Later, they'd change shifts again and three marshals would move into her den for the night

The next morning, the new shift would arrive and everything would start all over again.

On weekends, they went with Bonnie to the gym, for pedicures, and to the supermarket, where there were always two marshals walking her from aisle to aisle.

When one of the marshals learned that Bonnie had spoken about the detail to another female lawyer—who'd agreed with Bonnie's assessment that a few of the marshals were "hot"—the detail gave their protectee the code name, "Flirting With Danger," and that's how they referred to her for the rest of the time they were with her.

When Bonnie and her husband went to visit their older son at his school, and showed up with the marshals, they had to explain to him about the death threats. But they were very quick to reassure him that the marshals were really just a precaution, that the threats were probably nothing. They were careful not to panic him.

He looked at his parents, then at the marshals, then back at his parents, and wanted to know, "What if I'm in the line of fire?" He made a face, "You know what," he said, "maybe I should ride with Daddy in the other car."

Those three months would have been scary, Bonnie says now, "if I hadn't found so much of it funny. I baked cookies for my marshals every evening. Checkers, my diabolical Havanese dog, bit two of them. The other Havanese thought the marshals were there to scratch their bellies all night."

Some people who are being protected object to such a massive intrusion in their lives. They try to pretend it's not happening. There are stories about federal judges who were protected while trying terrorist cases. And some of them were so adamant that they didn't want the marshals in their lives, they insisted that the security detail live out of their cars in the driveway. When one of the marshals had to go to the bathroom, he had to use a nearby gas station. Some judges' wives used the marshals to carry shopping bags.

But that's not the way it worked at Bonnie's house. The marshals became part of the family. They ate meals together at home, and when she and her husband went to a restaurant for dinner on a weekend, the marshals were invited along to sit at the table with them. Bonnie's husband always paid.

Typically, she tried to put a funny spin on everything, but her husband knew that, deep down, she was concerned.

For her sake, he, too, tried to make light of it at times. He'd say to her, "I'm glad they're here. At least you have somebody to talk to while I'm traveling."

And, he'd remind her, "This is like having instant buddies. On Sunday afternoons, I have someone to watch football with."

Bonnie's husband even added a sports channel to their cable TV so the marshals on duty all night had something to watch.

But both of them knew there really wasn't anything amusing about this. And as nice as the guys were, the intrusion into their lives was stressful.

A Department of Homeland Security protection unit tried to take over Rooney's life, too.

But for Rooney, and for the four ICE agents who stayed with him round-the-clock wherever he went, it was different.

Maybe because he's a guy. Maybe because he had a gun. Or at least they thought he had it with him all the time but, more often than not, he left it home. Or maybe just because he didn't like the idea of playing along with them, the way she did.

Rooney insisted on driving his own car. And because each ICE agent insisted on driving his own car, too, everywhere Rooney went there were four agents in four cars chasing after him.

He'd stop every two days to buy cat food, and they'd go with him, and after a couple of times, they started to say, why can't you buy a month's worth at a time? And he'd make them understand that he cared more about his cats eating good food than he did about their discomfort of having to traipse after him.

ICE Intel, Department of Justice Intel, and El Dorado Intel, too, kept monitoring the state of play, constantly trying to update their threat assessment.

Rooney got a call one afternoon that some intelligence had come in to the Manhattan District Attorney's office, that was quickly forwarded on to ICE and the DoJ, that three paid assassins were now in New York to kill Bonnie and Rooney.

His detail was notified, and so was he, and when he called Bonnie, she and her detail knew about it, too. They were both brought quickly back to the office which was the safest place to be.

And there they sat, until someone determined that the source of the information was a paid informant in Florida who'd previously supplied a lot of bad information.

Both protection details nevertheless stayed on heightened awareness until there was no doubt that the information was false, until everyone was absolutely certain that there weren't three people who'd just arrived to murder Bonnie and Rooney.

As the months wore on, everyone seemed to agree that the threat diminished. The longer guys like Patemuro were in jail in America, the shorter people's memories were back home in Colombia.

People who worked for him, or were afraid of him, eventually started to think, he's gone and maybe I can take over.

The longer he was locked away, the more he lost his pull.

It was three months after the marshals first invaded Bonnie's life, and the ICE detail first invaded Rooney's, that they finally went away. The same people who felt that Bonnie and Rooney had needed protection—and it is now known for certain that the threat was real—decided that the threat had diminished.

One reason was because, along the way, they found Jaime.

He walked into El Nuevo Dorado International Airport in Bogotá one evening to check in for an Avianca flight to Madrid, Spain.

At the counter he produced a Colombian passport in his own name. That's when some men came up to him. They introduced themselves as policemen, and asked him to come with them. He objected. They said they were only going to ask nicely, once more.

He went with them to a small interview room behind their offices at the airport, where they questioned him for several hours—not always politely—about his travel plans. They knew he was going to change planes in Madrid for a flight to New York, and demanded to know why.

Jaime kept asking, what's this all about?

They told him that they suspected he was on his way to murder an American prosecutor and an American agent on the orders of Patemuro.

Of course, he immediately protested his innocence. He said he knew nothing about anything like that. He said it was absolutely untrue.

They said that the American Embassy was insistent he not be permitted onto the flight to Madrid.

He demanded a meeting with the ICE attaché at the embassy.

They said, be there at nine tomorrow morning. And then they said he was free to leave.

That surprised him, because he probably thought he was going to be held, at least, overnight.

But there was nothing to charge him with, and nothing they could do to retain him. He'd already missed the flight.

The ICE attaché was waiting for him at nine the next morning.

Jaime never showed.

And he hasn't been seen since. He's disappeared. Nobody seems to know where he is.

Maybe he understood that the Americans were on to him.

Or maybe he understood that, having promised Patemuro he would take the contract in exchange for having his debt erased, and then didn't fulfill it, the best thing he could do was go someplace where Patemuro would never find him.

Ultimately, it took two trials, but Patemuro was convicted in the Central Islip courthouse and is now facing jail for the rest of his life.

Out of the woodwork, a witness whom they had never interviewed came forward to say that he had some information on Patemuro.

Not knowing what to expect, Bonnie and her marshals, and Rooney and his ICE guys flew to Miami to interview him.

He was a nice enough older guy who explained that he was some sort of concert promoter.

"That's nice," Bonnie said. "And how do you know Patemuro?"

"Oh," he said, "Patemuro came to one of my concerts."

Bonnie smiled and waited to hear more.

But there didn't seem to be any more.

She looked at the man. "So?"

"So," the witness said, "that's all."

"That's all?" She couldn't believe it. "We flew all the way down here to find out he went to a concert?"

The concert promoter seemed genuinely embarrassed. "That's all . . . I'm sorry. But . . . doctora . . . you know what?"

"What," she asked, annoyed at him.

He said quietly, "Has anyone ever told you that you look just like Sophia Loren?"

25

Back in 1989, in a place called Sylmar, California, in the northern part of the San Fernando Valley, the police happened to stumble across a warehouse filled with twenty-one tons of cocaine.

It still ranks as one of the largest single busts in the States. But the really shocking thing about it was that this cocaine was the result of an early joint venture between the Mexicans and the Colombians.

No one is certain whether those joint ventures started with the Medellin Cartel doing a deal with the Guadalajara Cartel or if it was Juan Carlos Ramirez Abadia—Chupeta himself—who first hooked up with Amado Carrillo Fuentes of the Juarez Cartel. But however they started, the Sylmar cocaine signaled the beginning of what has become the full-blown Mexican invasion of America's southern border.

Today, the daily battle fought along that two-thousand-mile stretch is a ferocious reminder that Mexico has succumbed to civil war, waged between the last vestiges of the old economy it once had and the narco-state it has since become. All of the elements that have hurtled Colombia's democracy toward destruction are alive and well—and in spades—today in Mexico.

The war has been fueled by the forces of demand and market. Military might rendered near-impotent in the republic to the north has been trying to force a genie armed to the teeth with automatic assault weapons back into a bottle that has been smashed long ago.

The Mexican cartels, that now rule the world of cocaine, were born in the famine of the Depression when families, one on each side of the border, realized they could make money moving people and contraband back and forth. By the 1970s, marijuana had become their major cash crop. Ten years later the smugglers added Colombian cocaine to the load, and whatever they got from the Colombians for the service represented pure profit because they were going that way anyway.

Playing the mule made them rich, but it didn't give them power. To manage that, they took a percentage of the coke, to market as their own. Then, because business is business and loyalty has never been a strong suit among traffickers, they went in search of ways to cut the Colombians out of the picture. They started dealing directly with the Bolivians and Peruvians, which was fine until the Colombians started moving shipments through the Caribbean—catching American law enforcement looking the other way—then exerted muscle on the Bolivians and Peruvians to cut the Mexicans back down to size.

In those days there was a small mob operating out of Guadalajara. As they grew rich, jealousies and power struggles splintered the group, forming the Sinaloa Cartel. Then came the Tijuana Cartel, established by the Arellano-Felix brothers. From their Baja base, they violently guarded their monopoly on smuggling across the border into California.

Across the other side of Mexico, the Gulf Cartel was run by an egomaniac named Juan Garcia Abrego, who saw himself as heir apparent to Pablo Escobar. Like Escobar, he courted the media to turn himself into Robin Hood. Before long, he was handling one-third of all the cocaine used in the United States and was said to be worth, personally, $15 billion. He also holds the honor of being the first international drug trafficker to make it onto the FBI's "Ten Most Wanted" list.

But life as Abrego was living it came to an end for him in 1996 when he was arrested in Mexico and extradited to the United States on a technicality. Mexican law prohibited the extradition of its citizens. But Abrego had the misfortune of having been born in Texas.

His demise signaled the meteoric rise of the just-as-bizarre one-time head of the Juarez Cartel.

Originally set up in the early 1970s by his uncle, by 1993 Amado Carrillo Fuentes was turning it into a major power with the help of a former Mexican federal police commander. Operating out of Ciudad Juárez, in the state of Chihuahua, Carrillo staked out the middle of the border and controlled everything moving in both directions. He maintained a huge fleet of aircraft, including Boeing 727s, to fly drugs from Colombia to Mexico, then passed the drugs off to youth gangs who would smuggle them into the States. He came to be known as "El Señor de Los Cielos," the lord of the skies.

Within months of Abrego's capture, Carrillo was smuggling four times as much cocaine as all the other cartels combined, running a global enterprise that is said to have grossed $200 million a week.

Understandably, the bull's-eye shifted from Abrego to Carrillo, marking him as America's primary target. So, for the sake of old age, he decided he needed to become invisible.

On the morning of July 4, 1997, the thirty-nine-year-old Carrillo lay down on an operating table and expected, later that same afternoon, to wake up as a younger-looking gentleman named Antonio Flores Montes. Instead, eight hours of plastic surgery and liposuction later, he was dead, the victim of an apparent postoperative heart attack.

A power struggle erupted and his brother, Vincente, emerged victorious.

Vincente's friends were Chupeta and Bustamante, and the cocaine they were moving came through the Norte Valle.

The big map of Colombia that used to hang on the walls of Bonnie's office, has been taken down.

In its place there is a map of Mexico.

Today, there is enough cocaine being warehoused in Mexico, waiting to be smuggled into the United States, as to provide one line for every man, woman, and child on the planet.

When Bonnie and Rooney were first interviewing their Norte Valle cooperators, they didn't pay all that much attention to Mexico. They were well aware of the Norte Valle links to Mexico, but there wasn't much they could do with any fresh information. It was at a time when Mexico was not extraditing and, basically, not cooperating with the United States.

It was tough to find snitches in Mexico, and when you did you couldn't always trust them. Back then, the surest way to get someone killed was to ask Mexico for help. But in 2007, the U.S.-Mexican relationship really changed.

The civil war was now raging out of control and the narcos were clearly winning. Drug-related violence was killing the country. The government in Mexico City had no choice but to become considerably more proactive, and because the Mexicans needed help to make that work, they became that much more pro–U.S. law enforcement.

Realizing that the timing might now be right, Bonnie and Rooney went back to a lot of their Norte Valle witnesses, asking them if they had any information about the Mexican side of the business?

And many of them said yes.

"I felt a little stupid," Bonnie says, "that after all of those hours of talking to them, I'd never asked them about the Mexico side. Because Mexico wasn't extraditing, it just wasn't on our radar."

They couldn't talk about the logistics, because they weren't there on the ground, but they could give up the whole supply chain.

"The Juarez group is responsible for a tremendous amount of

border violence," Rooney explains. "Our border states are so flooded with murders and drugs that prosecutors there don't have the time to do very detailed and very complicated historical cases. They're inundated with bodies and seizures. We took the case because we have the whole supply side of witnesses and informants and coopera- tors. We have Bustamante's people telling us about the drugs that went to Vicente Carillo Fuentes."

He became the primary target.

Rooney notes, "Unlike the Bustamante case where we got all sorts of the people, our indictment just named Vicente Carrillo. The people who fed us information were so high up the ladder, that they didn't deal with his people, they dealt directly with him."

Ever since, ICE has been gathering information about who moved the drugs and who received the drugs, and have begun charging those people.

One of the people ICE now took an interest in was Maximillian Bonilla.

He'd started as a Bustamante transporter, and after Bustamante disappeared from the scene, he worked with a few of the others. But over the years he grew more and more important and was consid- ered the man who controlled the port of Buenaventura.

Anyone shipping from there, and a lot of traffickers were, had to pay him tax.

One day his lawyer phoned to say that he knew he'd been indicted and that he wanted to come in.

What generally happens when someone like this approached them, Rooney would arrange to meet the person outside the U.S., preferably in some country everybody could consider neutral. Many of these people are never going to show up in the U.S., and are very skeptical about a letter of safe passage. They worry that they'll be double-crossed and arrested.

The Dominican Republic is a good place, especially for Colom- bians, because they can get in and out easily. They don't need visas.

The routine is that an ICE agent would meet with these people two or three times, then make an assessment. He might suggest that they cooperate proactively. That means they're out on bail, meeting people, developing information, wearing a wire. But that option is usually only open to people when there is no violence in their past.

Or, the government can say, you're a nice guy and can cooperate, but you've got to come to live in the States. We're not letting you outside our jurisdiction.

Or, the government can say, sorry, you've killed too many people. If you want to cooperate you have to take up residence in the MDC.

Those are the three options.

With Bonilla, ICE was hoping it could work out a deal for option number one.

Among other things, he could help the government make a major corruption case against some Colombian port officials in Cartagena and Buenaventura who were allowing cocaine shipments to move through there. It was a grand scheme and would make a fabulous case.

So a meeting with Bonilla was set up for the Dominican Republic. But two days before, someone in the chain of command—now gone—decided that he wasn't going to have his people running around the Caribbean chasing ghosts when there was plenty of work to be done in New York and summarily pulled Bonnie's permission to travel internationally.

In the end, Rooney went. And, if nothing else, he was able to establish the truth behind a story about Bonilla. The rumor was that Bonilla had killed a man in a bar in Medellin, and after murdering him, he got drunk, climbed up on the table where the body was, and did an Irish jig.

Bonilla kept insisting that Rooney tell Bonnie the story wasn't true. He admitted to killing the man, and maybe, yes, he climbed up onto the table afterwards, but, he told his lawyer, "Tell her I never did the dance."

Meeting Bonilla, Rooney found a tough-looking fellow who never smiled. He just stared, very quietly, almost as if he was deliberately trying to stay detached. Born in 1972, Bonilla had been putting together multithousand-kilo shipments of cocaine for years.

And the big thing about him, that especially interested Bonnie, was his Mexican connections.

In 2007 there'd been a big seizure of his drugs, ten tons worth, in Tampico, Mexico. The cocaine was going to the man known as Z-40, head of Los Zetas.

A paramilitary organization, Los Zetas started life in the 1970s as mercenaries for the Gulf Cartel. But they since branched out to become a force in their own right, along the lines of the FARC and the AUC. The group has traditionally been made up of former elite Mexican Army soldiers and former police officers, as well as mercenaries from Guatemala. It's estimated that they are about four thousand strong.

Z-40 was Miguel Angel Treviño Morales. He is said to be a trafficker, mercenary, professional killer, and one of the reasons why there is so much savagery along the Mexico-U.S. border today. Under his leadership, Los Zetas are considered by the DEA to be highly sophisticated, technologically very advanced, and the single most violent group operating in Mexico.

Witnesses have told Rooney that Treviño liked to drive around in his car all day, pointing at people, saying kill this one and kill that one. One witness in particular told her that Z-40 once saw a dog in the road and ordered his driver to go out of the way to run it over.

"It didn't affect me that he was killing people," Rooney now says, "because he's a drug lord and that's what they do. But running over a dog for the sport of it? That's when I knew he was a truly evil guy."

Finding a way to get to him made Bonilla an attractive cooperator.

Rooney eventually worked out a deal to bring in Bonilla.

In one of the early interview sessions, he started talking about how drugs were moving out of Cartagena and going first to Panama, before being shipped to Mexico where they were smuggled into the United States.

Rooney was fascinated. He hadn't heard that before and decided that as a sideline to an investigation in Mexico, they should open an investigation into the Colombia-Panama connection.

At this point, Bonilla seemed aloof but not especially dangerous.

Maybe that was because no one had much information about his violence levels and didn't understand just how high up he was.

Yet, there was always some lingering doubt as to whether they could trust him enough to let him stay out, or if it would be better to hold him in jail until his trial came up.

In the end it was the link to Los Zetas and Z-40 that tipped the scales. The decision was made that if Bonilla stayed out, he might be able to get them right inside Los Zetas because he was talking directly to Z-40.

Another thing everyone felt they had going for them was Bonilla's family. He wanted them protected.

Rooney had even made a hobby out of getting cooperators' families out of dangerous situations, like being stuck in Colombia where they could possibly face retribution. He would arrange everything to bring them to the States, get them work visas, help them find a place to live, see that their kids got enrolled in school. He did what he could to keep them happy. It was a big administrative hassle.

Thanks to "Rooney's Ark," cooperators stayed loyal.

The decision was made to let Bonilla stay out.

In return, Bonilla cheated.

Instead of feeding information directly back to ICE, he brought in a subsource. He claimed it was because too many people wanted him dead. But the subsource was double-dealing.

Then, people related to Bonilla started to get killed.

Somehow, the Colombian press got wind of the fact that Bonilla was cooperating. Obviously Comba read the papers, because he was the one who declared war on Bonilla.

Making matters even more difficult, Bonilla wasn't keeping in touch the way he'd agreed to.

Word went out to him, "You need to come in."

He didn't.

Bonilla is still running around somewhere, doing his thing.

An arrest warrant in the United States awaits him.

ICE went back to setting its sights on Carillo Fuentes and the Juarez Cartel. A wave of indictments flowed from information provided by cooperators, but looked at activity that occurred subsequent to Bustamante's arrest in Cuba.

Among the people the government went after in those indictments are:

Luis Carlos Beltran Cristancho, known as "the Black Rambo." A Colombian, he was one of Bustamante's guys in Mexico. After Bustamante's arrest, he became the connection to Z-40. Arrested in Mexico in 2007, he was expelled to the United States and pleaded guilty.

An unnamed former Bustamante employee, who organized and invested in large shipments, until his surrender in 2007, pleaded guilty and is awaiting sentencing.

An unnamed shipment organizer out of Venezuela who arranged deliveries to Los Zetas, surrendered, pleaded guilty, and is awaiting sentencing.

Jimmy Herrera, another shipper working out of Venezuela, was arrested on a U.S. warrant in Colombia, was extradited, and pleaded guilty.

There is also Aldemar Alvarez and Otalvaro Castrillion, a pair of Colombians operating in Mexico, who were captured, extradited, and have pleaded guilty.

"You arrest people," Rooney says, "work out a cooperation deal, and they hand you other people. I guess we could continue to do this indefinitely. It goes on and on. We get one big guy, and another big guy comes along. We shut down the NVC, and there's the Juarez Cartel. We'll shut them down and another will come along."

Recently, a cooperating witness told Bonnie, "Your team did an incredible thing. You dramatically decreased the amount of cocaine going into the United States."

Bonnie asked, "So, we have reduced the amount of cocaine in the world?"

"No," the cooperator said, "we just send it to Europe now."

Epilogue

On December 31, 2009, Special Agent Romedio Viola of Immigration and Customs Enforcement, a legacy U.S. Customs officer who served for twenty-one years, retired.

On January 4, 2010, Assistant U.S. Attorney Bonnie Klapper went to her office and knew immediately why the place seemed so empty.

A sixteen-year partnership had come to an end.

In 2006, government auditors came up with what they believe is a complete list of the assets owned by or otherwise controlled by nineteen members of the Norte Valle Cartel. They include 1,294 businesses located in Aruba, the Bahamas, the British Virgin Islands, the Cayman Islands, Colombia, Costa Rica, Ecuador, Mexico, Panama, Peru, Spain, Vanuatu, Venezuela, and the United States.

These cartel members deal in agriculture, aviation, cattle, consulting, construction, horse breeding, distribution, financial management, hotels, industrial paper, investment, manufacturing, mining, pharmaceuticals, real estate, and shipping.

Of those, more than one thousand businesses and properties, plus hundreds of other assets, totaling well in excess of $1 billion, were seized.

Dozens of suspects and convicted felons went to prison or are still awaiting trial, or are cooperating with the U.S. government.

Of the three dozen men and women who made up the Norte Valle

Cartel, and had been targeted by her office, by the U.S. Attorney's offices in Miami and Manhattan, the NDDS in Washington, and a small handful of others, only three have not seen the inside of an American jail.

Varela is dead.

Carlos Alberto Rentería Mantilla, aka "Beto," was the last man who still had a $5 million price on his head. He was known to be in hiding somewhere in South America. The Colombians got in touch with him and made overtures for him to come in. But Beto, pushing seventy, sent a message back, "What's the difference to me if I get twenty or I get fifteen? The hell with you. Come and catch my ass."

In 2010, they caught his ass in Venezuela, and expelled him to Miami, where he sits, awaiting trial.

And then there is Jaime Rojas Franco, the one who got away from Rooney when they arrested Monsalve. He's out there somewhere. Bonnie heard he might be in Thailand. Or he might be driving an oil truck in Colombia. Or he might be living in the jungle with the last few stragglers of the AUC.

Rooney vowed to stay on the job until he brought Jaime back to America in handcuffs. Unfortunately, Uncle Sam was more concerned with drumming people out of service when they reach a certain age, than in keeping experience, passion, and desire on the job.

But then, the last that Jaime Rojas heard, Rooney was still out there looking for him.

And, in a funny way, he still is.

There is a "new Rooney," a young ICE agent named Doug, with whom Bonnie is now working.

And, there is still the old Rooney.

Bonnie arranged to have him hired as a contract investigator.

So a few hours after she came to work on the first Monday of the new year, he walked in, looking like his old self. He didn't have a badge and he no longer had a gun, but he still had that burning gut to bring in bad guys, especially Jaime Rojas.

Acknowledgments

There are many people to thank for this book.

It goes without saying that the top of the list belongs to two extraordinary people, and the stars of this story—Assistant U.S. Attorney Bonnie Klapper and special agent, now retired, Romedio Viola.

Having known them both for a long time, it is without any hesitation that I say, the words *extraordinary* and *stars* are befitting and appropriate. I am unabashedly proud to know them, grateful for their friendship and, as important, forever appreciative for their service to the country.

My thanks, too, to the men and women who served for those years in the El Dorado Task Force. Due to the nature of this story and, especially, information about ongoing criminal investigations and evidence that has appeared and/or is yet to appear in court, many of them spoke to me on the condition of anonymity. The same goes for various men and women at the Drug Enforcement Administration, Immigration and Customs Enforcement, the Criminal Investigation Division of the Internal Revenue Service, the U.S. Marshals, the Department of Justice, the United States Bureau of Prisons, and various federal court officers in Manhattan, Brooklyn, and Central Islip, New York. I add to the list, several contacts in Great Britain, who have been especially helpful to me in speaking with various people in Colombia, and contacts in Colombia, on both sides of the law.

For all sorts of reasons, I would like to thank Toby Barbero, Danny

Ming, George Soto, plus two of my great old pals, Ronnie Rose and John Forbes. I include them all in my list of personal heroes.

For cooperation and assistance, I wish to say thank you to the Office of the United States Attorney, Eastern District of New York (Brooklyn), the Office of the United States Attorney, Southern District of New York (Manhattan), Immigration and Customs Enforcement (ICE), and the Department of Justice in Washington. I value the time and effort spent on my behalf, the documentation made freely available to me, and the documentation I acquired through Freedom of Information requests.

I also spoke with a number of defense attorneys involved with these cases, to whom I am grateful, and in particular, the inimitable Oscar Rodriguez.

Very special thanks also goes to Robert Nardoza, at the U.S. Attorney's Office, Eastern District, and to my longtime friend Dean Boyd, formerly of ICE, now at the Department of Justice. You guys are the best in the business.

I am grateful as well to Tom Dunne for publishing me again, to Brendan Deneen for his superb editing, to Graham Jaenicke in Mel Berger's office and, in spades, to Mel Berger at William Morris Endeavor.

And, as always, to La Benayoun.

The Norte Valle Cartel

MAIN PLAYERS

Unlike Medellin and Cali, neither of which were cartels in the true sense of the word, the Norte Valle Cartel was a loose confederation of drug trafficking organizations that intermingled, intermarried, invested in each other's loads, fought with each other, and killed each other, but banded together to keep outsiders out.

The main traffickers in the Norte Valle Cartel were:

Luis Hernandez Gomez Bustamante (*aka Rasguño, "scratch"*)
His group included:
Jhonny Cano Correa—head of security and chief hit man
Jaime Maya Duran—money launderer
Orlando Sabogal Zuluaga
Carlos Arturo Patino (aka Patemuro)—transportation
Jose Aldemar Rendon Ramairiz—oversaw Tele-Austin

Involved with the Tele-Austin laundering business in New York were:
Juan Albeiro Monsalve
Ignacio Lobo
Hector Rivera

Juan Carlos Ramirez Abadia (*aka Chupeta, "lollipop"*)
Emerged out of Bustamante's group and formed his own organization.

Diego León Montoya Sánchez (*Don Diego*)
Arose out of an earlier creation of the Henao Montoya clan.

The Brothers Orlando and **Arcangel Henao Montoya**
This group employed:
José Dagoberto Florez Rios
Eduardo Restrepo Victoria (aka El Socio, "the partner")
Carlos Mario Jiménez (Macaco)

Wilber Varela (*aka Jabón, "soap"*)
He was head of the military wing for the Henao Montoyas but
staged a coup and took control, forming his own organization.

Dispositions of Selected People Named in This Book

Agudelo, Jose Ignacio: pleaded guilty to money laundering July 24, 2008; murdered in Cartago, Colombia.

Agudelo, Julia: apprehended in Colombia January 25, 2006; extradited December 6, 2007; pleaded guilty to money-laundering charges August 17, 2007; sentenced June 2, 2009, to time served.

Agudelo, Leonardo: pleaded guilty to drug charges May 15, 2008; awaiting sentence.

Agudelo, Marta: surrendered in Panama August 23, 2006; pleaded guilty to money-laundering charges November 2, 2007; sentenced May 29, 2009, to probation.

Bermudez, Pedro: arrested in Mexico and extradited August 19, 2010; arraigned August 20, 2010; awaiting trial.

Bustamante, Luis Hernandez Gomez: arrested in Cuba while entering the country using fake Mexican documents July 2, 2004; deported from Cuba to Colombia February 8, 2007; extradited to the United States July 19, 2007; pleaded guilty to drug charges June 26, 2008; awaiting sentence.

Cadavid, Nancy: sentenced September 24, 2004, to a term of time served.

Calle Serna, Luis Enrique (aka Comba): currently a fugitive from U.S. justice; indictment sealed.

Cano, Jhonny: apprehended in Colombia October 29, 2005; extradited to the United States in September 2006; pleaded guilty April 29, 2008, to drug charges, awaiting sentence.

Castaño, Edgar: pleaded guilty to money laundering July 24, 2008; awaiting sentence.

CW7: case sealed.

Flores, Jose Dagoberto: arrested in Colombia December 27, 2004; extradited August 31, 2006; pleaded guilty to drug charges October 5, 2007; sentenced October 20, 2009 to 66 months.

Giraldo Franco, Juan Carlos: apprehended in Colombia December 9, 2007; extradited March 24, 2009; pleaded guilty September 8, 2009; awaiting sentence.

Gomez, Davinson: apprehended in Colombia February 2, 2006; extradited March 2, 2007; pleaded guilty to drug charges October 5, 2007; sentenced May 14, 2009, to 72 months.

Guzman, Johnson (aka Franklin Lopez): pleaded guilty August 11, 1997, sentenced February 2, 2006, to 17 years.

Henao Montoya, Arcangel de Jesus: arrested in Panama January 10, 2004; expelled from Panama to the United States January 14, 2004; pleaded guilty to drug charges September 30, 2005; sentenced December 16, 2010, to 120 months.

Henao Montoya, Orlando: murdered in prison, October 1997.

Jiménez-Naranjo Carlos Mario (aka Macaco): pleaded guilty in Southern District, Florida, and Washington, D.C. Awaiting sentence.

Lobo, Doris: never charged.

Lobo, Ignacio: case sealed.

Lopez, Victor: pleaded guilty to money laundering July 15, 2008; believed to have been murdered in Colombia.

Maya Duran, Jaime: surrendered September 6, 2006, in Mexico; arraigned in the United States September 7, 2006; pleaded guilty to drug charges July 5, 2007; sentenced March 18, 2010, to 36 months.

Monsalve, Gilberto: apprehended in Colombia March 6, 2007, and extradited June 16, 2008; pleaded guilty to money-laundering charges June 26, 2008; sentenced November 20, 2008, to 46 months.

Monsalve, Juan Albeiro: arrested March 2, 2000; pleaded guilty to drug trafficking and murder; sentenced May 3, 2002, to life imprisonment.

Montoya, Gabriel: pleaded guilty to drug trafficking June 5, 2008; awaiting sentence.

Montoya Sánchez, Diego León (aka Don Diego): captured in Colombia September 10, 2007; extradited December 12, 2008; pleaded guilty to charges of conspiracy to import cocaine; sentenced October 21, 2009, to 45 years.

Patino, Carlos Arturo (aka Patemuro): apprehended in Colombia; extradited October 29, 2008; convicted April 7, 2011, and awaiting sentence.

Ramirez Abadia, Juan Carlos (Chupeta): captured in Brazil August 7, 2007; found guilty in Brazil of money laundering, corruption, conspiracy, and use of false documents; extradited to the United States August 22, 2008; pleaded guilty on March 1, 2010; awaiting sentence.

Rendón Ramirez, José Aldemar: apprehended in Colombia July 14, 2005; extradited March 2, 2007; pleaded guilty to drug charges October 5, 2007; sentenced March 23, 2009, to 84 months.

Rendón, Jair: apprehended in Colombia October 6, 2008; extradited January 26, 2010; pleaded guilty to drug charges October 15, 2010; awaiting sentence.

Rentería Mantilla, Carlos Alberto (aka Beto): captured in Venezuela July 4, 2010; extradited to the United States July 13, 2010.

Restrepo, Eduardo: pleaded on January 29, 2008, sentenced April 22, 2008, to 135 months.

Rivera, Hector: case sealed.

Rojas, Abelardo: apprehended in Colombia and extradited to the United States August 31, 2006; pleaded guilty to money-laundering charges December 8, 2006; sentenced March 27, 2007, to 41 months.

Sabogal Zuluaga, Orlando: apprehended in Madrid October 26, 2006; extradited to the United States December 18, 2006; pleaded guilty to drug charges August 3, 2007; sentenced July 17, 2010, to 72 months.

Salazar, Hector: surrendered in Panama April 17, 2008; arraigned in the United States April 18, 2008; pleaded guilty to drug charges August 22, 2008; awaiting sentence.

Trevino Morales, Miguel Angel (aka Z-40) indicted in the United States on various charges, June 19, 2009.

Uribe, Luis Escobar: apprehended in Panama July 28, 2008; extradited to the United States September 24, 2008; pleaded guilty February 27, 2009; awaiting sentence.

Vallejo Tangarife, José Luis: apprehended in Colombia August 16, 2007; extradited to the United States November 20, 2008; pleaded guilty to drug charges July 1, 2010; awaiting sentence.

Varela, Wilber (aka Jabón): murdered in Venezuela, January 2008.

Vega, Maria: never charged.

Villanueva, Gabriel: apprehended in Colombia June 9, 2007; extradited to the United States January 18, 2008; pleaded guilty to drug charges May 19, 2008; sentenced April 29, 2011, to 55 months.

Select Bibliography

BOOKS AND PAPERS

Burton, Fred and Scott Stewart. "Mexican Cartels and the Fallout From Phoenix," Global Intelligence, July 2, 2008.

Cronin, Audrey Kurth, Aden, Huda, Frost, Adam, and Benjamin Jones. "Report For Congress: Foreign Terrorist Organizations," Congressional Research Service, Washington, D.C., February 6, 2004.

Freedman, Michael. "The Invisible Bankers," *Forbes*, October 17, 2005.

Logan, Sam. "The Colombian Drug Trade: An Examination of Policy, Politics and War," Monetary Institute of International Studies, 2004.

Robinson, Jeffrey. *The Laundrymen*. London: Simon and Schuster, 1994.

Robinson, Jeffrey. *The Merger: The Conglomeration of International Organized Crime*, New York: Overlook Press, 2000.

——— *The Sink: Terror, Crime and Dirty Money in the Offshore World*, London: Constable, 2003.

PERIODICALS AND NEWS MEDIA

Agence France Press

——— "Colombian Drug Suspect Held In U.S. After Mexican Extradition," June 17, 2010.

———— "Top Colombian Cocaine Chief 'Jabon' Found Shot Dead,"
February 1, 2008.

Associated Press

———— "Drug Trafficking Suspect Wanted by U.S. Is Arrested in
Colombia," August 21, 2010.

———— "Army Captures Cartel Leader in Colombia," September
11, 2007.

———— "Brazil Extradites Colombian Drug Lord to U.S.," August 23,
2008.

———— "Brazil Nabs Colombian Drug Lord Wanted in U.S.," August
7, 2007.

———— "Brazil: Reputed Drug Lord Gets 30 Years," April 3, 2008.

———— "Brother of Colombian Drug Lord Pleads Guilty," January
23, 2009.

———— "Colombia Captures Boss of Norte Del Valle Cartel," September 10, 2007.

———— "Colombia Cartel Raid Nets $100m," March 11, 2004.

———— "Colombia: Drug Suspect Sent to U.S.," December 13, 2008.

———— "Colombia Extradites Suspected Drug Lord to U.S.," December 12, 2008.

———— "Colombia Extraditing Suspected Drug Kingpin to U.S.,"
July 19, 2007.

———— "Colombian Drug Baron Admits Guilt," October 18, 2008.

———— "Colombian Drug Lord's Brother Gets 30 Years in U.S.,"
April 28, 2009.

———— "Colombian Drug Kingpin Found Shot to Death," February
1, 2008.

———— "Colombian Police Capture Rebel Commander," March 17,
2004.

———— "Colombia Smashes Drug Ring with Hezbollah Ties,"
October 22, 2008.

———— "Cuba Deports Suspected Drug Baron," February 9, 2007.

———— "Cuba Seizes Colombia Drug Chief," July 9, 2004.

———— "Hezbollah Says Drug Allegations Target Its Image," October 25, 2008.

———— " 'I lost,' Top Colombian Drug Suspect Tells Captors," September 11, 2007.

———— "Kingpin Eugenio Montoya Sanchez Nabbed After Gunbattle," January 16, 2007.

———— "Submarine with Cocaine Seized off Costa Rica," November, 20, 2006.

BBC News

———— "Colombia Hit By Wave of Violence," August 6, 2002.

———— "Colombia Cartel Raid Nets $100m," March 11, 2004.

———— "Colombian Drugs Lord Found Dead," February 1, 2008.

———— "Cuba Deports Suspected Drug Baron," February 9, 2007.

———— "Cuba Seizes Colombia Drug Chief," July 9, 2004.

———— "Drug Submarine Found in Colombia," September 7, 2000.

———— "Mexican Navy Seizes Cocaine Sub," July 18, 2008.

———— "Rebelde De Las Farc Será Extraditado," May 8, 2003.

———— "Spanish Police Find 'Drugs' Sub," August 14, 2006.

———— "Top Colombian Drug Suspect Seized," January 11, 2004.

Boston Globe

———— "Trained By U.S. Colombia Unit Gains," May 5, 2003.

BusinessWeek

———— "The U.S. Is Wading Deeper into Colombia's War," March 16, 2003.

CNN

———— "Coast Guard Hunts Drug-running Semi-subs," March 20, 2008.

———— "Cuba Holding Colombian Drug Kingpin," July 10, 2004.

Colombia Reports

———— "Norte De Valle Cartel Is Finished: Naranjo," December 12, 2008.
———— "Venezuela Captures Last Norte De Valle Cartel Boss," July 5, 2010.

CounterPunch

———— "Bush and the Paramilitaries: Coddling Terrorists in Colombia," July 10, 2003.
———— "Training Colombia's Killers in the U.S.—Plan Colombia: Three Years Later," July 14, 2003.

Daily Mail (UK)

———— Malone, Andrew. "The Coke Father," September 12, 2007.

druglibrary. org

———— Schaffer Library of Drug Policy. "Major Traffickers and Their Organizations."

Economist

———— "Drug-trafficking Trends," May 1, 2008.

El Diario

———— "El Rasguño Speaks," March 23, 2007.

El Pais

———— "Comba: The Successor to Varela," January 5, 2010.

El Tiempo

———— "Rasguño Will Tell It to the Judge," July 20, 2007.

Jane's Intelligence Review

———— Galeotti, Mark. "Organised Crime Gangs Pose Threat to Cuban Development," February 2006.

La Semana

———— "The Battle for the Throne of the Fallen Narcos," March 3, 2009.

Los Angeles Times

———— "In Colombia, Peace Talks with Paramilitaries Don't Quell Fear," July 21, 2003.
———— Kraul, Chris. "Drug Traffickers Use Submersibles to Ferry Narcotics," November 6, 2007.
———— "New Colombia Drug Gangs Wreak Havoc," May 4, 2008.

McClatchy Newspapers

———— "At $2 Million Each, Subs Become the Drug Transport of Choice," July 18, 2008.

Miami Herald

———— Brodzinsky, Sibylla. "Colombian Drug Lord Captured," September 11, 2007.
———— "Colombian Cocaine Suspect in Cuba, Out of U.S. Reach," December 27, 2004.
———— Dudley, Steven. "Extraditions Play Role in Colombian Drug Cartel's Internal War," December 20, 2004.

The Nation

——— "Failed Plan in Colombia," July 31, 2003.

National Security Archives

——— "War in Colombia: Guerrillas, Drugs and Human Rights in U.S. Colombia Policy, 1988–2002," May 23, 2002.

New Colombia News Agency

——— "Army Increasing Cooperation with Paramilitary Death Squads," June 18, 2003.
——— "Colombian Security Forces Suffer Substantial Casualties," June 26, 2003.
——— "The Political Economy of a Narco-Terror State," October 2, 2002.

The New York Times

——— "Alleged Cocaine Kingpin on FBI's 10 Most-Wanted List Reported Captured By Colombian Troops," September 10, 2007.
——— Barrionuevo, Alexei. "Brazil: Court Backs Suspected Drug Lord's Extradition to U.S." March 14, 2008.
——— Barrionuevo, Alexei. "Brazil Extradites Suspect to the U.S." August 23, 2008.
——— "Bogota Sentences Drug Lord," February 15, 1994.
——— Brooke, James. "At Home (That's Prison) with Medellin's Ochoas," February 28, 1995.
——— Brooke, James. "Colombian Drug Chiefs Threaten War," March 30, 1990.
——— Brooke, James. "In Colombia, One Victory in a Long War," December 3, 1993.
——— Canedy, Dana. "Colombian Drug Figure Is Convicted in U.S. Court," May 29, 2003.

———— "Colombia Makes a Hero of Drug Cartels' Foe," January 24, 1993.

———— "Colombian Drug Leader Gets 17½-Year Term," December 22, 1992.

———— Forero, Juan. "Colombia Drug Lords Join Paramilitaries to Seek Leniency," November 27, 2004.

———— Forero, Juan. "Colombia Extradites 1980's Trafficker to U.S. to Face Drug Charges," September 8, 2001.

———— Forero, Juan. "Colombia—Top Cocaine Boss Arrested," July 16, 2005.

———— Forero, Juan. "Colombia's High Court Approves Extradition of Former Drug Leader," August 23, 2001.

———— Forero, Juan. "Surge in Extradition Of Colombia Drug Suspects to U.S.," December 6, 2004.

———— Janofsky, Michael. "Racketeering Charges Against Colombians in Huge Cocaine Case," May 7, 2004.

———— Kushner, David. "Drug-Sub Culture," April 23, 2009.

———— "Man Accused of Being Kingpin Is Arrested," January 15, 2004.

———— McKinley, James C. Jr., and Simon Romero. "Colombia Receives Drug Suspect Sought by U.S. and Jailed in Cuba," February 10, 2007.

———— "Mexico: Suspected Drug Kingpin Held," September 9, 2006.

———— Preston, Julia. "Cocaine Dealer Sentenced," May 13, 2005.

———— Preston, Julia. "Colombian Drug Suspect Extradited," March 17, 2006.

———— Romero, Simon. "Colombia: Drug Boss Killed in Venezuela," February 2, 2008.

———— "Suspect Tied to Medellin Cartel Leadership Becomes 3d to Surrender," February 17, 1991.

———— Treaster, Joseph B. "Drug Traffickers' Offer to Quit the Business Is Dividing Colombians," February 9, 1990.

———— Treaster, Joseph B. "Seven Indicted in 1992 Slaying of a Journalist," May 11, 1993.

——— "U.S. Strategy in Colombia Connects Drugs and Terror," November 14, 2002.

——— "Wanted by the US: 12 From Colombia," August 30, 1989.

——— Wren, Christopher S. "Keeping Cocaine Resilient—Low Cost and High Profit," March 4, 1997.

Reuters

——— "Another Cocaine-Laden Submarine Sinks off Colombia," January 3, 2008.

——— "Brazil: Cartel Leader Arrested," August 8, 2007.

——— "Brazil Nabs Colombian Drug Lord Wanted in U.S.," August 7, 2007.

——— "Colombia Arrests Senior Rebel Commander," January 3, 2004.

——— "Mexico Captures Submarine Loaded with Drugs," July 17, 2008.

The Scotsman

——— "New Super Strain of Coca Plant Stuns Anti-Drug Officials," August 27, 2004.

——— "Subs, Drugs and Killings," January 5, 2010.

St. Petersburg Times

——— Adams, David. "Special Report: A Scam in the Drug War," May 5, 2003.

——— "Danilo's War: The Story of One Officer's Rise and Fall in Colombia's Drug Wars Illustrates the Challenges Police Face," March 6, 2006.

Sydney Morning Herald

——— "Cali Cartel Leader Caught In Drug Swoop," January 11, 2004.

Time

—— Fedarko, Kevin. "Outwitting Cali's Professor Moriarty," July 17, 1995.

—— Gleick, Elizabeth. "Kingpin Checkmate," June 19, 1995.

—— Moody, John, Pablo Rodriguez Orejuela, and Tom Quinn. "A Day With the Chess Player," July 1, 1991.

—— "The Cali Cartel—New Kings of Coke," July 1, 1991.

The Wall Street Journal

—— Luhnow, David and Jose de Cordoba. "The Mexican Drug Lord Who Got Away," June 15, 2009.

The Washington Post

—— "Plying the Pacific, Subs Surface as Key Tool of Drug Cartels," June 6, 2009.

Washington Times

—— "Directing the Drug War," August 5, 2002.

USA Today

—— "Colombian Police Nab Reputed Leader of Drug Cartel," December 28, 2004.

ADDITIONAL SOURCES

National Security Archives

—— "U.S. Intelligence Listed Colombian President Uribe Among 'Important Colombian Narco-Traffickers' in 1991," August 2, 2004.

———— "The Role of Drug Trafficking in Colombia's Internal Political Conflict," April 4, 2004.

PACER: *Public Access to Court Electronic Records*

United States District Court

———— Washington, District of Colombia.
———— Eastern District of New York (Brooklyn).
———— Eastern District of New York (Central Islip).
———— Southern District of Florida (Miami).
———— Southern District of New York (Manhattan).
———— Western District of Virginia (Roanake).

Court Documents

04-CR 1064: *U.S. v Juan Carlos Ramirez Abadia*

02 CR 1188: (includes all superseding indictments) *U.S. v Luis Hernando Gomez Bustamante, Arcangel de Jesus Henao Montoya, Orlando Sabogal Zuluga, Jaime Maya Duran, Jhonny Cano Correa, Aldemar Rendon, Jose Dagoberto Florez Rios, Gilberto Sanchez Monsalve, Juan Carlos Giraldo Franco, Davinson Gomez O'Campo, Jaime Rojas Franco, Marta Agudelo Castano, Julia Agudelo Castano, Carlos Alberto Gomez, Jose Luis Vallejo, Ariel Rodriguez, Juan Carlos Patino Restrepo, Gabriel Villanueva, Abelardo Rojas, Hector Alonso Salazar Maldonado, Carlos Arturo Patino Restrepo, Jair Rendon, Luis Escobar, Jose Luis Vallejo, and others.*

01 CR 945: *U.S. v Hector Rivera, aka Hector Lucas*

99 CR 804: *U.S. v Diego Montoya Sanchez*

97 CR 791: *U.S. v Juan Albeiro Monsalve, Ignacio Lobo*

97 MJB 00011: *U.S. v Tele-Austin*

96 CR 613: *U.S. v Johnson Guzman*

Also, *U.S. v Wilber Alirio Varela, U.S. v Diego León Montoya Sánchez, et al.*

UNITED STATES GOVERNMENT

Department of Defense

—— Joint Interagency Task Force South—Self-Propelled Semi-Submersible Fact Sheet, 2008.

Department of Homeland Security

—— Borja, Elizabeth C. "Brief Documentary History of the Department of Homeland Security 2001–2008.

Department of Justice

—— "The Attorney General's Guidelines Regarding the Use of Confidential Informants," September 2005.

—— "The Drug Enforcement Administration's International Operations, Audit Report," February 2007.

—— "High-ranking Colombian Drug Traffickers Sentences on Cocaine Charges," February 27, 2006.

—— "Leader of Colombian Drug Cartel Pleads Guilty to Racketeering Charges," October 17, 2008.

—— "Leader of Norte Valle Colombian Drug Cartel Extradited to United States," July 20, 2007.

—— "Leader of Norte Valle Colombian Drug Cartel (Luis Hernando Gomez Bustamante, Also Known As "Rasguno") Extradited to United States," May 20, 2007.

—— "Norte Valle Cartel Leader Extradited to Face Charges in the United States," December 12, 2008.

—— "United States Announces Rico Charges Against Leadership of Colombia's Most Powerful Cocaine Cartel," May 6, 2004.

—— "United States Announces Rico Charges Against Leadership of Colombia's Most Powerful Cocaine Cartel, State Department Announces Reward for Suspect Apprehension," May 6, 2004.

—— "Violent Colombian Drug Kingpin Sentenced To 45 Years In Prison For Importing Thousands Of Kilograms Of Cocaine Into The United States From Colombia," June 3, 2008.

Department of State

—— Bureau of International Narcotics and Law Enforcement Affairs: "International Narcotics Control Strategy Report: The Caribbean," March 2005.
—— Bureau of International Narcotics and Law Enforcement Affairs: "Narcotics Rewards Program."
—— Bureau of International Narcotics and Law Enforcement Affairs: "Narcotics Rewards Program—Target Information." List of Foreign Terrorist Organizations.
—— "Narcotics Rewards Program—Target Information."

Department of the Treasury

—— "Cali Cartel Financial Network," September 2004.
—— "Federal Indictment Narcotics Trafficking," May 2004.
—— Financial Crimes Enforcement Network (FINCEN): "Treasury Acts Against Flow of Dirty Money to Colombia," December 23, 1996.
—— "North Valle Cartel Financial Network," May 2005.
—— "North Valle Cartel Financial Network Specially Designated Narcotics Traffickers," November 2006.
—— Office of Foreign Assets Control: "Organizational Chart, North Valle Drug Cartel," October 2006.
—— Office of Foreign Asset Control—"Overview of the Foreign Narcotics Kingpin Act," January 15, 2008.
—— Office of Foreign Assets Control: Recent OFAC Actions, October 25, 2006.
—— Office of Foreign Assets Control: "Specially Designated Narcotics Traffickers," August 2006.

———— Office of Foreign Assets Control: "Varela Drug Trafficking Organization, North Valle Drug Cartel," November 2005.

———— "Transcript of Press Conference Announcing Guilty Pleas by Cali Cartel," September 9, 2006.

———— "Treasury Designates Financial Web of Colombian Drug Lords," September 14, 2004.

———— "Treasury Designates North Valle Drug Cartel Traffickers," October 14, 2004.

———— "Treasury Designation Targets Elusive North Valle Cartel Leader," August 29, 2006.

———— "Treasury Further Assails the Financial Infrastructure of the Cali Drug Cartel," November 17, 2004.

———— "Treasury Names Colombian Drug Kingpins To Traffickers List," February 23, 2000.

———— "Treasury Names Colombian Drug Kingpin to Traffickers List," April 24, 2001.

———— "Treasury Names Colombian Drug Kingpins To Traffickers List," August 18, 2000.

———— "Treasury Takes Action Against Major Medellin-Based Trafficker and His Financial Empire," March 28, 2007.

———— "Treasury Targets Financial Network of Ramirez Abadia," August 15, 2007.

———— "Treasury Targets North Valle Cartel's Next Generation of Leaders," October 25, 2006.

———— "U.S. Treasury: Report on Narco Impact," May 4, 2007.

Drug Enforcement Administration

———— "Colombian Norte Valle Cartel Leader Arrested," April 14, 2010.

———— "Defendant in Colombian Norte Valle Drug Cartel Extradited to the United States," October 21, 2005.

———— "Indictments Charging Leaders of the Norte Valle Colombian Drug Cartel Unsealed," May 6, 2004.

—— Secret Memorandum to Chief International Operations from Country Attaché, Bogotá Country Office: "Operation Millennium: January 20, 2000."

Federal Bureau of Investigation

—— "Norte Valle Cartel Kingpin and Former FBI Top Ten Fugitive Diego Montoya Sanchez Sentenced to 45 Years for Cocaine Trafficking, Murder, and Racketeering Charges," October 21, 2009.
—— "Leader of Colombian Drug Cartel and Former FBI Top Ten Fugitive Pleads Guilty to Drug, Murder, and Racketeering Charges," August 11, 2009.

Federal Deposit Insurance Corporation

—— "Bank Secrecy Act and Anti-Money Laundering History of Anti-Money Laundering Legislation," June 3, 2004.

Immigration and Customs Enforcement (ICE)

—— "Extradited Colombian Money Launderer for Norte Valle Cartel Sentenced to Ten Years in Federal Prison," March 28, 2005.

United States Customs Service

—— "History of the U.S. Customs Service Investigation into Colombia's Cali Drug Cartel and the Rodriguez-Orejuela Brothers"

United States House of Representatives

—— "Testimony of R. Richard Newcomb, Director Office of Foreign Assets Control U.S. Department of the Treasury Before the House Financial Services Subcommittee on Oversight and Investigations," June 16, 2004.

——— John Ashcroft, Attorney General of the United States—Statement before the Committee on the Judiciary Concerning Oversight of the Department of Justice, July 25, 2002.

——— Thomas A. Constantine, Administrator, Drug Enforcement Administration—Statement Before the Committee on Foreign Relations Committee, Subcommittee on the Western Hemisphere, Peace Corps, Narcotics, and Terrorism: "International Organized Crime Syndicates and their Impact on the United States," February 26, 1998.

——— R. Richard Newcomb, Director Office of Foreign Assets Control U.S. Department of the Treasury—Statement Before the Committee on Governmental Affairs United States Senate Hearings on Terrorism Financing: "Origination, Organization and Prevention," July 31, 2003.

——— Bonni Tischler, U.S. Customs Service—Testimony Before the Senate Caucus on International Narcotics Control, June 22, 1999.

Index